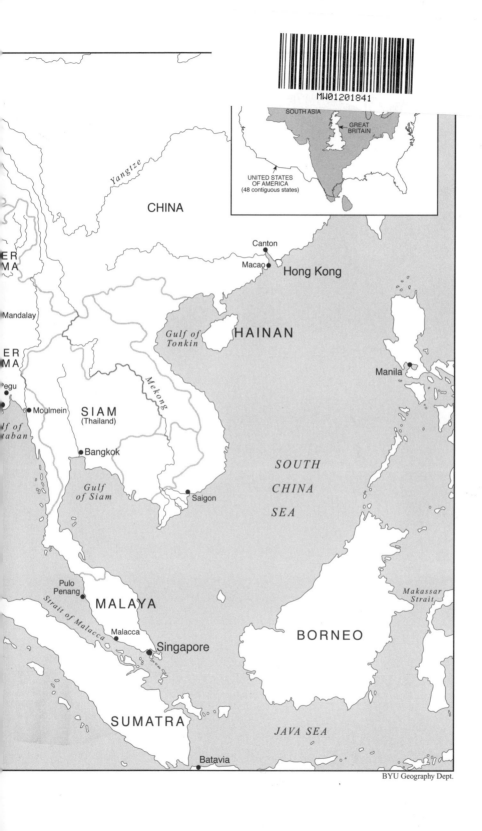

SOUTH ASIA

GREAT
BRITAIN

UNITED STATES
OF AMERICA
(48 contiguous states)

CHINA

Yangtze

Canton

Macao●

Hong Kong

ER
MA

Mandalay

Gulf of
Tonkin

HAINAN

ER
MA

Manila

Pegu

Moulmein

SIAM
(Thailand)

Mekong

lf of
taban

Bangkok

Gulf
of Siam

Saigon

SOUTH

CHINA

SEA

Pulo
Penang

MALAYA

Strait of Malacca

Makassar
Strait

Malacca

Singapore

BORNEO

SUMATRA

JAVA SEA

Batavia

Dear David & Karen,

   This book tells the amazing stories of the first missionaries called to preach the Gospel in India in this dispensation. Their stories of courage & dedication are amazing! It is a privilege to be able to share in this mission today, in even the smallest way!

   Thanks for your kind help & encouragement!

                    Love,
                    Becky

NOTHING
MORE
HEROIC

NOTHING
MORE
HEROIC

THE COMPELLING STORY OF THE FIRST LATTER-DAY SAINT MISSIONARIES IN INDIA

R. LANIER BRITSCH

DESERET BOOK COMPANY
SALT LAKE CITY, UTAH

The author gratefully acknowledges the courtesy of the following institutions and individuals for providing the illustrations on the pages below:

Archives, Historical Department of The Church of Jesus Christ of Latter-day Saints, Salt Lake City, Utah: 32, 43, 85, 134

Bancroft Library, University of California–Berkeley: 16

British Library, by permission, X666 PL17 and X666 PL27: 4, 28

Charleen Cutler: 42

Hobart Caunter, *Lives of the Moghul Emperors,* The Oriental Annual Series: 39

Hobart Caunter, *Scenes in India,* The Oriental Annual Series: 75

Frank Esshom, *Pioneers and Prominent Men of Utah:* 69, 105, 133

Lynn M. Hilton, comp., *Levi Savage Jr. Journal:* 157

Andrew Jenson, *LDS Biographical Encyclopedia:* 70

Jagmohan Mahajan, *The Raj Landscape: British Views of Indian Cities:* 124, 130

Gerald Phillips: 30

Photographic Archives, Harold B. Lee Library, Brigham Young University, Provo, Utah: 6, 106, 153, 236

W. Urwick, *India Illustrated,* New York: Hurst and Company, 1891: 57, 60, 66, 90, 92, 95, 104, 182, 250, 259, 262

Utah State Historical Society, by permission, all rights reserved, photo no. 12901: 215

All other illustrations and photos are the property of R. Lanier Britsch: 26, 62, 68, 73, 83, 89, 96, 110, 128, 142, 192, 202, 204, 209, 275

Library of Congress Cataloging-in-Publication Data

Britsch, R. Lanier.
   Nothing more heroic : the compelling story of the first Latter-day Saint missionaries in India / R. Lanier Britsch.
      p.   cm.
   Includes bibliographical references.
   1. Church of Jesus Christ of Latter-day Saints—Missions—India—Burma—Siam—History—19th century.   2. Church of Jesus Christ of Latter-day Saints—Missions—South Asia—History—19th century. 3. Musser, A. Milton.   I. Title.
BX8661.B75   1999
266'.9354—dc21   99-35842
                                                          CIP

Printed in the United States of America   72082-6502

10   9   8   7   6   5   4   3   2   1

To the missionaries to India, past and present

There is nothing more heroic
in our Church annals than the labors and sufferings
of these brethren of the mission to India.

ELDER B. H. ROBERTS

CONTENTS

PREFACE

I have chosen to recount this history in the voice of Amos Milton Musser, who has been one of my heroes for thirty-five years. Amos Musser was one of the first missionaries to serve in India and spent a number of years working at the Church historian's office, where he was an assistant Church historian from 1902 until 1909. Thus he was probably familiar with the primary sources I have used and in fact could have written this book, fleshing out many areas that journals, letters, and histories have glossed over. Amos Musser died on September 24, 1909, seven years after the 1902 jubilee of the sending of the Utah part of the mission to India. I have not fantasized conversations or created imaginary scenes. Every event is as true to the story as if Amos Milton Musser himself had really written it.

In 1964, I completed a master's thesis on the 1850s mission of The Church of Jesus Christ of Latter-day Saints in India, Burma, and Siam (Thailand). Although it was a satisfactory study, it was based on a slim body of original sources. The journals of Amos Milton Musser were my prime documents. Also of great importance were the Manuscript History of the East India Mission, which was compiled under the direction of Andrew Jenson at the Church historian's office, and the letters from the India missionaries that were published in the *Millennial Star* in England. Thirty-five years have passed, and to my good fortune a number of

additional materials—diaries, journals, reminiscences, and so on—
have been published by families or submitted to the Archives of
The Church of Jesus Christ of Latter-day Saints in Salt Lake City
or to Manuscripts and Special Collections at the Harold B. Lee
Library at Brigham Young University in Provo, Utah. Descendants
of the India missionaries have contacted me and shared precious
documents and materials. I have also met a number of descendants
of the India missionaries by accident, or so it appeared at the time,
who have given me copies of journals, diaries, letters, and so on, or
who knew someone whom I should contact who could supply
information to fill out the story. In quoting from such primary
documents I have retained the spelling and punctuation of the
originals.

A few important journals are still missing, most notably those
of Nathaniel Vary Jones, who served as president of the India
Mission. But every part of the mission is well documented and the
story as I have presented it here is quite complete. I'm grateful that
with the passing of time the fuller history of this remarkable undertaking has gradually been revealed.

Many friends, relatives, and co-workers have contributed to
this project. My wife, JoAnn, has cheered me on while wondering
whether the completed manuscript would ever be published. I'm
grateful for a professional development leave and financial support
provided by Brigham Young University's College of Family, Home,
and Social Sciences during the 1997–98 school year. I am also grateful for generous financial grants from the BYU Religious Studies
Center and the David M. Kennedy Center for International
Studies that made it possible for me and my wife to visit India and
retrace the steps of the early missionaries. We will long have wonderful memories of our weeks in India (trains, airplanes, taxis, auto-
rickshaws) with Sarah and Shahram Paksima, our talented,
thoughtful, and energetic guides.

I extend special thanks to the following for providing docu-
mentary materials on their ancestors who served in India and
Burma: Philip K. Folsom on William F. Carter; Charleen Cutler on

William Willes; Frank J. Earl (deceased) on Truman Leonard; Ross Findlay on Hugh Findlay; Carol Lloyd on William Fotheringham; George M. McCune on Matthew McCune and family; Julie Taylor Peterson on James Patrick and Mary Ann Meik; and Gertrude Musser Richards (deceased) on Amos Milton Musser.

Two archives hold most of the original source materials used for this study: The Archives of The Church of Jesus Christ of Latter-day Saints in Salt Lake City and Manuscripts and Special Collections at the Harold B. Lee Library at Brigham Young University, Provo, Utah. Gratitude is extended to Randall Dixon, Ronald G. Watt, and William Slaughter at LDS Church Archives and to Russell Taylor, Brad Westwood, and David J. Whittaker at the BYU Library.

I'm grateful to professor emeritus Ted J. Warner for reading and critiquing the manuscript; to my son-in-law, David J. Frantz, for helping with graphics; and to Aaron Gleave for checking footnotes and quotations for accuracy. One of the most stressful times of any writer's life is the period between submission of a manuscript to a publisher and receiving a reply regarding its fate. At Deseret Book two of the most important decision makers are Ronald A. Millet, president and general manager, and Sheri L. Dew, vice president of publishing. Fortunately, they are my friends. They have supported my work even though they have recognized that the audience for such writing is relatively small. I'm grateful that they believe in the worth of history and that some books deserve a place on library and family bookshelves simply because the information is important and enlightening, rather than because it will sell enormous numbers of copies. I thank them for supporting this project and letting it see the light of day. I express gratitude to Suzanne Brady, my editor at Deseret Book, for her good work and careful production of this book and to Richard Erickson for layout and design.

Few things are more disturbing to an historian than to realize that his work is not perfect. But things come up and prove our fallibility regularly. I've tried to get it right. Unfortunately, I'm sure errors of fact or judgment will surface with time. Even though many people have helped with this project, I must accept responsibility for the final product.

The history recorded in this book is true, it is important, and it is inspiring. Missionary work has always demanded the best of men and women. Meeting new and different peoples and cultures with the intention of positively changing lives demands humility, respect, honesty, self-sacrifice and self-mastery, sincerity, tenacity, courage, and faith in the Lord Jesus Christ. To my knowledge, there has never been a mission that demanded more of all the cardinal virtues (and others) than the Church's early mission to India. Truly, as Elder B. H. Roberts wrote in his *Comprehensive History of the Church*, "There is nothing more heroic in our Church annals than the labors and sufferings of these brethren of the mission to India" (4:72–73).

Introduction

THE EAST INDIA MISSION IN CONTEXT

The mission of The Church of Jesus Christ of Latter-day Saints to India and South Asia in the 1850s came at the end of the so-called Company Raj ("rule"). From the early seventeenth century the power of the East India Company in India, including the territory now part of the modern states of Pakistan and Bangladesh, had grown to almost total subjugation and domination of the subcontinent by the 1750s. But in 1813 the East India Company lost its trade monopoly, and in 1833 Parliament did away with it altogether as a trading company. The British government took control of the administration of most of India. The army, which was by the mid-nineteenth century composed mostly of *sepoys* (Indian soldiers) was the foundation of British power. Even though the East India Company was largely gone, India remained a place of opportunity for Europeans who desired civil, social, or military rank and privilege. Many Anglo-Indians, Caucasian sons and daughters of English residents of India, had grown accustomed to the blessings of social and economic position. They remained in what was now their homeland and became part of the elite fabric of the country. Other men from the British Isles came to India as soldiers or government employees. Some women emigrated to India in quest of husbands. Whether

1

male or female, they hoped to find position and to get gain. The British governmental administration grew steadily, and by the 1850s it was an enormous machine run mostly by English clerks and headed by civil servants of skill, experience, and knowledge. Parliament in England devoted considerable time and discussion to matters related to India. Governors-general varied greatly in quality but overall attempted to direct matters with acceptable British skill and acumen. Over the decades, in addition to others' efforts, various of the governors-general attempted to stamp out some of India's most obvious social ills—gang robbery, thugs, suttee (widow burning), and female infanticide.

In January 1848, the Marquess of Dalhousie, known simply as Lord Dalhousie, became governor-general over all British interests in greater India. He was governor-general during the entire period of the Latter-day Saint mission. Dalhousie was energetic and focused. And he was a convinced westernizer. He was concerned not only with peace and social stability, but also with the administrative and institutional modernization of India. Dalhousie shared the view of most Europeans that western ways and social norms were simply superior to those of India. During his rule from 1848 to 1856, he oversaw the introduction or the development of the railroad, telegraph, road enlargement and development, improvement of *cantonments* (military municipalities), and development of other parts of the country's infrastructure. He was also determined to enlarge the geographical area of British control. His most debatable policy was the doctrine of "right of lapse," which held that Indian territories whose rulers had no male heir would lapse into the control of the British. Following the takeover of a number of small territories, the large kingdom of Oudh, with its court at Lucknow, was annexed in February 1856. This act was part of the cause of the tragic war of 1857, which was centered in that area. The war of 1857 was the cause of Parliament's decision to make India part of the British Empire in 1858.

Much of this was going on while Latter-day Saint elders were traveling the roads and rivers of India. For the most part they were above the fray. The name Dalhousie is not mentioned once in the journals and writings of the Mormon missionaries. The counsel of the leaders of the Church was to remain aloof from political, social, and economic matters. The elders had no trouble accepting this counsel, partly because they were so far removed from those who controlled government and society.

In a way, India was two countries: the India of the Indians, and the India of the British. Although the British Raj controlled and conditioned to some degree what was going on at all levels, the Indians lived their lives much as they had done through the ages. The British saw it otherwise, but the Indians did care who ruled them. They preferred their own leaders. They wanted a king or prince or raja to honor and revere. But most of all, they wanted to be left alone to follow their own religious, social, and economic traditions.

The other India, that of the British and other Europeans, made up an elite stratum of society that was almost impenetrable by any who were of the wrong blood and breeding. Native Indians could not enter; neither could Mormon missionaries.

The story that follows tells of seventeen set-apart missionaries and their efforts to penetrate the almost unbreakable social and religious shell of the British in India. The elders attempted in every area to teach the Gospel to native Indians, but the main effort of the missionaries was to find Europeans who would listen to their message. At times the missionaries complained that the type or class of people who were so freely accepting the Restored Gospel in England and Scandinavia were simply not in India. This was largely true. The mission proved to be a most trying missionary experience. But it is a wonderful story of adventure, faith, faithfulness, and courage.[1]

NOTE

1. For further reading in the history, religions, and cultural background of India, I recommend two books by Stanley Wolpert, *A New History of India*, 5th ed. (New York: Oxford University Press, 1997), and *India* (Berkeley: University of California Press, 1991). More information regarding recent history of The Church of Jesus Christ of Latter-day Saints in India and Asia is contained in my book *From the East: The History of the Latter-day Saints in Asia, 1851–1996* (Salt Lake City: Deseret Book, 1998).

Custom House Wharf, by Sir Charles D'Oyly, c. 1835

1

CALLED TO SERVE IN EAST INDIA

Apr. 25 P.M.[1] we arrived opposite Fort William about 6 o'clock, the beauty of scenery surpasses anything I ever before beheld on both sides of the river as we passed along its shores, about noon we took a Customs House Officer aboard, the tide has been in our favor, its assistance in addition to a smart breeze enabled us to make our destined haven before the tide commenced to recede, my feelings while beholding the beautiful scenes as we passed along the muddy channel of the Hoogly, which presented themselves as I stated before is indescribable.[2]

Those are the words I used to describe our arrival as missionaries of The Church of Jesus Christ of Latter-day Saints in Calcutta, India, fifty years ago. My name is Amos Milton Musser. In my position at the Church historian's office, I've been able to peruse the journals and diaries of my fellow laborers in that distant land. It is an amazing story, a story of heroic courage and complete faithfulness to a call from the Lord. Some of my companions have told part of the story. Now, after piecing together my experiences with theirs, I have learned enough to tell almost the entire epic.

I was born at Donegal, Lancaster County, Pennsylvania, on May 20, 1830. This year as I write being 1902, that's seventy-two years ago. Like Nephi of old, I was born of goodly parents. My father, Samuel, died when I was only two years old. My mother,

Amos Milton Musser

Ann, married again, but her second husband, a man much older than she, passed away when I was eleven. My uncle, John Neff, took care of us in those days. He was a warm and generous man all of his life. In his later years, he frequently shared flour from his mill with widows and others in need. Even though he was generous with us, life was far from easy.

In 1842, Uncle John was baptized. Being a careful, serious, and religious man, he had studied the doctrines and practices thoroughly before gaining his testimony that the heavens truly had been opened again as the Prophet Joseph said. Before long, almost the whole family was baptized. But I wasn't ready. I was still quite young, and I had some questions. With the encouragement of other members in our branch, Uncle John, wanting to be part of the building of Zion and desiring to gather with the Saints of God, visited Nauvoo early in 1844 to investigate moving all of us there. He liked what he saw, but before he could move us, the Prophet

Joseph was murdered, and our plans to migrate were delayed by almost two years. After tarrying for a time, in August 1846 we moved to Nauvoo but found that most of the Church members had already left. The Saints were going west not because they wanted to but because they had been driven out. There was tremendous tension and fear and disappointment among those who were fleeing. I felt it and wanted to bring some justice for the Mormons.

After helping our combined families across the Mississippi, I went back to Nauvoo. Matters became very agitated. On September 10th, 11th, and 12th, a mob (they called themselves a posse) of about eight hundred people under the leadership of Thomas S. Brockman attacked a small army of around three hundred Latter-day Saints and others who had lately moved into Nauvoo. The pretext for the attack was the slowness of the Saints' departure from Nauvoo. The battle itself lasted only three days, but three good men (Captain William Anderson, his son, August, and David Norris) were killed, and we all decided that defending what little was left was not worth the sacrifice of others. At the conclusion of the battle, representatives from the Church and the anti-Mormon forces signed the "Nauvoo Treaty of Surrender." With this conclusion, the Saints moved out of Nauvoo as quickly as they could.[3]

I decided to stay on in Nauvoo and find work. I hadn't been baptized yet, and because I was a boy of only sixteen years, even with my relationship with the Mormons, nobody considered me a threat. Living in the environs of Nauvoo wasn't hard for me. Mother had pushed me to write clearly and well, and I had become a pretty good penman and bookkeeper. For someone with my skills, getting a job as a clerk in a business was fairly easy.

In September 1848, Mother married for the third time. Her husband was a widower named Jared Starr. After spending that winter together at Winter Quarters, Mother and Brother Starr were able to emigrate to Utah in 1849. Once they were settled, she wrote to me (I was in Eddyville, Iowa) and encouraged me to come to the Valley. I decided it was time. In the early months of 1851, I gave up my job and traveled to Kanesville (Council Bluffs), Iowa, to be with the Saints. I realized there that I had a testimony of the Restored Gospel and was baptized by James Allred and confirmed by Elder Orson Hyde. In April, I left for the Valley, where our company arrived on September 22, 1851. Mother, my two sisters, Elizabeth and Susanna, their families, and my half-brother and sister had been there for two years before I arrived. To my delight, Mother and Brother Starr's baby girl was now almost two years old. We had a great reunion.

Looking back over decades, I can still visualize how beautiful Salt Lake City looked in the early fall that year. Many pioneers have written about how things were. It was a lovely, growing city. The streets were wide and straight, and most houses had orderly fences to demarcate their boundaries. Only four years had passed since Brother Brigham and the first company arrived. What a miracle had been accomplished.

With my skill and experience as a clerk, it did not take long to find work. Edward Hunter had been called to replace Bishop Newel K. Whitney as Presiding Bishop of the Church on April 7, 1851. Fortunately, Bishop Hunter was a shoestring relative of sorts. That did not hinder my getting an introduction to him. He needed clerks at the Tithing Office, and I was happy to work there. Some people have suggested that such work must have been boring. Nothing could have been futher from the truth. People came from miles around to offer their tithes. And emigrants heading for California often stopped by to ask for directions and help. A new Tithing Storehouse was under construction when I arrived in town. No, the Tithing Office wasn't boring. It was the center of much of what went on in those days.

MISSION CALL AND PREPARATION TO SERVE

I was getting settled and somewhat knowledgeable about the work of the Tithing Office when the Brethren called a special conference that was held August 28 and 29, 1852. Two thousand elders and many of their wives were assembled in the Old Tabernacle. I was mostly surprised when I heard my name called out from the pulpit, but I cannot say I was comfortable sitting there. Why shouldn't I be called? I was twenty-two years old with no prospects for marriage. The Brethren laid out a powerful position regarding the responsibility, the honor, and the blessing it would be for an Elder of Israel to serve a mission in the world at that time because many nations had not yet received news of the Gospel's Restoration.

President Young made clear the necessity of doing this work in the proper order. He asked what would have happened if the Church had sent missionaries to the four quarters of the earth six years earlier, shortly after leaving Nauvoo? Where would the converts have gathered? We needed to build up Zion first as a gathering place. Now we were ready as a Church to carry out this important step.

At the end of the morning session, President Brigham Young asked his counselor, President Heber C. Kimball, to read the names of those who had been selected. The list seemed to go on and on of missionaries who were being sent almost everywhere: Washington, Iowa, New Orleans, Nova Scotia, Texas, England, Wales, Ireland, France, Germany, Gibraltar, Denmark, Norway . . . Then came the calls to Asia—Hindustan was first. My name was the third to be called. Although others received calls to China, Siam [Thailand], Africa, Australia, and the Sandwich Islands [Hawaii], my thoughts immediately centered on Hindustan . . . India . . . East India . . . Calcutta. Ninety-six names were read at that time. That night I wrote:

> Sat. 28th [August]
> This morning our special conference commenced, opened with singing and prayer, & after a few good remarks by Bro. H. C. Kimball, there were 107 [actually 108] Elders chosen for Missions to Nations of the Earth, to preach the Gospel, &c &c 8 others with myself was chosen to go to Calcutta East India

the following are the names Bros N. V. Jones, S. A. Woolley, Richard Ballantyne, T. Leonard, W. Fotheringham, R. Skelton, R. Owens, W. F. Carter & myself.[4]

I was somewhat acquainted with all of these brethren. A few of them, particularly Brother Leonard, I had known since the battle at Nauvoo. But we got to know each other considerably better before we all returned home. I have never known a more devout, courageous, dedicated group of men in my life.

People have wondered why the Brethren decided to send out so many missionaries at that time. First, the Church and the Saints were prospering. In 1851, the First Presidency stated publicly in a General Epistle that the Church had never been in a more prosperous condition. This must have stimulated their confidence to send out more elders to preach the Restored Gospel. But, without doubt, the most important reason was the strong dedication the Brethren held that the fulness of the Everlasting Gospel had to be preached to all the world. In September 1851, in the Sixth General Epistle, the First Presidency spoke positively regarding the Lord's opening the doors of nations that had heretofore been closed. They wrote, "The way is fast preparing for the introduction of the Gospel into China, Japan, and other nations, which for ages have sat in darkness, and stood aloof from celestial science and foreign intercourse." I don't know how the Brethren could have known other than by the Spirit that American Commodore Matthew C. Perry would open Japan in 1853 and 1854. Maybe the "other nations" they mentioned included India, Siam, Burma, and Ceylon [Sri Lanka].

After what we had been through in Nauvoo and coming west, going to India did not seem particularly daring or courageous, but we knew it would be very demanding. At that time, most Mormon missionaries were married. I had it easy because I was young and single. Leaving wives and children behind, as most of our group did, was terribly difficult. In addition to the emotional strains, it placed financial and other burdens on families that took years to overcome. I still remember watching Richard Ballantyne sitting with his wife, Huldah, during the conference. He gripped her hand, and both of them looked shocked when they heard his name called from the pulpit. But he accepted the Lord's call, and despite poor health and hostile adversaries in Madras, he served a strong mission. And Nathaniel Vary Jones . . . what a man! He died so young, only forty, but had done so much to build the kingdom. Before coming to Utah he had served as an officer in the Mormon Battalion. Levi Savage, Jr., and Robert Owens were also in the Battalion. Some of our group of elders had helped build the Old Fort in Salt Lake City, and many had fought the battle of the crickets. Elder Ballantyne had already founded the first Sunday schools in the Church. He had also been kidnapped for the Gospel's sake while in Illinois. Of course, all of us had walked or ridden in wagons across the plains to get to the Valley. Walking again to new fields of labor did not seem out of the ordinary.

I do not believe most of us India-bound missionaries had thought much about India before we received our calls. I later learned that articles about Elder Lorenzo Snow sending missionaries from Britain to India had appeared in the *Millennial Star* in England as early as August 1851. While in England, as part of his mission to Italy, Switzerland, and Malta, he had discussed with other members of the Twelve the wisdom of sending missionaries to India. They sanctioned his idea, and he sent William Willes, an Englishman, to Calcutta, and Hugh Findlay, originally from Scotland, to Bombay. Evidently they were making some headway, for branches of the Church were reported in both cities. Elder Snow was also responsible for Joseph Richards returning to India to be Elder Willes's companion. While in Malta in May 1852, he had asked Church leaders in England for an additional missionary to join Elder Findlay in Bombay.[5] Elder Snow had returned from Europe at the end of July 1852, only a month before the special conference. Although I never asked him about it, I am sure he immediately enlarged on his India efforts to the First Presidency and the Twelve and recommended that additional missionaries be called to serve in that field.[6] Certainly Elder Snow shared with them the successes Elder Willes was enjoying as late as March 1852 and perhaps into May and June. At that time the work was moving well, and baptisms had numbered almost two hundred. We newly called missionaries were pleased with Elder Snow's positive reports and eagerly looked forward to our arrival in Calcutta.

Most of us had little access to much information regarding India or Siam, but after August 28, 1852, we read everything we could get our hands on concerning India or Hindustan,[7] as it was often called. We also learned what we could about Hinduism and the other religions of India and how other missionary societies were faring among them.[8] Plans to create the University of Deseret had been announced before the date of our calls, and the Church had acquired a few high-quality books and encyclopedias. Occasionally, people have suggested that we were operating in the dark about what we should expect in India. That was not entirely true. We studied the history, geography, and weather of the subcontinent. Nothing we read was very positive or encouraging, and most of what we learned warned us that our work would be demanding.

In addition to my call to India, there is another reason why I remember the special conference so well. Within the Church, we had known, believed in, and practiced the principle of plural marriage for almost a decade. Brother Joseph had taught the principle clearly, and most Latter-day Saints in Utah understood and accepted it. That Brigham Young had many wives was not a well-kept secret. Worldwide the Mormon practice of polygamy and the "Gold Bible" seemed to be the only things known about the Church, even before August 1852. Nevertheless, polygamy was not a public doctrine.

Then on Sunday, August 29th, the First Presidency assigned Elder Orson Pratt to deliver an extensive lecture on the principle. He went on at great length and covered almost every facet of the matter. Later, his lectures on plural marriage were published in a series called the *Seer.* When he finished and others had said more on the subject, Elder Thomas Bullock, clerk of the conference, read the revelation given through the Prophet Joseph Smith earlier in Nauvoo and recorded July 12, 1843. This revelation was published in the *Deseret News* and wherever the Saints published newspapers.[9]

After January 1, 1853, knowledge that plural marriage was a doctrine of the Church was abroad in Great Britain and wherever the *Millennial Star* and the *Deseret News* were distributed. It is now recorded in Section 132 of the book of Doctrine and Covenants.[10] Polygamy was the shout heard round the world. Everything any enemy of the Church could conceive in anger and hatred was heaped against the members of the Church because of this practice. Even before we arrived in Calcutta, word of polygamy went before us. There was no escaping its effects even in the most distant villages and camps of India, Burma, Ceylon, Singapore, Siam, and Hong Kong.

I continued working at the Tithing Office and did most of my preparatory work after hours. I sold my cow for thirty dollars and bought a pen, some new clothes, a watch, and some other useful items. We held several training meetings in which various topics were discussed, and plans were developed. Our leaders decided we should travel by wagon train by way of southern California, as had been suggested by Elder Willes in a letter from India. This plan required us to buy wagons, horses and mules (ox-drawn wagons were too slow), harnesses, and all that went with such travel. Of course, we would be camping along the way so we had to take cooking gear and utensils, food, blankets, tents, and everything one needs for minimal comfort on a long journey. I was invited to travel, cook, and sleep in company with Nathaniel V. Jones, Truman Leonard, and Samuel Amos Woolley. All of them were married and returned missionaries. As we traveled, they told me how to speak to an audience, which parts of the Gospel generally gained the most interest, and how best to deal with anti-Mormons. They also taught me a good deal about the Gospel.

On October 16th, most of us were set apart as missionaries. The spirit of the occasion was positive, and we were promised heavenly protection, the ability to bring many into the Church, the ability to heal the sick, withstand sickness, and overcome evil people and influences wherever we went. Brother Skelton's blessing particularly enumerated the gifts of the Spirit, which he and his companions would enjoy. He was promised that the Spirit would warn him of secret works, even attempts to take away our lives. The Spirit would "dictate to thy mind who to bless, and who to curse, but curse no man unless the spirit of the Lord command thee."[11]

During the next two weeks, we assembled ourselves into a wagon company, and on October 24th, we met at Peteetneet.[12] While on our way, we stopped at the Point of the Mountain to take one last look at the Great Salt Lake Valley. Wanting to be as much like the Apostles of old, I sent my purse and my only money, four dollars, back to my mother. I was truly "without purse or scrip." So were my companions. The group that gathered at Peteetneet consisted of thirty-eight missionaries called to Calcutta, Siam, the Sandwich Islands, Hong Kong, and Australia. China-bound Hosea Stout was elected captain, Bishop N. V. Jones became chaplain, Burr Frost acted as sergeant of the guard, and I was asked to serve as clerk. I continued so to serve when we arrived in India. We had the usual difficulties that were associated with travel in those days: some sickness (Brother Jones became so sick with a fever near Las Vegas that we had to delay travel for two days), lack of water while traveling across the desert, blacksmithing when a horse lost a shoe or something broke on a wagon, and that kind of thing. The Saints along the way greeted us warmly and cared for our needs.[13] It made good sense for us to travel as a group. If we ran into foul weather, difficult terrain, or other problems, there were sufficient numbers to get us out of most kinds of trouble.

The trip to California took about six weeks. We followed a route that took us through Parowan and then to Cedar City.[14] From there it was on to Mormon Mesa, Las Vegas, across the Mojave Desert, over the Cajon Pass, and down to San Bernardino, California.

San Bernardino was a new but thriving Latter-day Saint colony of more than one hundred families. We stayed there for two weeks, from December 3d[15] to the 17th, and then moved on through Los Angeles to San Pedro. Moving on to San Pedro sounds so easy, but it took five days' travel in a terrible winter rainstorm that seldom abated. The mud and chill winds made our movements very uncomfortable. The kind Saints in San Bernardino hauled us there and would take no money in reward. San Pedro wasn't much of a port, having no natural harbor. Ships were forced to anchor a mile or more from shore and transfer passengers and freight by boat to and from shore. There were only five small houses there at that time.

Over the years people have asked why we went to San Pedro and then sailed up the coast to San Francisco instead of going directly west to San Francisco. We feared that an early winter storm through the Sierra Nevada might cause serious problems. The southern route was warmer, but even then we encountered some snow as we crossed Cajon Pass.

On Christmas day 1852, we found a small two-masted ship, the brig *Col. Fremont* under Captain John Erskine, Jr., to take us to San Francisco and arrived there on January 9, 1853.[16] The ocean was rough, and we could hardly hold down anything we ate. The crew had brought four Spanish steers on board for fresh meat while en route, but even before we sailed, two of the beasts became enraged, driving passengers to the hold or cabins and the sailors to the rigging. The steers were killed immediately. While at sea, the other two cattle broke loose and were similarly disposed of.

The weather was still blowing a gale when we arrived at the Golden Gate and San Francisco harbor. Brother Fotheringham described our arrival in these words:

> When within a mile of the wharf . . . the captain ordered the sailors to let go the starboard anchor. The chain jammed in the windless; at the same time the tide was running at the speed of a mill race. The sails being in a condition to render the brig no assistance, she drifted down with the tide, running against a large ship lying at anchor in the bay, carrying away the

San Francisco about 1850. This picture, the oldest daguerreotype photo of San Francisco, is often called the Forest of Masts

ship's flying jib-boom and martingale, and her own try-sail-boom and gaff. She got clear of the ship without any further damage, still drifting astern, when they let go the starboard anchor, which brought her up.

Our vessel might have had her quarter stove in, and sunk before assistance could have been rendered; also we were in danger of the falling of the broken spars, chains, blocks and ropes down on our heads.[17]

Needless to say, we were grateful to the Lord for His deliverance and for sparing our lives.

At San Francisco, we decided to combine forces with the Siam-bound elders, Benjamin F. Dewey, Elam Luddington, Levi Savage, and Chauncey Walker West, for our voyage to India. We had traveled as one unit to that point, but it became clear that ships bound for Siam were few and far between. So our numbers swelled from nine to thirteen. From that time on, we worked as one missionary unit.

San Francisco was a terrible city. Every vice imaginable was available: gambling, drinking, prostitution, brawling. No one seemed to keep the Sabbath. Businesses remained open on Sunday as though it were any weekday. The city's sinful temptations were not a problem for us, however. Our problem was to raise enough money to sail to India. We had sold our wagons and horses in southern California, and most of us had sent the proceeds home to our families. We were, after all, called as missionaries, and we intended to serve without purse or scrip. We did not believe we could prove the nations without providing them with the opportunity to serve the Lord's servants.

Fares for the thirteen of us totaled about three thousand dollars, or about two hundred dollars per person. To raise this sum of money, we divided San Francisco into districts and went door to door asking for donations. Largely failing in San Francisco, some of the elders went to Sacramento and many gold mining towns nearby, Santa Cruz, and other towns to see if they could do better. But after three weeks of collecting funds, we had raised only around six hundred fifty dollars. At that point, John M. Horner of San Jose, a Church member who had traveled to California on the ship *Brooklyn* and who had amassed some wealth in farming, came forward and along with his non-member brother contributed the remainder of the needed funds. Another Church member, Thomas S. Williams, who was in business at Sacramento, contributed five hundred dollars.[18]

Before I recount our voyage to India, I want to say a couple more things about the thirteen of us who served in India together. I mentioned earlier that most of the missionaries, ten of the thirteen, were married. Elder Carter had three wives, and Elder Owens had two. Fotheringham, Skelton, and I were the only single elders. We were also the youngest, ages twenty-six, twenty-eight, and twenty-two, respectively, when we were called. The average age was thirty-one years, with forty-six-year-old Luddington being the eldest. The married elders left a total of at least forty children behind. There were many tender feelings when we left the Salt Lake Valley, feelings that were not quickly assuaged.

We did not know it at the time, but on January 11, 1853, two days after we arrived at San Francisco, Hosea Stout's wife, Louisa, died in Utah after childbirth. The infant had passed away a few days before. Brother Stout was, as I have said, the leader of our company until we parted at San Francisco.

THE VOYAGE AND LIFE AT SEA

The necessary money to pay for our fares having been generously provided, we were now ready to procure passage on an India-bound vessel. After making many inquiries along the wharves, our group finally arranged cabin passage on the clipper ship *Monsoon*, Captain Zenos Winsor, Master. As we talked with Captain Winsor, we learned that he had sailed from Boston the same day we received our calls, August 28, 1852. He had arrived at San Francisco on the same day we did. We felt strongly that he had been guided our way by the hand of God.[19] As we continued our association with him and later with his brother, Alexander, who also commanded ships, our conviction became ever surer that he was a good man raised up to give us assistance.

The *Monsoon* was an exceptional ship. Brother Carter said it was "the finest ship I ever saw and with the best accommodations in the cabin of any ship that I have ever seen."[20] It had been constructed in Bath, Maine, in 1851, and weighed 774 tons.[21] We were assigned to suitable cabins when we boarded on January 27, 1853.

The vessel hauled out of the wharf the next day and anchored in the bay for the night. Using the ebbing tide the following day, we sailed safely through the Golden Gate and into the open sea. From the first night on board, Captain Winsor gave us the privilege of meeting in his cabin every evening to sing hymns, speak, and offer prayers. He frequently met with us and showed considerable sympathy for us and for our work. At the first meeting, we elected

Elder Ballantyne president of the group, with N. V. Jones and C. W. West as counselors. They occupied these positions until March 3d, when Jones was selected to serve as mission president of the East India Mission.[22] West had been called to lead the Siam-bound group and assumed that position when we arrived at Calcutta.

Only four days into our voyage, or about 825 miles out from San Francisco, we were alarmed that Ballantyne and Savage were becoming much sicker than the others of us who were suffering from seasickness. It was soon evident that they had contracted smallpox while in San Francisco.[23]

"The brethren were placed in a vacant state room," Brother Fotheringham later wrote, "and Elder Skelton was appointed to be their nurse; and through the faith and prayers of their brethren, and the blessing of God, they soon recovered, and that, too, without the contagion spreading, or afflicting any other person on board. Shipboard is a close place to have the smallpox."[24] On February 21st, twenty-four days after showing their first signs of smallpox, I noted in my journal that the two men had completely recovered. Most of their clothes were thrown overboard, as was their bedding. Two good results came of this frightening episode: first, our faith in God was strengthened;[25] and second, Ballantyne and Skelton developed a warm friendship that carried through their missions and into later life.[26]

With favorable winds, the *Monsoon* made rapid progress. We sighted the island of "Owyhee of the Sandwich Islands," as we spelled it then, on the twelfth day. Hawaii had not become the tourist attraction then that it has become now at the turn of the century. By early March we were sailing between the northern Philippines and the Island of Formosa [Taiwan]. And two weeks later we were becalmed near Cochin-China [Vietnam]. But things changed quickly. Two days later we found ourselves in heavy weather. The captain called us on deck during the storm to see the "mariner's light" or "Saint Elmo's fire," a condition caused by the buildup of static electricity in the air. "It had the appearance of large balls of light, which kept flitting about the tops of the ship's masts," wrote Fotheringham. Saint Elmo being the patron saint of sailors, they considered Saint Elmo's fire a hopeful sign. After passing through the China Sea, we came in full view of Singapore. We could see "some fine buildings and a good deal of shipping in the harbor."[27] Although we didn't stop, several of our group later spent time there while returning home. On March 21st, we entered the Straits of Malacca, just north of the Dutch East Indies island of Sumatra, and six days and six hundred miles later we were in the Bay of Bengal.

On a map it would appear that our journey was about over when we had only twelve hundred miles to go, but stiff headwinds brought slow progress, and almost a month passed before we reached the sand heads where the Hoogly River meets the bay. The voyage had been a relatively long one, but by the standards of that day, it had been fast and comfortable. Elder Ballantyne captured our thoughts when he wrote:

> A good cheerful spirit also seems to prevail on the vessel from Captain to crew, and scarce a profane word has been heard since we came on board. The Captain allows us every privilege that we can desire, is sociable and furnishes excellent, healthy diet three times a day. We have fresh bread morning and evening with potatoes, meat, butter, cheese, with tea and coffee morning and evening to those who drink it. Many of the brethren don't use it, preferring to observe the Word of Wisdom.[28]

In reviewing Brother Carter's journal, I note a comment he made when we came through the Straits of Malacca. It captures an important truth regarding our situation not only en route, but also while we labored in India. He wrote: "The God of Israel has managed affairs in our behalf and what we ask for in faith, we receive, and we have never asked for anything we needed but what we have received it. God is witness and has blessed us ever since we left our homes."[29]

Brother Carter's health did not hold up well in India, he being the first to return home, but what he said was true. God did provide our every need. Miraculously, although some of us spent days very ill, none of us died. Generally, we had our health and strength.[30] Many Europeans were not so fortunate. God blessed us with life, food, clothing, money, places to stay, means of transportation, and safety. But, as you will see, God did not provide many converts. As is always true, He did not take away any man's agency, nor did He allow us such power.

We had practiced preaching sermons to one another from the beginning of our voyage. Also, Brothers Ballantyne and West lectured us on English grammar. Now, as we drew near the conclusion of our journey, we were thrilled with the prospects that lay ahead.

On April 24th, we dropped anchor off Sagar Island, about 120 miles south of Calcutta. Part of the Sunderbans, Sagar Island is the southwesternmost landmass created by the silt dropped by the distributaries of the Ganges (Indians call it the Ganga) and Brahmaputra Rivers. The island was flat, sandy, and swampy; in those days it was infested with alligators, crocodiles, and Bengal tigers. Also, there were hyenas, jackals, and birds that survived on carrion, mostly human bodies that had been ritually placed or dumped in the river after death. The bay held many ships that had come down from Calcutta. When the pilot came on board, we learned that the citizens of Calcutta who occupied the ships were fleeing a cholera epidemic. The Hoogly River was the most sacred of the distributaries of the Ganga, India's most sacred river. I shared my version of our arrival at the beginning of this chapter. Elder Savage penned a more detailed account with these words:

> April 25, 1853, Monday. This morning early, our anchor was raised and we commenced proceeding up the river with a favorable tide and light breeze.[31] We soon arrived where the land appeared on either side. It is thickly scattered [with] dwellings and small villages situated on the river banks[,] composed of buildings which are only small huts composed of mud walls and roofs thatched with straw. Domestic animals are quietly feeding in the green fields or strutting up and down at the

waters edge. All presented to us a peculiar but pleasing prospect, the beauties of which were more enhanced by our just arriving from a long voyage at sea. We passed this day very pleasantly in viewing the different scenes (and to us strange ones) that were presented to our view as we passed up the river. We arrived in Calcutta all safe and in good spirits, and at six o'clock P.M. dropped our anchor at Cooley Bazaar Island, a little below Fort William, being [three months] since we sailed from San Francisco. Elders N. V. Jones and C. W. West [president of the Siam Mission] went on shore to search for the residence of some of the Saints and remained overnight.[32]

So began our mission to India.[33]

NOTES

1. Actually April 26, 1853. The missionaries had crossed the international dateline but had not adjusted the date in their journals and diaries.

2. Amos Milton Musser, Private Journals and Memos, 2:51; copy in possession of the author. Typescript available at the Archives of The Church of Jesus Christ of Latter-day Saints, Salt Lake City, Utah. See also B. H. Roberts, *A Comprehensive History of the Church of Jesus Christ of Latter-day Saints, Century One*, 6 vols. (Salt Lake City: The Church of Jesus Christ of Latter-day Saints, 1930), 3:1–22.

3. Karl Brooks, *The Life of Amos Milton Musser* (Provo, Utah: Stevenson's Genealogical Center, 1980 (rev. ed. of Brooks's M.A. thesis, Brigham Young University, 1961), 6–7.

4. Musser, Journals, 1:7.

5. Lorenzo Snow, "The Malta Mission: Letter from Lorenzo Snow" [to Samuel W. Richards, May 1, 1852, Malta], *Millennial Star* 14 (June 5, 1852): 237; and Samuel W. Richards, "Editorial: Call for Elders for Gibraltar and Bombay," *Millennial Star* 14 (June 12, 1852): 250.

6. Roberts, *Comprehensive History*, 3:388–89.

7. There are a number of spellings for this word. Most typical today is *Hindustan*, but *Hindostan* and *Hindoostan* are still quite common. Specifically, *Hindustan* refers to the northern parts of India, but it is sometimes applied to the entire subcontinent.

8. After his mission to India, Elder Samuel Amos Woolley wrote, "When I first went to that land I of course had a favorable opinion of those people, as I had seen the reports of the Gentile Padres (priests) that they had made so many 'hopeful conversions.'" He said he had high hopes to convert both natives and whites. Thus Elder Woolley was somewhat informed regarding the work of other Christian groups before he arrived in India. See Samuel Amos Woolley to John Taylor, April 1855, Centerville, Delaware, in *The Mormon* 1 (April 28, 1855): 2.

9. "Supplement, 1853," *Millennial Star* 15 (January 1, 1853): 32ff. It is now recorded in Doctrine and Covenants 132.

10. "Supplement, 1853," *Millennial Star* 15 (January 1, 1853): 9–10. The "Supplement" was attached to *Millennial Star* 15 (January 1, 1853). The "Revelation" was reprinted in both parts of the publication.

11. Robert H. Skelton, Journal and Papers, Manuscripts and Special Collections, Brigham Young University Library, Provo, Utah, transcript of blessing. Skelton's journal is

actually a combination of writings from his original journal and elaborations that he added at a later date. It is difficult to discern which parts are original and which were added later as commentary or correction.

12. Present-day Payson, Utah.

13. William F. Carter, "Incidents from the Life of William F. Carter," in Kate B. Carter, comp., *Heart Throbs of the West* (Salt Lake City: Daughters of Utah Pioneers, 1943), 4:204–5. See also William Furlsbury Carter, Journal, October 1852–December 1853, Archives of The Church of Jesus Christ of Latter-day Saints, Salt Lake City, Utah; William Fotheringham, "Travels in India," *Juvenile Instructor* 11 (December 15, 1878): 284–85.

14. The Mormon settlement farthest south in Utah at that time.

15. Musser's journal has the group arriving on December 3. Fotheringham published another account in the *Juvenile Instructor* in which he used the 5th as the date of arrival. Because Musser's journals are still available and Fotheringham's are not, as of 1999, I have honored Musser's date.

16. Conway B. Sonne, *Ships, Saints, and Mariners: A Maritime Encyclopedia of Mormon Migration, 1830–1890* (Salt Lake City: University of Utah Press, 1987), 50.

17. Fotheringham, "Travels in India," *Juvenile Instructor* 11 (December 15, 1878): 285.

18. Horner actually paid the fares of the Australia, Hawaii, and China-bound elders as well, at a cost between five and six thousand dollars. See Musser, Journals, 2:16; Andrew Jenson, *Church Chronology*, 2d ed., rev. and enlarged (Salt Lake City: Deseret News Press, 1899), 47; and Amos Milton Musser, "East India Mission," *Juvenile Instructor* 6 (April 1, 1871): 55–56. For further references to Horner, see Susan Easton Black, comp., *Early LDS Membership Data* in *The LDS Collectors Library* (Salt Lake City: Infobase, 1995). Regarding Williams's contribution and other attempts to obtain donations, see Fotheringham, "Travels in India," *Juvenile Instructor* 11 (December 15, 1878): 285.

19. Musser, Journals, 2:16.

20. Carter, "Incidents," 4:207.

21. Sonne, *Ships, Saints, and Mariners*, 146.

22. Carter, "Incidents," 4:207.

23. Musser, Journals, 2:21.

24. William Fotheringham, "Travels in India," *Juvenile Instructor,* 12 (January 15, 1877): 16.

25. In 1871, Musser wrote: "Notwithstanding we had ate, slept, walked, sat, sang and prayed together, from the time we left San Francisco till after the disease broke out upon them no other person took ill. Here was another striking interposition of the Lord in our behalf, for which we were indeed thankful." By the time the missionaries reached India, "scarce a mark could be seen on their faces." See Musser, "East India Mission," *Juvenile Instructor* 6 (April 1, 1871): 55–56.

26. Conway B. Sonne, *Knight of the Kingdom: The Story of Richard Ballantyne* (Salt Lake City: Deseret Book, 1949), 76. The 1989 revised edition is essentially unchanged.

27. Carter, "Incidents," 4:207.

28. Sonne, *Knight of the Kingdom*, 78. In the early 1850s, the Church placed greater emphasis on obeying the Word of Wisdom. For example, in the Sixth General Epistle to the Church, the First Presidency (Brigham Young, Heber C. Kimball, and Willard Richards) included the following: "The conference voted to observe the words of wisdom, and particularly to dispense with the use of tea, coffee, snuff, and tobacco, and in this thing as well as others, what is good for the Saints in the mountains, is good for the Saints in other places" (James R. Clark, comp., *Messages of the First Presidency of The Church of Jesus Christ of Latter-day Saints*, 6 vols. [Salt Lake City: Bookcraft, 1965–75], 2:90). The epistle was dated September 22, 1851.

29. Carter, "Incidents," 4:207–8.

30. In 1871, Musser wrote: "The Lord preserved his servants from all the plagues of

that country. Do you not think that our temperate habits and our moral and devoted lives had something to do in promoting this preservation? I am sure they had." See *Juvenile Instructor* 6 (April 1, 1871): 55–56.

31. The tide that runs up the Hoogly River acts much like a funnel, pushing ever more water into the narrowing margins of the river. At Calcutta, the tide rises eleven feet.

32. Levi Savage, *Levi Savage, Jr., Journal,* comp. Lynn M. Hilton (Salt Lake City: John Savage Family Organization, 1966), 11.

33. Elder Savage mentioned that they had been gone from San Francisco for three months, but they had been away from Salt Lake City for six months.

2

OUR LABORS BEGIN IN CALCUTTA

Nothing we might have heard or read could have prepared us for life in India. Calcutta, where we first encountered India, was a remarkable mix of European and native, rich and poor, high and low, magnificent and degraded. We soon learned that Calcutta, "the City of Palaces," was not ancient, as were most of India's great cities. Calcutta was founded in 1690, on the site of several very small villages, one of which was called Kalikata, hence, the English name Calcutta. The name Kalikata honored the Hindu goddess Kali, the most fearful and dreaded consort of the god Shiva, the destroyer aspect of the Hindu *Trimurti*, or Trinity. Calcutta became the capital of British India in 1833.[1] From its humble and feeble beginnings, it had grown to a large metropolis boasting government buildings of such grandeur that they might have been in London, Paris, or Washington, D.C. But the streets of the native sections were "generally narrow and run irregularly through the city," wrote Elder Savage. "The European buildings are composed of brick and cement. They are generally large, two or three stories high, with flat roofs, and have the appearance of long standing."[2] According to Fotheringham's writings, Calcutta had a populace of 400,000, mostly natives, only 23,000 being Europeans or part-European.[3] More recent information leads to the conclusion that Fotheringham's

A street in Calcutta, about 1855

numbers were off by at least half, the population being around one million. Emigrants, artisans, and traders from "every nation under heaven" were seen in the streets of the great metropolis. But almost all of the power and social positions were in the hands of Europeans.

Calcutta was not a hospitable place. Why anyone had chosen to rule an empire as vast as India from such an insalubrious location, I do not know. The city was miserably hot and humid most of the year, infested by diseases of a most wretched variety: malaria, typhoid, cholera (there was a serious epidemic in progress at our arrival), dysentery, and so on. Hardly above sea level and almost under water during the monsoon season, Calcutta was a miserable place.[4]

Even its elegant grandeur had a negative side. The poor, and most of Calcutta's residents were poor (most of the native men wore nothing more than a loincloth), were cowed and demeaned by the offices, bungalows and mansions, carriages, and general haughtiness of the elite classes. The British in India had done much to elevate life for themselves and to ennoble themselves in their own eyes, but their efforts were focused on mammon, position, prestige, comforts, luxuries—the "fleshpots of Calcutta." Probably a more stiff-necked people never walked the earth than the *nabobs*, the pretentious Europeans of Calcutta and India. In their own eyes, their theaters, their evening carriage rides along the Strand (the road beside the Hoogly River) near the Maidan (parade park) surrounding Fort William, and their unending concern for protocol, manners, and impeccable behavior elevated them high above other men. Few Europeans walked anywhere. Most reclined in luxury while they were carried about in palanquins (Hindustani, *palki*), a covered litter, by two or four natives. The hard coldness of many of these people was unmatched throughout the world.

OUR FIRST FEW DAYS IN CALCUTTA

Elders Jones and West went ashore shortly after we docked at Calcutta. After asking directions and being carried in a palki a mile

View of the Bazaar Leading to Chitpore Road, *by James Baillie Fraser, 1819*

and a half through winding, crowded, noisy streets, they found number 2-1/2 Jaun Bazaar Street, the address where I would spend a significant part of my time over the next eight months. They remained there overnight and returned to the *Monsoon* with discouraging news. Their host for the night, Sister Sarah McCune, was "much disaffected"[5] by the news of the Church's announcement regarding the doctrine of plural marriage, which had been made public at the special conference in August 1852. Word of this doctrine and practice had arrived in India before our coming. "It appeared that while entering the Straits of Malacca," wrote Brother Fotheringham, "the mail steamer on her voyage from China to Calcutta, spoke [to] our ship, learning her name, where from and where bound to, and that there were thirteen 'Mormon' Elders on board, for India. The steamer arrived in Calcutta three weeks ahead of us, and gave the alarm. The newspapers published far and near that we were coming." We did not know it at that moment, but upon hearing of our imminent arrival, "Bishop [Daniel] Wilson, the Lord Bishop of Calcutta, called the clergy together, informing them that several 'Mormon' Elders would shortly arrive in India, and his counsel was to hold no converse with them, but to treat them with silent contempt, which counsel, as subsequent experience proved, they kept to the letter."[6] That's the way Fotheringham said it; and he said it correctly.

"We put our trunks into a boat which conveyed them and ourselves to the shore where considerable strife ensued among the natives who stood on the shore like a numerous army, all wanting the privilege of carrying our trunks to the place of deposit, for pay of course." Thus did Elder Savage describe our first encounter on Indian soil. He went on, saying, "But, we hired a cart which took them all safe at Sister McCune's, who occupies a portion of a large commodious house which is [owned] by Brother James P. Meik."[7] Robert Skelton wrote, "[Sister McCune] lives in a private compartment of the James Meik dwelling." The Meiks lived permanently at Acra Farm, a plantation on the Hoogly River eight miles south of Calcutta. Their large home was right on the river.

James Patrick Meik

Although our quarters in the Meik-McCune home were comfortable, the intelligence we gained upon arriving was discouraging. Elder Carter wrote, "We find the Church here in bad condition."[8] He was correct. We had expected to find a flourishing branch of around one hundred members or more. To our disappointment we found only eight. I noted, "of about 180 members, 170 natives, there is but about 6 or 8 left."[9] Most of the former members had fallen into apostasy, and one or two, like Sarah McCune's husband, Matthew, had been assigned duty in different parts, such as Rangoon, Burma, where he was engaged in the Second Anglo-Burmese War. Further, we learned that our fellow servants, Elder William Willes and Elder Joseph P. Richards, whom we had expected to meet and orient us regarding affairs and conditions, had departed Calcutta to teach the Gospel at cantonments up the Ganges plains. At latest mail, they were eight or nine hundred miles upcountry. And to make matters worse, the native converts had walked away from the Church as soon as they found that there was no material reward for membership. (Incidentally, when they heard of our arrival, they sent a delegation to Elder Jones to attempt to negotiate a settlement for becoming Mormons. Jones quickly despatched them.) I'll place all this in context a little later.

Without doubt, the greatest stumbling block in our way to success was plural marriage. Sister McCune said the doctrine of plural marriage had upset the branch and almost all the members had fallen away.[10] Fortunately, although Sister McCune was shaken, she did not fall, and neither did her noble husband. Matthew McCune was the first to introduce the Restored Gospel in Burma. I'll share his Burma experiences later.

James Patrick Meik and his wife, Mary Ann, proved to be among the stalwarts in the faith. "The kindness of himself and wife toward us was unbounded, and I trust it will never be forgotten by the Elders. His house was like [an] oasis in a desert to us during our stay."[11] They did everything in their power and according to their considerable means to further the work of the Lord. Brother Meik had been ordained to the Melchizedek Priesthood by Elder William Willes prior to our arrival. We always referred to him as elder, just like the rest of us. Although he was not set apart as a missionary, he was our companion until the last of us returned home to Zion. He emigrated later.

By three o'clock on April 27th, our first day on Indian soil, Brother Meik had arrived from Acra Farm. He knew the exact condition of every member and all who had fallen away. Our first decision was to call a conference of the missionaries and members to be held two days later, April 29th. Elder Meik's wife was among those who "had withdrawn from the communion table on account of the principle of plurality." This problem was resolved on April 30th during a meeting in which Elders Jones, Ballantyne, and West preached on the order of celestial marriage. "She made a good confession" and "was restored to fellowship."[12]

We busied ourselves acquiring clothing that was suitable for

Nathaniel Vary Jones

the climate. Fortunately, although most of us were almost destitute financially, the Siam elders had been given one hundred dollars beyond their needs in San Francisco. They shared these funds with the rest of us, and we were able to gain some comfort from the oppressive heat by donning new tropical apparel.[13]

THE FIRST CONFERENCE IN ASIA, APRIL 29, 1853

Our conference was in reality an organizing meeting for the East India Mission. We met at the "Latter-day Saints Lecture Hall," a chapel Elder Meik had constructed at 2-1/2 Jaun Bazaar Street. Meik, of Scottish descent, had been born in India. In various locations, we met one or another of his relatives. He had "a large number of businesses in Calcutta." Among them, he was a "civil architect" and "builder," which probably contributed to his ability to get the chapel built. This small chapel was undoubtedly the first Mormon chapel constructed anywhere in India or in East Asia. The "47 feet by 17" building was quite functional, having "a font at one end, a raised platform above, and provided with backed seats at the sides, and arm chairs in the centre, with large folding doors at both ends, in a public part of the city."[14] N. V. Jones presided over and conducted the meeting, which commenced at 10:00 A.M. My minutes of the meeting follow:

> At 10 o'clock our conference commenced. Present were Bros. [J. P.] Meik, Elder Saxton, also two sisters, including the Elders from America. Bro. Jones was unanimously appointed President of this branch of the Church in India.[15] I was appointed clerk for the conference. Had a good time. P.M. Came together again to continue our meeting. The following distributions of the Elders was made, viz Bros. Ballantyne, Skelton, and Owens for Madras, Bros. W. F. Carter and Wm Fotheringham for Dinapore about 260 miles from Calcutta, Bros. T. Leonard and S. A. Woolley for Chinsura about 30 miles from Calcutta, and Bro. Jones and myself to tarry at Calcutta. The brethren were all well satisfied and feel well.[16]

Elder Fotheringham noted in his *Juvenile Instructor* articles that Leonard and Woolley were to remain at Chinsura only until they heard from Hugh Findlay in Bombay regarding his need for assistance. As the story played itself out, I, Amos Musser, eventually went to Bombay with Leonard, not Woolley.

The situation among the Siam-bound elders was somewhat problematical. Chauncey W. West continued as president of the Siam Mission, but there was some tension among the four of them. That mission seemed doomed to failure from early on. Although I did not know of Elder Savage's thoughts at the time, I noted in reading his journal that he had wanted the Siam elders to leave the *Monsoon* at Singapore:

> March 20, 1853, Sunday. . . . Sometime previous to this, Brother Chauncey W. West, the President of the Siam Mission, said that he did not know but it might be best for the Siam Mission to disembark at Singapore and then re-embark on some vessel bound up the Gulf of Siam to Bancock, the capitol

of Siam. But there was little said upon the subject as far as I know until the day we should arrive at Singapore. Then the Siam Mission was called together to deliberate upon the subject of whether we should stop at Singapore or go on to Calcutta. But as we could get no particular information of the place, we concluded to continue our journey with our brethren to Calcutta. I must confess that at the time we were passing Singapore, I was very strongly impressed that was the place that we ought to have stopped, but I said nothing then for the ship was sailing along briskly, and we were too far along to effect such a landing.[17]

Elder West took some time at our conference to explain the plans of the Siam elders. He said they had "concluded to go to the island of Ceylon [modern Sri Lanka], and introduce the Gospel to that people; and in the Fall, or as soon as the way opens, two of us will go to Siam and introduce the Gospel there."[18] Elder West had visited the American consul, Dr. Charles Hoffnagle (the accepted spelling, although the elders spelled it at least four different ways), who showed himself a true gentleman and offered to help in any way possible. He also told West that because of the Anglo-Burmese War it would be impossible to travel overland to Siam. Furthermore, the winds were wrong until fall when the monsoons would shift and make passage possible. After surveying the transportation situation in Calcutta for a week or so and visiting Chinsura with Elders Woolley and Leonard, West returned to Calcutta (with Elder Joseph Richards, who had just returned from his travels upcountry) and called a meeting of the Siam-bound elders. It was held on Thursday, May 12th, to "decide upon some plan that would enable us to go to Siam or some other place." The four elders decided "that Elders West and Dewey should take sufficient money to pay their passage to Ceylon (for we had not enough money [to pay] all of our passages to any place) and precede directly there. Elder Ludington and myself [Savage] were to remain here until the way should open up for us to go to Burma, Siam, or to follow them to Ceylon. I now, more forcefully than ever feel the impropriety of our not stopping at Singapore."[19] Funds being low, they paid full fare for one elder and the other had to go as his servant, at half price. In hindsight, Savage was probably right. Considering Luddington's lack of success when he did teach the Gospel in Bangkok, perhaps four missionaries would have failed there instead of one if they had all reached that place. We will never know.

Three days later, on Sunday morning, May 15th, Elders West and Dewey left for Ceylon. Elders Luddington and Savage "accompanied them to the river and saw them safe on board a Lighter [a large open barge used primarily to load and unload ships anchored in a harbor]."[20] They sailed forty-one miles down the Hoogly to Diamond Harbor, where they met the steamer that took them to Ceylon. I'll return to West and Dewey later.

I mentioned that Elder Joseph Richards returned to Calcutta with Elder West on May 11th. With his arrival, it was possible to learn more of the history of our mission. Elder Richards and Elder Willes had done many good works before the *Monsoon* delivered us to those strange shores.

NOTES

1. In 1912, three years after Musser's death, the capital of India was moved from Calcutta to New Delhi. New Delhi has continued as the capital of the Republic of India since independence in 1947.

2. Savage, *Journal*, April 27, 1853, 17.

3. William Fotheringham, "Travels in India," *Juvenile Instructor* 12 (March 1, 1877): 52.

4. In 1971, Geoffrey Moorhouse wrote in *Calcutta* (New York: Holt, Rinehart and Winston, 1971; new afterword, 1983): "The truth is that almost everything popularly associated with Calcutta is highly unpleasant and sometimes very nasty indeed" (5). "It was, all the same, lunacy for anyone not born and bred in Bengal (or, at least, in India) to settle down here and make an Empire from it. Everything in Nature was against it, the climate most of all" (10).

5. Skelton, Journal, April 27, 1853 (typescript, 53). Brigham Young University Library, Provo, Utah. Robert Skelton wrote further, "Sister McCune feels very much opposed to Polygamy, not only in modern days but nearly finds fault with Abraham the devout Patriarch of old, with his twelve sons" (Journal, April 28, 1853, 12 [typescript 53]). It should be noted, however, that Sarah McCune had been baptized on July 14, 1852, by her husband, Matthew, at Acra Farm. Their son Henry Frederick McCune was baptized at the same time. Only twelve days later, Matthew left for Rangoon, where his military obligations took him. He was the first convert in the family and the stronger advocate of the Latter-day Saint faith. Chances are that if he had been at home to support her and examine the new doctrine with her, she might have responded differently. See Matthew McCune, Journal, 1851–56, Daughters of Utah Pioneers Library, Salt Lake City, Utah; microfilm, Archives of The Church of Jesus Christ of Latter-day Saints, Salt Lake City, Utah.

6. William Fotheringham, "Travels in India," *Juvenile Instructor* 12 (February 1, 1877): 28.

7. Savage, *Journal,* April 27, 1853, 12. The impression has existed that Matthew and Sarah McCune owned or controlled the large bungalow at number 2-1/2 Jaun Bazaar Street. This impression was probably founded on the memories of Henry Frederick McCune, who reported that while age thirteen at the time of the Utah missionaries' arrival in Calcutta, he met the missionaries at the dock and with a group of servants and carts escorted them to the McCune bungalow (forty rooms) where a room and a servant were assigned to each missionary. He also mentions that Chauncey Walker West "took me in his arms and said, 'Brethren, this is the little man I saw in my vision last night.'" This seems questionable because West was in the McCune home that night and hardly needed a vision of the boy, who must have been there for West to see. Yet journals mention young Henry meeting and guiding the elders to the McCune home. He served as interpreter for the group. In an article by Henry F. McCune that appeared in ["Life Sketch"], *Utah Genealogical and Historical Magazine* 6 (October 1925): 144–52, Henry refers to himself and the family as aristocrats. The choice of words is interesting: *nabobs* would probably be more accurate. The McCunes were not of the British aristocracy but rather of that segment of society that elevated itself in India because it was possible to hire servants of all kinds for a pittance. Matthew McCune was not a commissioned officer but a sergeant major, a noncommissioned rank. His posterity has sometimes spoken of him as "major," a military rank he did not hold. See also George M. McCune, "Henry Frederick McCune, Autobiography and Biography of His Life and Works, A.D. May 31, 1840 to December 15, 1924," typescript, 1971, Archives of The Church of Jesus Christ of Latter-day Saints, Salt Lake City, Utah.

8. Carter, "Incidents," 4:208.

9. Musser, Journals, 2:54.

10. Fotheringham, *Juvenile Instructor* 12 (February 1, 1877): 28.

11. William Fotheringham, "Travels in India," *Juvenile Instructor* 12 (February 15, 1877): 44.

12. Carter, "Incidents," 4:209.

13. Savage, *Journal,* April 29, 1853, 12. Temperatures during April are typically among the hottest of the year. The thermometer sometimes stands at 120 degrees Fahrenheit with humidity near 100 percent. Most of the elders noted their suffering in their journals. For example, Carter wrote: "The heat here is very oppressive; the coldest place that I can find in the shade, I sweat like a man over a furnace. We will not see a white man in the streets from ten in the morning until five in the evening; they cannot endure it" (Carter, "Incidents," 208–9).

14. William Willes, "Letter from William Willes: The Gospel in Calcutta" [To Samuel W. Richards, January 7, 1852, Calcutta], *Millennial Star* 14 (March 15, 1852): 90–91. See also Skelton, Journal, 81 [typescript, 53]. Number 2-1/2 Jaun Bazaar Street is close to the heart of the busiest part of Calcutta. Nothing remains of the chapel or of Meik's home, which was probably taken down and built over even while the mission was underway.

15. Several of the elders recorded this point differently. Savage wrote, "[Jones] was unanimously sustained as President of the Calcutta Branch." Carter recorded, "Brother Jones was appointed to be President of the Calcutta Mission and over Saints in India." And Fotheringham said, "Elder N. V. Jones was unanimously chosen by the brethren to be the President of the East India Mission." Suffice it to say, Jones presided over the mission's activities as well as those of the Calcutta Branch until he departed for home.

16. Musser, Journals, 2:54; see also N. V. Jones to S. W. Richards, *Millennial Star* 15 (August 20, 1853): 558–59.

17. Savage, *Journal,* March 20, 1853, 9.

18. East India Mission Index, Minutes of Conference Held in Calcutta, April 29, 1853, Archives of The Church of Jesus Christ of Latter-day Saints, Salt Lake City, Utah.

19. Savage, *Journal,* May 12, 1853, 14.

20. Savage, *Journal,* May 15, 1853, 14.

3

FOUNDING THE EAST INDIA MISSION

On April 19, 1849, Private Thomas Metcalf of the 98th Regiment of the Queen's forces in India wrote to the *Millennial Star* in England. He had "received a tract, entitled 'Divine Authority,' on the question was Joseph Smith sent of God." The tract, written by Elder Orson Pratt, "struck me with astonishment," he wrote, "its words were so powerful and unquestionable, agreeing with the scriptures, revealing things that have been so long hidden." Metcalf had first heard of the Latter-day Saints while serving in China. In Lahore, India,[1] he had read *Divine Authority; or, Was Joseph Smith Sent of God*, and another tract concerning the kingdom of God. He believed what he read and asked "what [he] should do to be saved from the wrath to come." He closed by asking for a "few tracts which will instruct me in the things concerning the kingdom of God, and concerning the prophecies of the scriptures that have been fulfilled, and of those which have to be fulfilled."[2]

Metcalf had a salutary effect on the East India Mission. Before our missionaries arrived in India and while he was stationed in Peshawar, Northwest Frontier Provinces, he was struck down by fever and ague, usually malarial, in November 1850. Prior to his death, however, he received additional LDS literature from the Church in England, and, having read it and believed, he distributed the tracts and other materials among his friends and fellow soldiers. He could be counted the first missionary for the Church in India, but he had not been baptized. He died unbaptized but accepting the Gospel. One of his friends, Lance Corporal Edward Jones, corresponded with Church representatives in England, and when Elders William Willes and Joseph Richards were sent to India, they continued correspondence with him until Willes found him at a cantonment at Dugshai, in the foothills of the Himalayas.

Private Metcalf's letter was part of the impetus that brought our missionaries to India, but he was not the only enquirer. The records we have gathered at the Church historian's office, where I have worked for some time, reveal another interesting incident leading to the opening of Latter-day Saint missionary work in Calcutta. For example, a letter from Benjamin Richey of Nephi, Utah, to George A. Smith, Historian and General Church Recorder, tells of his arrival along with fellow Mormon George Barber at Calcutta in late 1849. They knew nothing of Thomas Metcalf, but they did meet others who were seeking the truth.

Having been baptized on January 27, 1849, by Elder Henry Savage, and being as yet unordained to the priesthood, Barber and Richey embarked as seamen on the bark *Sharp* on February 8th. Their voyage took them to Calcutta and then on to Singapore, Penang Island (famous for nutmeg, mace, and sugar) off the coast of Malaya, and back to Calcutta. They docked there in December 1849. The crew was discharged because the ship needed repairs. Barber and Richey found temporary quarters at a sailors' home.

There they became acquainted with a "city missionary and scripture reader," an older man named Maurice White. They regularly joined him in praying and reading and pondering the Bible. According to Richey's letter, one morning White read a chapter from Corinthians by the Apostle Paul. Richey asked him what he thought it meant. Unable to answer, White returned the question. Richey's answer, based on Latter-day Saint doctrine, satisfied

Boats on the Ganges, by J. C. Armytage from a drawing by William Daniell

White, and he invited Richey and Barber to join him that night in a meeting of a group who were leaning toward the theology and doctrines of the Plymouth Brethren. An evangelical sect, the Plymouth Brethren rejected the formality of high church practices. Like their brethren elsewhere, this group had no minister or set organization, but they loved and sought after the truth. Barber and Richey were warmly accepted, but they found themselves short of knowledge regarding the Restored Gospel. Fortunately, they did have the Book of Mormon, Elder Parley P. Pratt's *A Voice of Warning*, Orson Pratt's *Remarkable Visions*, tracts on baptism and priesthood, and Orson Spencer's *Letters*.[3] As often happens, some of the group soon rejected their testimony and teachings, but James Patrick Meik and his wife, Mary Ann, Maurice White, William A. Sheppard, and a few others developed a strong interest in the Latter-day Saint message. When Richey and Barber sailed for London, they carried the request and a few rupees from this group for more printed literature and missionaries.[4]

Shortly after they arrived in England, they found a letter in the *Millennial Star* from William A. Sheppard, writing for the group, asking for more information about the Church and placing various theological problems before Elder Orson Spencer.[5] It had been written February 6, 1850, not long after the young sailors embarked for home. Barber and Richey soon met with Elder Franklin D. Richards in London, he being very interested in the enquirers at Calcutta, and shared what they knew. They also forwarded the desired tracts and literature to the group in India.

Details are sketchy, but around the time Barber and Richey likely reached London (we don't know the actual date), the combined effect of the letters and the information from these young sailors might have led Elder George B. Wallace to call Elder Joseph Richards, who was on his way to India as a sailmaker on a large merchant ship, the Indiaman *Gloriosa*, as a missionary to East India.

Elder Richards arrived in Calcutta in mid-June 1851, made contact with the Plymouth Brethren, and on June 22d, baptized

James Patrick and Mary Ann Meik, Matthew McCune, and Maurice White, in the tank (reservoir) at Acra Farm, Meik's home. These four were the first converts baptized in India and Asia.[6] William A. Sheppard did not accept some of Elder Richards's explanations of the Gospel. His baptism was to await a later time.

The three brethren were soon ordained to offices in the priesthood. Richards ordained White an elder and made him branch president over the Wanderer's Branch on June 29, 1851, a week after his baptism.[7] Elder Richards turned the care of the little flock over to White and within a few days embarked on the *Gloriosa* and sailed for England.

ELDER LORENZO SNOW CALLS WILLES AND FINDLAY TO INDIA

With the exception of the references in the *Millennial Star* and a few items Elder Hugh Findlay has supplied for my perusal, I, Brother Musser, don't have much information with which to re-create Elder Lorenzo Snow's involvement with India. In October 1849, eight months after Elder Snow was called as an Apostle, he was sent to open missionary work in Italy. His trip to England, like ours to India, took six months. He made his way to Italy by July 1850 and set to work. Eventually, he had the Book of Mormon translated and printed in Italian. But he ranged over a larger field than Italy alone, for he also included Switzerland and Malta, a small island south of Italy in the Mediterranean Sea, in his mission. It was his intention to make Malta a center for the distribution of Latter-day Saint literature and scriptures. Although Elder Snow eventually visited Malta, this plan never came to fruition. He did part of his work in England, particularly the printing of the Italian language Book of Mormon, and this placed him in touch with developments in India. He decided to include India in his mission's jurisdiction.

Sensing that India offered a large unharvested mission field, Elder Snow called two additional British elders to serve there.[8] In

William Willes

addition, he called William Willes to Calcutta to continue Joseph Richards's work. And to Bombay and the western side of India, Elder Snow called Hugh Findlay. It was Elder Snow's intention from the beginning to travel home by way of India when the time came. Unfortunately, even though both elders planned for Snow's visit and needed his encouragement, because of transportation delays and a deadline to reach the Valley by mid-1852, Elder Snow was forced to return home by the Atlantic rather than by way of India, the Pacific, and around the world.

In his writings, Brother Willes commented on the circumstances of his call. In the spring of 1851 he felt moved to do more for the Church, and hearing that Elder Snow was going to be in attendance at the Deptford Branch where he resided, Willes implored the Lord to inspire Elder Snow if he, Willes, were appropriate "for a more extensive sphere of usefulness." Following the meeting the next Sunday, Elder Snow talked with Willes about possible mission service and his ability in languages. The next day Elder Snow extended to Willes a call to missionary service in India. "On arriving home to my wife," wrote Willes, "and telling her I was called to go to India on a mission, she clinched her hands, became red in the face, and jumped across the room with much emotion. She soon became reconciled to my leaving and went to work to get employment . . . and Fred, my eldest son [age twelve], obtained employment at a candy and confectioner's establishment, and Harriet [age eight] staid at home and took care of little John [age three] and Anney [age seven]." Clearly, Willes's call demanded sacrifices of the entire family.

On August 30, 1851, three days before he sailed for Calcutta on the *Queen*, an East Indiaman, William Willes wrote a farewell letter to the *Star*, as the *Latter-day Saints' Millennial Star* was often called.[9] Almost four months later, on December 25, 1851, he disembarked at Calcutta. For several days, the *Queen* had stood at anchor off the sand heads before sailing up the Hoogly and finally being pulled to anchor by a "steamer" tug. His voyage had been long, but he had been fully engaged. While on board, he had taught the Gospel to many soldiers and sailors, and an elderly woman from India had given him a few lessons in the Hindustani language.[10]

Upon his arrival, Willes found six Church members to greet him. He also found that Maurice White, branch president, had left for London to be with a larger congregation of members. Before leaving, he had baptized John Grundy and his wife, Maria, and an Indian woman named Anna. Before long, Willes baptized "nine natives—five Christian, and four Pagan." He was already arranging for the translation of Elder Lorenzo Snow's tract *Ancient Gospel Restored* into "Bengalee and Hindoostanee."[11]

On January 7, 1852, when Elder Willes wrote his first report to the *Star*, he was "bounding with grateful emotions of thanksgiving that He has made me and my brethren the instruments in His hand for spreading such glorious tidings in a land filled with

Hugh Findlay

'darkness, selfishness, and cruel habitations.'"[12] For the moment, matters were moving forward in a positive way.

Elder Hugh Findlay received first notice of his call to Bombay in a letter from Elder Snow, dated September 1, 1851, one day before Elder Willes sailed from England. In a kind and un-demanding manner, Elder Snow wrote: "How would it suit your feelings and circumstances to perform a Mission to Bombay, India? Could you raise the means from your Conference [district], that you would need to perform such a mission, provided it should be wisdom for you to go?" Elder Snow asked for an answer later that week.[13] Despite another realistic letter from Snow—"I should like you to go on this mission if circumstances are favorable and you think you could *live* through it. You must be well aware that it is no easy mission. A strange country, a hot climate, pestilential diseases, &c., &c., are no pleasant things to encounter"—Findlay soon accepted the call.[14]

Brother Findlay, a widower who had lost his first family to disease, possibly diphtheria, in 1847, was serving in 1851 as president of the Hull Conference. He had previously shown his ability and zeal as a missionary for the Restored Gospel. Born in New Milns, Scotland, in 1822, Findlay had developed the ability to wield an effective pen.

Elder Franklin D. Richards, president of the European Mission, which included the British Isles, released Findlay from his calling and encouraged him to raise in his conference the twenty-five pounds needed for his passage. The funds were quickly raised. The twenty-five pound figure was based on Willes's cost. As matters worked out, however, Findlay was given passage on a steamship at a much-reduced rate. The voyage, which began on October 20th, took only three weeks. Passage was by way of the Isthmus of Suez in Egypt. The canal that now serves so well was not completed until 1869 (the same year that the transcontinental railroad in Utah was finished), but with a short overland passage of 107 miles, one's trip by sail was reduced by thirty-five hundred miles and two or three months.

WILLES LABORS ALONE FROM DECEMBER 1851 TO JULY 1852

In many ways, the work Elder Willes performed as a lone missionary was representative of what was done and how affairs were going to move through the remainder of the mission. He ranged over a fairly broad territory, setting up teaching stations wherever conditions appeared promising. Although he (and later we) directed his proselytizing first to the English-speaking populace, he almost immediately shared the Gospel message with native Indians of any caste. His mode of teaching was similar to that used in England and elsewhere; that is, he came to India armed with tracts and other literature and shared such information with all whom showed an interest in his message. He even placed a copy of the Book of Mormon and other books and tracts in the Calcutta library.[15] A well-educated man, Willes regularly used the hall Brother Meik had constructed for long series of lectures (forty, twenty, twelve, and so on) regarding the principles and doctrines of Mormonism. Seeing that most interested natives were unable to read his literature in English, Willes immediately set about getting tracts translated into the local languages. In this he was greatly assisted by Brother Meik, who had been born in India and knew some local languages. Even Willes's relationship with other Christian ministers and missionaries was a sample of our later experience throughout the country. Initially, his antagonists were few, but as he achieved a measure of success, he was verbally attacked in his lecture meetings and in the press. And his disappointments with Indian "converts" proved to be the universal pattern of our mission.

As I have said, when Elder Willes wrote his first letter home to President Franklin D. Richards in England, he was "bounding with grateful emotions" that he had been called to preach the Gospel in India. His words revealed a man who might have believed he could single-handedly, with the Lord's help, conquer all of India with the message of the Restoration. Matters were progressing well. Several soldiers, who had sailed to India with Willes on the *Queen*, were ready to be baptized; Meik's lecture hall was about completed; the Indian woman named Anna, who had been baptized by Maurice White, was promising interest among her people; and William Sheppard, who had written to the *Star* for more information, was again showing interest in the Gospel message.[16]

Willes was still positive four months later. His lectures were well attended; he was baptizing regularly, mostly natives; and his translation work was progressing. He was gaining some use of the Bengali language. But he was experiencing steadily increasing harassment from the Christian ministerial corps.

On May 15th, Willes reported Church membership of 189: there were 170 *ryots* (native farmers and cultivators) and 19 others, including several high-caste Indians and some Europeans. Most of the Indians were already Christians. Their desertion of their previous churches "caused a great stir" among the Protestant missionaries. No small wonder. The native Christians of that area, Calcutta and the surrounding territory, had been hard won from their Hindu origins.

Willes mentioned more than once the famous Baptist missionary William Carey and his associates William Ward and Joshua Marshman. When Carey began his work in the Danish colony at Serampore, twenty miles north of Calcutta, in the 1790s, he struggled not only against the power of local religious and social traditions and an enervating climate but also against the displeasure of the English East India Company that wanted no "missionaries and school teachers" in the country. But Carey and his colleagues persisted and did a tremendous work. Among his greatest accomplishments was his gift as a linguist and translator. From his pen came translations of the Holy Bible into many Indian languages. From his devotion to Jesus Christ came many converts to Christianity.

As missionaries of the Restored Gospel, we considered the *padre* (the name universally used for Christian priests and ministers in India) to be teachers of incorrect doctrine. But we knew that when we taught our version of Christianity and baptized members of their congregations, we invited warfare at the pulpit and in the press. Time and experience proved that the established Christian denominations had the upper hand, but for the moment, Willes was excited with prospects for our Church's future.

Willes's work with native Indians seemed to hold great promise. Anna, the first Indian convert, was the daughter of Christo Paul, a high-caste Brahmin who had reportedly been the first fruit of William Carey's ministry. Anna was baptized by Maurice White before he sailed for London but was confirmed by Elder Willes shortly after his arrival in Calcutta. She had struggled for four years to understand the conflicts among the various Christian groups and the lack of evidence that they exhibited of the spiritual gifts and powers of the Primitive Church. On the day after her confirmation, she became sick and asked for the administration of oil and the laying on of hands by Elder Willes. She was miraculously healed. According to Willes, "she exclaimed, '*Esso Mussee, such ah hay*' (Jesus Christ is true)." She told Willes that "a whole church of native Episcopalian Christians . . . desire to be baptized as soon as matters can be arranged in relation to their social position, &c." Elder Willes may not have fully understood what was meant by his own words: "as soon as matters can be arranged in relation to their social position, &c."[17] India has the most complex and restrictive social system in the world: caste, or as the Indians call it, *jati*. Willes noted converts from various Brahmin castes, writers and doctors, in particular, as well as ryots, who were of the *Vaisha*, the third caste, which also included merchants. Even though converts from such disparate castes claimed to be Latter-day Saints and even took on names of LDS Apostles (Brigham, Orson, John, Parley, Thomas, Wilford, Amasa, George, Lorenzo, Erastus, Franklin, and William[18]), they hardly associated with one another. Because of caste traditions, taking the sacrament from one another's hands was difficult. While caste should have been set aside when these people became Christians, the residue of the past was not quick to slip away.

Castes traditionally number four: *Brahmin* (priests and scholars), *Kshatriya* (warriors, politicians, and public servants), *Vaisha* (merchants, businessmen, and farmers), and *Shudra* (servants, serfs, and menials). But in practice there are several thousand different castes and subcastes that are divided according to occupation, ritual practices, marriage, eating restrictions, and so on. In addition, a large number of Indians, the untouchables, have no caste and are not allowed entry into Hindu temples. Their shadows are said to defile and pollute any upper-caste person on whom they fall.[19] Caste controls every action of those under its rule. But like these first missionaries from Utah, those who live under the influence of the caste system seldom consider its authority. Indians, like members of many other cultures, simply live and accept the influence of their ways as proper and right.

The power of tradition and caste is so strong that if a person leaves Hinduism to join another religion, such as Christianity, that person is stripped of any rights to occupation, family, and home. For this reason, the Protestant missionaries who baptized early converts soon recognized that if provision were not made for their welfare, they would perish. Some newly baptized Christians were hired to do such tasks as cooking, cleaning the mission compound, gardening, and the like. Those who were literate and of higher caste were appointed as catechists, teachers, and writers. Others helped with translation projects. As time passed and numbers of converts increased, finding jobs for every new member became difficult, and what had begun as a legitimate means of sustaining the disenfranchised deteriorated into a dole. Wherever Christian missionaries served, they found that Indians generally became Christians in mass movements. That is, entire communities or segments of a community converted together; thus no one lost their relationships and position.

By the 1850s, some dishonest Indians had learned to play the various Christian missions off against each other to see which church would offer the most sustaining help. Unbeknownst to us, we Latter-day Saints were made part of this game. Several converts manifested intelligence, translation ability, and the willingness to teach Willes and others the local languages, and they seemed to be sincere in their newly found faith. But when they learned that we had nothing of material worth to offer, whether former Brahmins or ryots, they walked away, and we didn't see them again. In late 1852, after Willes and Joseph Richards left for northern India, Elder J. P. Meik and his counselors in the Calcutta Branch presidency "cut off" the native members of the Church when they demanded "money and blankets" or they "would not remain in the Church any longer." Throughout the country our experience was the same.[20] Anna seems to have been about the only exception.

By May and June 1852, Elder Willes was still excited by his apparent success. His Indian congregation, consisting primarily of farmers from miles around, was growing, and he needed reinforcements. His enthusiasm at that time was largely responsible for the call of the Utah missionaries in August 1852. What Willes didn't know was that the dirty springs and rivulets of opposition that he had been experiencing during his first few months would grow into a fetid river of resistance and abuse. Brother Willes's experience among the Anglo-Indian population of Calcutta was tragic. In his first letter to England, he mentioned lecturing to "about 100 respectable Europeans and half-castes or *Eurasians*, among which were some editors, missionaries, and ministers, who conducted themselves very respectfully."[21] The large numbers in attendance did not continue, but interest remained quite high for several months. Many native *baboos*, native clerks who write English, attended and expressed interest. Even the newspapers were willing to print evenhanded articles about Mormonism.

But in March "one of the dissenting ministers . . . commenced to shew his teeth." Various slanderous anti-Mormon stories were circulated, and the debate heated up in the newspapers. For example, the Solomon Spaulding story regarding the supposed origins of the Book of Mormon was preached from some Protestant pulpits, and the mouths of our detractors blasted polygamy. One Indian, Dwarkinath Bans, a member of the Royal College of Surgeons, London, came to Willes for correct information regarding our doctrines. He had seen "reports in the Newspapers about Brigham Young having driven through the streets of Deseret in a long van, with sixteen wives, and fourteen of them with infants at the breast, and also that he had ninety wives in all, and another of the brethren thirty."[22] Elder Willes lent him *The Voice of Warning* and labored with him for a time. In June 1852, Elder Willes reported angry reprisals by "Sectarian Missionaries" who told their congregations of native ryots that "if they join us, they will become *Mussulmen* [Muslims], and be obliged to have many wives, &c., and that *Joe Smith* bought three hundred thousand Mormons with the gold he found in California, &c. &c."[23] Even in far-off India, the great hatred of Joseph Smith, our doctrines, and especially our practice of plural wives was well known and slandered in churches and newspapers throughout the area where Willes worked.

Mormonism became a lively topic in Calcutta. A number of articles, pro and con, appeared in the *Citizen*, the *Hurkaru*, the *Morning Chronicle* and other newspapers. Even some of Elder Findlay's newspaper articles from Bombay made their way into the Calcutta press. Willes said he had never seen such "bitterness of spirit" manifested by the priests and ministers at home in England. Through all this, Elder Willes continued his lecture meetings, his preaching trips into the countryside (twenty miles in any direction from Calcutta, often on roadless tracks), and his work with a Brahmin convert named Brigham Prankisto (who soon fell away) and J. P. Meik on various translations into Bengali and Hindustani.

During the summer months and early fall, India's monsoon season, anti-Mormon attacks continued, and Willes reported disturbances in his meetings. He took this problem to the police superintendent who sent four *chokidars* (policemen) to the next meeting, and the previous disturbers sat silent. Generally, however, the reaction of Willes's opposition was argument, anti-Mormon articles in the newspapers, and cold indifference.

ELDER JOSEPH RICHARDS RETURNS TO INDIA

On July 20, 1852, Elder Joseph Richards arrived at Calcutta, having been sent by Elder Lorenzo Snow to assist Elder Willes. Richards had commenced LDS missionary work in India a year before. Now he returned with a call for an extended period of service. He had left London in January on the bark *Elizabeth*, but the voyage was slow, taking almost seven months. Fortunately, not all of that time was at sea. The *Elizabeth* anchored at the Cape of Good Hope in South Africa for a month. Richards took full advantage and did some teaching of the Gospel and distributed tracts and pamphlets, initiating LDS missionary work in that land. A day following Richards's arrival at Madras, he took ship on the *Lucknow* and worked his way during the ten-day passage to Calcutta. When he arrived, Richards was in good health and high spirits. He had enjoyed good weather during the entire journey.[24]

On July 25th, Richards's first Sunday back in Calcutta, he heard his friend and convert Matthew McCune offer his farewell sermon prior to leaving the next day for military service in Burma. Richards was pleased to find that William Willes and J. P. Meik had ordained McCune an elder on April 11, 1852. Only a few days before Richards arrived, on July 14th, McCune had baptized his wife, Sarah Elizabeth, and son, Henry, in Meik's tank at Acra Farm.[25]

Although he felt McCune's loss, Willes was inspired with fresh courage and hopes by Richards's presence. Their companionship proved to be strong and energetic. During August, September, and October, they continued to labor in and around Calcutta. As the monsoon rains slackened, audiences at their lectures increased somewhat. But from September, they were receiving promptings of the Spirit, dreams and the "still small voice within," encouraging them to move to other cities. Although the Church members in Calcutta felt weak and hesitated to face alone the hostile pressures coming from antagonists, they ultimately concurred with the missionaries' decision. J. P. Meik accepted the call as presiding elder in Calcutta, and John Grundy and Eldred Saxon agreed to serve as his counselors.[26]

On November 10, 1852, while we Utah missionaries were traveling by wagon train to southern California, Elders Willes and Richards departed on foot from Calcutta on a trip that would extend well over a thousand miles into the northern part of India.

NOTES

1. Lahore is in present-day Pakistan.

2. Thomas Metcalf, "Letter from a Sincere Enquirer," *Millennial Star* 11 (August 15, 1849): 252.

3. Full titles of these pamphlets and books are as follows: Parley P. Pratt, *A Voice of Warning and Instruction to All People, Containing a Declaration of the Faith and Doctrine of the Church of the Latter-day Saints, Commonly Called Mormons* (New York: W. Sandford, 1837), 216

pages; Orson Pratt, *Interesting Account of Several Remarkable Visions, and of the Late Discovery of Ancient American Records* (Edinburgh: Ballantyne and Hughes, 1840), 31 pages; and Orson Spencer, *Letters Exhibiting the Most Prominent Doctrines of the Church of Jesus Christ of Latter-day Saints* (Liverpool: Orson Spencer, 1848), 244 pages.

4. Benjamin Richey to George A. Smith, December 2, 1865, Nephi, Utah. This letter is cited and quoted in Manuscript History of the East India Mission, Archives of The Church of Jesus Christ of Latter-day Saints.

5. W. A. Sheppard, "Letter to Orson Spencer" [February 6, 1850], *Millennial Star* 12 (May 15, 1850): 155–57.

6. Joseph Richards, "Introduction of the Gospel to Calcutta.—Baptisms, &c." [Richards to Elder Savage, June 24, 1851, Acra Farm, Calcutta], *Millennial Star* 13 (September 1, 1851): 283–84.

7. Journal History of the East India Mission, Branch Record, Friday, December 26, 1851, 1, Archives of The Church of Jesus Christ of Latter-day Saints.

8. "Mission to the East Indies," editorial note, *Millennial Star* 13 (August 15, 1851): 250.

9. William Willes, "Departure of Elder Willes for Calcutta" [August 30, 1851, London], *Millennial Star* 13 (November 15, 1851): 348–49.

10. William Willes, Journal and Reminiscences, 1851–1885, by date, Archives of The Church of Jesus Christ of Latter-day Saints.

11. "East India Mission," *Millennial Star* 14 (May 1, 1852): 153. This brief notice carried information garnered by the *Star* from a letter from Willes to William Cook in London.

12. William Willes, "The Gospel in Calcutta" [Willes to Samuel W. Richards, January 7, 1852, Calcutta], *Millennial Star* 14 (March 15, 1852): 91.

13. Lorenzo Snow, Birmingham, England, to Hugh Findlay, Hull, September 1, 1851, in Hugh Findlay, *Missionary Journals of Hugh Findlay, India–Scotland,* comp. Ross and Linnie Findlay, (Ephraim, Utah: n.p, 1973), 1.

14. Ibid.; Lorenzo Snow, Preston, England, to Hugh Findlay, n.d.

15. During his voyage to India, Willes noted lending to fellow passengers the following: Tracts, 1st and 2nd series, *The Voice of Warning, Divine Authority, Remarkable Visions,* the Book of Mormon, *Kingdom of God,* and the Doctrine and Covenants. He mentioned other literature later. The Calcutta library was a large Greco-Roman style building that could have been comfortably situated in any large Western European city.

16. See Willes, *Millennial Star* 14 (May 15, 1852): 90–91.

17. Ibid.

18. William Willes, "Rapid Spread of the Gospel in Hindoostan" [Willes to Franklin D. Richards, March 24, 29, and April 6, 1852, Calcutta], *Millennial Star* 14 (June 26, 1852): 285–87.

19. Mohandas K. Gandhi focused much attention on this large segment, perhaps twenty percent, of India's populace. He called them *harijan,* the children of God. With Indian independence in 1947 and the implementation of the constitution in 1950, caste was made illegal and all social groups were granted access to places of worship. More recently, the word *dalit* has come into use to designate the untouchable or repressed classes.

20. William Willes and Joseph Richards, "The East India Mission" [Willes and Richards to Samuel W. Richards, February 1853, Agra], *Millennial Star* 15 (May 21, 1853): 331–32. This letter confirms facts widely observed in mission literature concerning India.

Following his mission, Elder Samuel Amos Woolley wrote somewhat regarding this problem. In his series in *The Mormon* 1 (June 9, 1855): 3, he insists that the natives were merely bought to be Christians. He says they were "measurably honest and sincere in their religion, and now they are sincere in nothing." He derides the Protestants for spending so much money buying converts. "I have talked with them for hours at a time, and told them over and over again that if they were Mormon Christian (as that is the way they designate, by calling them Baptist Christian, Mormon Christian, &c., and some time 'I am a Christian for Padre Sahab,' so, and so, calling him by name) they must be so for the love of truth, and not for money, and still they would come time after time and try to get some price to be Christians, and some have said, 'how can we be Christians for you if you will not pay us anything' and others would come hearing we were just from America (as the American Missionaries are generally the most flush with money for that purpose) and say we are getting eight rupees a month of Padre Sahab, so and so, for being a Christian, now if you will give me just one rupee in advance of their present pay let that be five, eight, or ten rupees." He said that the group of natives that Meik sent away came back when the American elders arrived. Jones sent them away again.

21. Willes, *Millennial Star* 14 (May 15, 1852): 91.

22. Willes, *Millennial Star* 14 (June 26, 1852): 286.

23. William Willes, "Glorious Success of the Truth in Hindoostan" [Willes to Samuel W. Richards, May 2, 1852, Calcutta], *Millennial Star* 14 (July 10, 1852): 316.

24. William Willes and Joseph Richards, "The Work in Hindostan: Extracts of Letters From Elders William Willes, and Joseph Richards" [Letters to Samuel W. Richards, 3 and 4 August 1852, Calcutta], *Millennial Star* 14 (October 16, 1852): 541–42.

25. McCune, Journal, by date.

26. Willes and Richards, *Millennial Star* 15 (May 21, 1853): 331.

4

TRAVELS TO DELHI AND BEYOND BEGIN

William Willes and Joseph Richards had chosen the best time of year to begin their missionary travels. November, December, January, and part of February are usually the most comfortable months in India and are the main growing season. Rice, wheat, barley, oats, and other grains move rapidly toward maturity. Vegetables and fruits, too, grow in great variety during this season of the year. Nights are chilly in the north, but daytime temperatures are pleasant. There is some rain but nothing like the monsoon season. There is some heat, but it is much more bearable than during late February to June or July. And the harsh, dry, dusty winds of the hot season are still not persecuting everyone from the Punjab to Bengal.

Just before their departure, Willes and his associates published one thousand copies of an eight-page English language tract that explained some principles of the Restored Gospel. It consisted of writings from Parley P. Pratt, Orson Pratt, Orson Spencer, and others. They also printed five hundred copies in Bengali of Lorenzo Snow's *The Only Way to Be Saved*. The Hindustani version was expected off the press soon. Armed with this and other literature, they were ready to visit as many English settlements and cantonments as they could find.[1] They also hoped to influence native Indians.[2]

Willes, Richards, and others of us traveled the route to Delhi at a favorable time in history. The governor-general of British India, Lord Dalhousie, was a progressive man with aggressive designs to modernize India. He was also eager to expand British control over parts of India that remained under Indian maharajas, princes, nawabs, nizams, and other such local rulers, and he did so. Among his public works projects was construction of a macadamized hard surface road from Calcutta to Delhi, the Punjab, and beyond. This road, the Grand Trunk Road, was completed between Calcutta and Delhi by the time Willes and Richards walked and rode along it.[3] During the hot season, the tar in the hard surface melted and stuck to the wheels of wagons and carts and to the draft animals' feet, but during the first few months of the missionaries' journey, it provided a comfortable means of travel. In 1853, Lord Dalhousie initiated construction of railroads, but the Mormon missionaries didn't use any of them.

A REMARKABLE MISSIONARY JOURNEY UPCOUNTRY

Traveling without purse or scrip, Willes and Richards set out on foot carrying everything they needed: clothing, scriptures, tracts and pamphlets, blankets, and water. The first day took them through Dum Dum, Barrackpore, and to Serampore. They were hosted by a kindly woman who made them forget for a moment that they were of the "sect which is everywhere spoken against." They spent the second night in the French settlement of Chandernagore. The third day they reached Chinsurah, about thirty miles north of Calcutta. Before they could find friends to care for them, they spent two nights in a native hut and slept on a mat on the ground. Their description follows:

> While W. W. went out to distribute tracts and find a preaching station, J. R. staid at home, praying for success, which was followed by the Lord opening the hearts and houses of two Queen's pensioners, Messrs. John Saukey and Thomas

Travelers' bungalows

Wells, where we were fed, housed, clothed, and blessed; and where we lifted up our warning voices seven nights in succession to soldiers, pensioners, and civilians, who heard the Word gladly—this ended in the baptism of our above-named friends and their wives and families, and the organization of the Chinsura Branch, Elder T. Wells presiding, and Elder J. Saukey, Counselor.[4]

Two-days' walk and forty-five miles brought them to Burdwan, where they found the entire city celebrating the local raja's birthday. The size and grandeur of the palaces and the beauty of their illumination at night impressed the missionaries. But they were unable to find a place to stay and spent two nights sleeping on bamboo leaves and boughs before meeting friendly hosts. They were unable to find any interested hearers of the word at Burdwan. Five days later, Willes and Richards walked on toward Benares,[5] 421 miles away.

Their steps initially took them through the Rajmahal Hills, which later missionaries found to be difficult terrain by bullock (ox) wagon, but the journey was new and the hills were no problem for Willes and Richards. They then entered the eastern part of the Gangetic plains, part of India's most fertile and populated country. Generally the terrain is flat: the elevation rises only seven hundred feet from Calcutta to Delhi. Hiking was not as strenuous as in other parts of the country. They passed through hundreds of villages and nearly unending verdant fields. Neon-green rice fields almost bragged about their new growth.

The watery patchwork looked like miles of mirrors, placed side by side with belts of beige and red dirt dividing them. But they also passed through "jungle and desert, abounding with all kinds of wild beasts, putting up each night at the native *chokeys* [sheds or stations] or *serais* [an enclosed yard for animals with rooms around it for travelers to sleep in], sleeping on the ground, wrapped up in our blankets, often aroused by the howling of our noisy four-footed neighbors, who, thanks be to the guardian care of our Heavenly Father, never came nigh our dwelling."[6] All this to say nothing about the deadly king cobra that annually took the lives of many throughout the country.

In every village and town, the people considered them a strange curiosity. Englishmen simply never walked ("pad the hoof" was the way they said it) or carried their own *traps* (luggage), especially during the heat of the day. Indians commented on their strange ways and offered to carry their bundles for a price, but the elders simply replied that they were humble servants of Jesus Christ who were traveling without money. They were completely dependent on the people and the Lord for their sustenance.

As they walked, India revealed its fascinations and beauties. In the bazaars and on market days, the elders saw and heard raspy-voiced hawkers selling melons, tangerines, bananas, pineapple, guava, coconuts, mangos, starfruit, dates, onions, cauliflower, asparagus, herbs with wonderful aromas, pumplenoses, jackfruit, custard-apples, garlic, gooseberries, plums, figs, tamarinds, almonds, beetroot, artichokes, mangosteens, sour-sops, green grapes, potatoes, ginger, tomatoes, persimmons, pomegranates, turnips, cabbages, cucumbers, beans, lentils, peas, teas, rice of various shades and grades, brown cakes of sugar, sugar cane, cashew nuts, blue cones of powdered dye (they also traveled through fields of indigo), Fuji-like mountains of turmeric, coriander, cumin, cayenne pepper (capable of causing fire on one's tongue), curry (ocher, orange-red, tan, saffron, brown, and black), salt, baskets, pots and pans (brass, pewter, tin, steel, and earthenware), cottons (muslin and calico and occasionally chintz), and silk fabrics of exuberant color and great variety, bangles, earrings, necklaces, pins and trinkets, dusty-black coal, milk and cream from goats, buffalo, or Brahma cows, coffee, beer, wine, tobacco, and on and on.

In larger towns and cities, snake charmers and bear trainers fascinated and frightened wary onlookers. On side streets or in second story rooms, astrologers, palm readers, and numerologists pondered and pronounced the future for believing patrons. Quick-footed, thieving goats scampered among market-goers and into dark alleys. A sea of white dhotis[7] typically flowed through the market places and the centers of towns accented with an occasional saffron, blue, purple or maroon sari sailing by. Along the Grand Trunk Road and on dusty or muddy side roads and paths, or in the fields, the elders saw water buffalo working or lolling in streams or ponds while their loyal herders splashed water on their backs to prevent sunburn to their tender skin. Women and children gathered dung from cattle, mixed it with straw, shaped it into balls, and smashed it into flat disks on walls to dry. Indians cook over what western Americans call buffalo chips. Elephants occasionally tramped these roads but were more common in locations farther west. Stubborn donkeys teased their owners as ponies quickly moved past, pulling small unpainted carts carrying goods for sale or recently purchased.

In the towns and villages, almost every trade was carried on in small stalls, under sagging shelters, or on the road. Barbers shaved and cut the hair of their clients while squatting near the curb (if there happened to be one). The missionaries saw shoe repairmen cutting, gluing, sewing, and tacking while their customers stood by barefoot chatting with friends and neighbors. Occasionally, they,

Hindu temples at Benares

too, stood by waiting for their own shoes to be refurbished. Tailors fashioned shirts and pants with quick stitches and constantly looked for more business, promising finished products almost instantly.

To Hindus, Benares is "the centre or heart of the earth." It is their holiest place and most sacred space in the world. From times immemorial, Indians have believed that those who die beside the Ganges go straight to heaven, or Nirvana. "The streets [are] very narrow," wrote the elders, "and houses very high, in many cases richly sculptured, and curiously and fantastically ornamented." They continued:

> Benares is the sanctum sanctorum of the Hindoos, of great antiquity, swarming with devotees from all parts of India, having innumerable shrines, temples, idols, sacrifices, Brahmin bulls, painted and besmeared pilgrims, maimed, halt, and blind—in many cases wantonly effected in sacrifice to their idols. The shrines and idols, where they offer small portions of rice, flowers, and other matters, on which they sprinkle water, are extremely filthy, the dust and decaying matters mingling and forming a decoction which the strong stomach of a Hindoo god, or the sectarian god "without parts," alone could entertain with any degree of comfort—these are certainly choice quarters for the residence of the gods. "Birds of a feather flock together."[8]

Truly, Benares is one of the most extraordinary cities in the world. Hundreds of Hindu temples and a few Muslim mosques of great size and renown thrust their respective spires and minarets heavenward. The focus of most attention was the theater-like *ghats* (flights of steps that descended to the riverbank) that occurred from place to place throughout the entire length of the city. Pilgrims and priests, as well as local residents, moved down the sacred steps and into the waters of the Ganges in greatest numbers at sunrise and sunset, but at all times of the day the elders saw thousands of religious seekers rinsing, splashing, dunking, drinking, praying, chanting, and smiling in the polluted river that washes all mortal sins and filth away. Along the banks of the Ganges, *sadhus* (wandering holy men) and *Brahmins* (professional priests) offered

Bathing ghats at Hindu temples at Benares, or Varanasi, a modern view

prayers and gave counsel beneath large, mushroom-shaped umbrellas.

In temples and shrines nearby, images of Shiva and Rama attracted the adoration of orange or white-robed pilgrims with ocher sandalwood paste smeared on their foreheads and those who had come to Benares to die. In the temples and shrines, beside the besmeared images gleamed oil lamps and waxy candles that gave off their faintly flickering glow. "Those living at a distance of three hundred miles will exclaim: 'Gunga, Gunga, atone for the sins committed during three previous lives.'"[9] Hindus believe firmly in reincarnation or transmigration of souls. All life forms (gods, humans, animals, vermin, demons in hell, and so forth) have inhabited many, perhaps countless, prior bodies, and unless they have the good fortune of being saved from rebirth by a Hindu god or through working out their own salvation through *karma* (works), *yoga* (meditation), *bhakti* (devotion), or some other path, they can expect many more rebirths after this one. *Samsara,* the eternal wheel, the law of time and rebirth, imposes its demands without ceasing. Karma, the moral law of accumulating deeds (thoughts, words, and actions) is ever bound to samsara in equitably determining one's place in the next life. Most Hindus hope ablutions in the Ganges, prayers and offerings to one or another of their gods, or keeping caste laws perfectly will positively affect their future.

People come from throughout India to die at Benares. At the burning ghats, untouchables who have been born to serve in charnel houses spend their days and nights preparing corpses for cremation. Although Hindu tradition strongly suggests that a man's eldest son should light the fire to his funeral pyre, more frequently, after the family has delivered the dead body to the charnel house, they retreat and leave the final work of burning to those of no caste whatsoever. Sometimes families of the dying brought them to the river or the burning ghats even before death, hoping their souls would receive a better rebirth because of close proximity to the sacred river.

Being "unsuccessful in obtaining an opening to preach" in

Benares, Elders Willes and Richards crossed the Ganges to the south bank and walked on to Chunar, sixteen miles away. Chunar is a place of no great importance, but it boasts a hilltop fortress, a cantonment, and a Hindu temple that attracts worshipers from throughout the country. (It is questionable whether many pilgrims would visit there if it were not located so close to Benares.) The missionaries arrived there exhausted and sunburned on December 28, 1852, and found room in a serai. Willes had been away from home for sixteen months and Richards for almost a year. Our party of missionaries from Utah sailed the same day from San Pedro en route to San Francisco. Four months passed before our two units were to be welded into a single mission by the heat of the Indian sun. In the meantime, Elders Willes and Richards continued their remarkable labors.

On the evening following their arrival, the elders implored the Lord, asking for someone to invite them to his house. Almost immediately an elderly gentleman named Green came to the door of their shanty. He had been informed of their coming and desired to talk with them. Mr. Green was employed by the East India Company, but in his private life he believed in the teachings of the Swedish mystic and religionist Emanuel Swedenborg. He arranged a little place for the elders close to his and furnished it as a living quarters and a small chapel. In that place they "had numerous and attentive audiences, who 'hung on our lips' as though we were beings of another sphere."[10] They also held meetings in the Baptist chapel, arranged by Mr. Green. At Chunar, the brethren baptized eight people, the first being John Bromley, the district road overseer from Mirzapore, twenty miles away. Formerly of the East India Company horse artillery, he had been badly wounded multiple times in the Anglo-Sikh wars of the late 1840s. His dedication to the Restored Gospel seemed firm. Willes and Richards ordained him an elder in the priesthood and expected him to be a leader in the Church. He spoke of his eagerness to emigrate to Salt Lake City. Two days later "six females and a youth, the son of Mrs. Thompson, who herself came forward, being the first female who has been immersed in that river (the Ganges) [by Mormon elders]."[11]

Nearly four hundred retired Europeans, either by birth or by extraction, lived at Chunar Fortress. Many of those people offered to write letters of introduction to friends and acquaintances in other cities. But at that time, the brethren began teaching some deeper points of doctrine, and their previously friendly and helpful audiences dissipated quickly.

Only five months later, in May and June 1853, Elders William F. Carter and William Fotheringham traveled by Ganges steamer as far as Chunar and Mirzapore. To their great disappointment they found only two members in Chunar, Sister Goodyear and Sister Scott, and neither of them showed much warmth or interest. When they reached Mirzapore, they learned that John Bromley had fallen away. Carter and Fotheringham had sent a letter ahead announcing their imminent arrival, but when they found his home, he was not there and was not expected for several days. "The engineer [who delivered the letter] told me," wrote Fotheringham, "that when he delivered the letter to him, he stated that he was too fast in being baptized, that he had not counted the cost in receiving doctrines that were so unpopular. It had caused a current to set in against him that he could not stem, and which was likely to imperil his chances of gaining a living." Fotheringham continued:

> It is an easy matter to comprehend the situation of an isolated person, naturally weak and with no experience, who there embraced the Gospel. . . . It required one to be grounded in the truth to withstand the combined influences of Hindoo idolatry, Moslem superstition, and, what is more blighting than either, Christian bigotry and unbelief.[12]

Not knowing what was going to happen in the coming months to their newly baptized associates, Willes and Richards continued on their way. At Mirzapore, they baptized a former Brahmin scholar and teacher named Peter Perkarse. Even though they ordained him an elder and held great hope for his future in the Church, his name does not show up in the historical records at a later date.

Elders Willes, Richards, Fotheringham, and Woolley traveled in wagons similar to these

From Mirzapore, they traveled on through Allahabad, Futtehpoor (Fetehpur), and to Cawnpore (Kanpur), 626 miles on foot from Calcutta. They were now in the middle of the area where the Indian War of 1857 (the Sepoy Mutiny or Sepoy Rebellion, depending on your point of view and loyalties) raged most aggressively. At Cawnpore, they became aware that they could travel more cheaply by taking the government-operated bullock-drawn wagon train. The wagons of the train moved on around the clock, stopping every twelve miles to change draft animals and occasionally to deliver or pick up freight. Taking their places uncomfortably amidst the dusty freight, luggage, and boxes, they were soon at Agra, city of the world-famous Taj Mahal, arriving there before the end of February 1853.

It was at Agra that Willes and Richards first received word that the Church had acknowledged the principle of plural marriage. Years later Willes wrote:

> One of our visitors was a Mr. Warren, a Presbyterian priest who was the first to tell us of the Church acknowledging the

practice of Polygamy, and when Joseph Richards heard him say so, he said, "If that be the case I shall never want to go to Utah," but, I felt like defending the principle to Mr. Warren, and while we were talking our native servant came in with our mail matter, and when we opened it found a copy of the revelation on the subject in the Deseret News extra, when Richards saw this he began to repent of having spoken against it, and begged my pardon. He began to search the Bible, and soon found plenty of evidence in its favor.[13]

Although I was in Calcutta to hear most of his reports when Elder Richards returned from Agra, I don't have the exact dates of Willes's and Richards's movements over the next two or three months. Briefly put, they worked together in Agra for about a month, until the second half of March. Their situation was favorable because Elder Willes contacted a distant relative who was hospitable and generous. This kind man, William Cushier (Crawford), rented a house for them for a month. They lived there, held meetings, and answered questions, "which [i]nquiries [were] numerous and earnest." Their first few meetings were well attended, and they expected to preach regularly for the duration of their stay.[14]

At that time, Elder Richards was enduring ill health. He did not have the energy to continue on to points farther north. Willes and Richards were also worried about how their converts in Calcutta and along the Ganges were accepting the announcement of the doctrine of plural marriage. Richards was also eager to meet the Utah elders and learn from them concerning doctrinal changes. Therefore, he and Elder Willes decided it would be best for him to return there.[15] Having discovered the economy and relative speed of the bullock train, he traveled back to Chinsura and joined us in Calcutta on May 11, 1853. By the time I met him, he had regained his health. At the time of their separating, Willes and Richards had baptized sixteen people. In a letter, they reported that new members at "Chinsura, Chunar, and Agra, are prepared to receive and maintain two Elders a-piece, as soon as they arrive."[16] Unfortunately, these brethren didn't realize that their work was already crumbling behind them as they moved on. Elder

The elders occasionally rode in large, four-wheeled wagons similar to these military bullock-drawn wagons designed to carry heavy freight

William F. Carter

Richards labored with us for a short time before accepting his release. On June 19, 1853, he embarked for Boston.[17]

When Elder Richards returned to Calcutta, he gave a fairly positive account. But soon after, President Jones began receiving reports from Willes regarding the unkind treatment he was receiving at various cantonments. President Jones had already assigned Elders William F. Carter and William Fotheringham to go to Dinapore, but after that effort failed, he sent Elders Fotheringham and Samuel A. Woolley to join Willes near Delhi, to replace him, and to allow him to return to mission headquarters at Calcutta.

ATTEMPTS TO ESTABLISH THE CHURCH AT DINAPORE AND NEARBY CITIES

While Elder Willes continued his journey north from Agra through Delhi, the Punjab, and into the foothills of the Himalayas, Carter and Fotheringham, who had accepted the assignment to teach the Gospel at Dinapore, were making preparations to begin

William Fotheringham

that expedition. Unlike Willes and Richards who walked, Carter and Fotheringham sailed by river steamer to Dinapore. Both men were a little upset that the captains of coasters and steamers were not as willing as the American captains had been to reduce fares for men of limited means, especially ministers of the Gospel such as they were. To raise money for steamer fare, they sold their watches to their brethren. At the same time, Sister Meik generously gave them enough cloth to make five garments apiece, and her good husband donated some clothing and an umbrella to the cause. On May 16, 1853, they were ready and boarded the steamer *Benares*.

The route to Dinapore by steamer was much longer than by land, 875 miles versus 376 miles, respectively, but much faster and more comfortable. The following day the *Benares* hoisted anchor and sailed down the Hoogly toward the Sunderbans, the sand islands where the distributaries of the Ganges meet the Bay of Bengal. The Hoogly grows much too narrow and shallow north of Calcutta to support boats displacing a greater draft, so it was necessary for steamers to sail south, then east toward Burma, and finally north on the course of the Ganges.

"We stopped and took in coal," wrote Carter three days later. "Both sides of the river are lined with native villages. They swarm out of their huts to see us pass, like bees out of their hives. I could not compare them to anything else. The shores of the river are literally alive with men, women and children, and thousands of cattle. Many of the natives are busy putting in their rice. The principle wood is coconut trees, mangoes, teak and bamboo."[18]

The following morning everyone on board heard three or four hundred natives screaming and yelling from the shore. An alligator or crocodile, called a *muggur* by the natives, had caught a man. The beast was twenty feet long and immensely powerful. "He went down with the man and just before we got to him, arose without the man. Close to us, he went down and we saw no more of him. Soon after we passed, the man arose, but was dead," noted Carter.[19] These waters were infested with muggurs. A man had been lost the day before. To prevent such incidents, the natives drove bamboo poles into the water like picket fences to create protected areas for bathing and doing laundry. Evidently, the muggurs had discovered a hole in the protective barrier, and the natives were paying the price.

Unlike Willes and Richards, who had begun their journey while the weather was mild, Carter and Fotheringham were traveling in the height of the hot season. Day by day Carter noted the thermometer reading: On May 24th it stood at 102 degrees at 4:00 P.M. Other days were considerably hotter. The humidity was especially difficult for Carter. As the steamer moved northwestward, the air was often filled with hot wind and dust.

Boat travel was interesting to the two missionaries. Ever-shifting sandbars complicated movement up the river. New pilots came on board every twenty miles who were acquainted with the movements and changes in the riverbed. Carter compared the Ganges to the Mississippi, and Fotheringham compared it to the Missouri. Boat traffic was thick and constant. The Ganges was like a major highway. Not only were the elders amazed at the number of alligators and crocodiles, but also they were shocked at the number of human corpses that floated by or which they viewed on the riverbanks or on sandbars. Most of these bodies were those of the poor who could not afford proper cremation, but some were from areas where local droughts or crop failures created higher-than-normal death rates. Asiatic cholera was also at epidemic levels when we arrived in Calcutta. As many as six hundred deaths were registered in Calcutta daily. Who knows how many were occurring along their route? Thousands?

After being grounded on sandbars and weaving slowly up the river, the *Benares* finally made Dinapore at evening on May 30th. Dinapore was the elders' appointed objective because it was a large military cantonment. They came armed with a letter of introduction from Brother Meik to his uncle, General Young, evidently the ranking officer at the camp. They immediately found Young's residence, a distance of two or three miles. He was not in, so they returned the next day.

Their encounter with General Young was instructive for all of our activities for the remainder of the mission, especially our encounters with the military. Largely because he was Brother Meik's uncle and the elders were Meik's friends, Young received them courteously. This was almost the last time a high-ranking military officer received any of us courteously. Carter and Fotheringham hoped to preach the Restored Gospel to the regiment of European soldiers assigned at Dinapore (there were also three regiments of sepoys), but aside from handing out some tracts, they did not succeed in holding a single meeting.

The elders had two encounters with Young, one at this point and a second while they were en route back down the Ganges toward Calcutta. He told them he had no interest in considering a new religious system. He was set in his path, wanted to follow the traditions of his fathers, and had no desire to change. But he expanded his own opinions to include others. According to Fotheringham, "He thought the army officers and the civilians

Protestant church at Dinapore, which Elders Fotheringham and Carter walked past

holding offices from the government would very likely cling to their present religious notions." The general said, "We would find India a very hard country in which to disseminate our doctrines, as the most of the Europeans in the north-west provinces were military characters, and were so situated that it made it a difficult matter to reach them."[20]

As for preaching to the soldiers, the government had provided for their religious needs by building Protestant and Catholic chapels, many of them substantial, providing ministers and priests to man them, and even marching the troops to church each Sunday. "He said before we could preach to the people [soldiers]," wrote Carter, "we would have to consult the commanding officer and he would have to consult him and get permission from them before we could preach to the soldiers. He told us we could not have any of their meeting houses to preach in." Off-duty soldiers were free to hear us, he supposed, but they were quite taken with other activities. Most difficult for us as missionaries was his next statement: "It was contrary to the government regulations to allow any religious propagandist, other than those supported by the government, a place at the cantonment in which to hold forth." Carter wrote that Young described "how strictly they had to obey the laws and discipline of the military departments of India."[21] There were many variations on Young's themes, but as Elder Fotheringham wrote years later, "Our subsequent experience in India proved to us that General Young's ideas were tolerably correct."[22]

Within only a few days, Elders Carter and Fotheringham encountered even stiffer military opposition to their missionary efforts. Realizing that they would not be allowed any success at Dinapore, they paid six rupees each to the captain of the *Benares* and sailed on to Chunar, where they landed June 11th. The weather was extremely hot, more than 110 degrees in the shade. Elder Carter was suffering greatly from the sun and dust-filled wind early in the afternoon. As the hours passed, his condition worsened. Not having a place to stay, they placed their trunks under a large tree near the river. Fotheringham spent the next four

Chunar Fortress on the Ganges, *by J. C. Armytage from a drawing by William Daniell*

hours walking from place to place trying to find Mrs. Goodyear and Mrs. Scott, whom Willes and Richards had baptized. When he found them, neither was friendly. But worse, while Elder Fotheringham was at Mrs. Goodyear's home,

> there came a Sergeant and asked Brother Fotheringham if he belonged to the same society that Mr. Willes did. He told him he did. "Well," he said, "I am sorry to inform you that your stay in this place will have to be very short," because he had orders from his superior not to allow any of that order to stay in the place. Brother Fotheringham told him that we were missionaries from America sent to preach the Gospel to the people. He told the sergeant we calculated to obey the laws of the country wherever we traveled, consequently if the authorities would not allow us to preach, we would leave them.[23]

Hoping to get to the source of the orders, Elder Fotheringham visited Colonel Blake, the cantonment commander. After Fotheringham explained the nature of his mission to him, Blake, in an imperious manner, "replied that we could not be permitted to hold forth in the cantonments, and wanted to know what had brought us there to preach, where there were so few people. Then he added, 'You have your belief, and I have mine; and why not stay in your own country, instead of coming and troubling us here?'"[24] Following a short exchange, Blake closed the door on Fotheringham.

Fotheringham returned to the place where Carter was waiting by the river. Together they asked the Lord to provide a place for them to stay. They remembered Mr. Green, who had treated Willes and Richards so kindly. On finding his place, he allowed them to stay for a night. He also sent three bearers to haul their belongings from the river to his house. Green and his wife provided supper and "plenty of filtered water to drink." The Greens' generosity was much appreciated.

As I mentioned earlier, finding no permanent place at Chunar, the elders moved on to Mirzapore. Their trip there took two and a half days by dingy. The weather was so hot and dry that "when

Elder Carter would dip a silk handkerchief in the river and put it over his face to shelter him, it would be dry in two minutes." When they made Mirzapore, they found the steamer *Benares*. By this time, the captain and crew had become good friends with the elders and were happy to see them. Finding that they were very hungry, the captain had the cook prepare a lunch, "which was greatly relished."

We have already discussed their unhappy discovery that Mr. Bromley had fallen away from the Church. There was nothing else to do but return to Calcutta. "Elder Carter's health being much impaired," wrote Fotheringham, "he felt that he could not stand the fatigue and exposure which we would have to endure if we proceeded farther up the country, especially as the rainy season was setting in; hence we concluded to return to Calcutta."[25]

They made their desires known to Captain Elder of the *Benares*, and he welcomed them as passengers. Carter gratefully described how their mission to Dinapore ended:

> The captain of our boat said, "You are moneyless, but you shall not be left here." Said he, "You take a deck passage down and when you get to Calcutta, if you can't get the money to pay it, I will pay it, and as for your board, that is in my hands. I will board you and make you welcome." And he said to me, "If you offer me any money I will take it as an insult." He said that he had taken us up here and we acted the part of gentlemen and "I find no fault of your doctrine, and you have been badly treated by the people and I will not see you left here, but I will see you safely conveyed to Calcutta."
>
> We felt to thank the Lord our God for raising up friends for us when we were destitute and among strangers and in a strange land, amongst everything that calculated to try the souls of men, such as the scorching sun and hot blasts of winds that blow a gale from the sandy deserts and where the dead were floating by the boats every hour, and sometimes two or three together day and night.[26]

Another captain who was docked at Mirzapore also offered to carry Carter and Fotheringham down to Calcutta. They had started their journey somewhat upset at the captains for not giving them a reduced fare; now they were grateful to the Lord that such men had come to their aid.

The *Benares* docked at Calcutta in the evening of June 25th. The entire trip had taken thirty-nine days. Elders Carter and Fotheringham had performed no baptisms, though Charles Booth, second engineer on the *Benares*, along with his wife, his mother, and her sister, later accepted the Gospel and emigrated to Utah. Meanwhile, I was disturbed and discouraged with their report. Following are the words I penned in my journal that day:

> They gave an awful report of the officers, and priests etc., up the country. They could not get one chance offering to any. The officers would turn them off and tell them they could not be protected, and would not dare to preach to the soldiers. The Brethren have had quite a trying time. They say the soldiers are under the dictations of the officers, the officers under the dictations of the priests, and the priests under the *Devil.* In going to preach to the inhabitants of India (Europeans), is like going to England and America and selecting none but the aristocracy or upper ten to preach to as all the European inhabitants of this country are living in the greatest ease, having many servants to wait on them. They care nothing for the servants of God.[27]

What made matters more difficult was that the "aristocracy" of India were not originally of the aristocracy of England. Those who acted as though they had a high place in English society were in India largely because they wanted to be of that higher station. Few are so hard to take as the newly rich.

Several days later, on June 27th, all of the missionaries in and near Calcutta met to discuss the future of the mission. Decisions that had been made two months earlier needed updating and revising. As we met, we received a letter from Elders West and Dewey stating their intention to go on from Ceylon to Bombay to work with Elder Findlay. The Calcutta elders had considered sending Elder Fotheringham to help Findlay in Bombay, but with West and Dewey's plan to go there, the group decided to send

Fotheringham and Elder Woolley upcountry to work with Elder Willes.

Elder Carter wrote: "Brother Jones asked me where I wanted to go; I told him I thought that I would have to go to some colder climate, to live long. Says he, 'I suppose you would rather go to America than anywhere else.' I told him if I had my choice I would rather go to America than anywhere else. Said Brother Jones, 'You can go where you have a mind to.' Brother Musser motioned that I go home to the Valley of the mountains. It was seconded and carried unanimously." Brother Jones then explained to the rest of us that Carter's health had been failing ever since we arrived. "He said that I was too far advanced in years [he had turned forty-two years of age on May 1st] and had been through too many hardships to stand the climate of India, for it was as much as they that were young and full of nerves could do to stand it; and he was satisfied were I to stay I would not live a great while." Carter probably suffered sunstroke at Chinsura. It is also possible that he had contracted malaria for he "had the ague sweat on [him] day and night"[28] and was very feeble.

With the financial assistance of Dr. Charles Hoffnagle, the American consul in Calcutta, Carter arranged for passage on the American clipper ship *John Gilpin* and sailed from Calcutta on July 9th. Hoffnagle was a true friend and support to the missionaries. On several occasions he gave financial assistance and moral support.

Carter's voyage was long but not particularly arduous. The *John Gilpin* sailed past the Cape of Good Hope, across the Atlantic near Brazil, and north to Boston, where it docked on November 10, 1853, 126 days out of Calcutta. After visiting friends and relatives in the eastern United States, Elder Carter eventually crossed the plains and arrived in Utah in September 1854, almost two years after leaving for India. He had circumnavigated the globe "without purse or scrip."

NOTES

1. Cantonments played a large role in the lives and work of the missionaries to India. The word *cantonment* is peculiar to India. Its meaning is somewhat synonymous with "base, fort, camp, and garrison." The Oxford dictionary defines cantonment as "the lodgings assigned to troops; in India, it means permanent military stations." Cantonments provide not only lodgings but also administrative offices, warehouses for arms, munitions and other material, parade grounds, chapels, mess halls, medical facilities, and other offices and facilities necessary to operate what could be called military towns. Although there were some cantonments by the late eighteenth century, military camps were not generally permanent until peace was established in the mid-nineteenth century. The government and the military command saw the necessity of establishing permanent military stations for quartering troops and for providing for the health, safety, discipline, and general welfare of the soldiers and their families. At the high point there were eighty-seven cantonments throughout India. In the 1990s, sixty-two cantonments served as the principal bases of the Indian army. The British government originally established all contemporary cantonments in India. See Veena Maitra, *The Cantonment Administration in India* (New Delhi: by the author, 1996.)

2. William Willes to Lorenzo Snow, September 1852, *Deseret News* 3 (May 14, 1853): 4. In this letter Willes told Snow that he believed it wise to do most printing in India because the cost was more reasonable than shipping literature from Liverpool or London. In another letter, dated September 4, 1852, to Samuel W. Richards in England, Willes writes of wanting to obtain a press and also of "extending" his labors "up country." See "Introduction of the Gospel in the Birman Empire" [Willes to Samuel W. Richards, September 4, 1852, Calcutta], *Millennial Star* 14 (December 11, 1852): 670.

3. In the 1990s, the Grand Trunk Road remains the most traveled highway in India. It has been widened slightly but is basically a two-lane road with narrow or no shoulders. All forms of traffic use its constricted space: enormous trucks, cars, handcarts, carts and wagons of all sizes drawn by animals of all descriptions–donkeys, mules, camels, horses, goats, bullocks–motorcycles, bicycles, and so on.

4. William Willes and Joseph Richards, "The East India Mission" [Letter to Samuel W. Richards, February 1853, Agra], *Millennial Star* 15 (May 21, 1853): 331–32.

5. Nineteenth-century writers usually used the name Benares, whereas post-Independence writers almost always refer to the city as Varanasi. There is only a slight phonemic difference between the consonants *B* and *V*, thus accounting for the earlier British spelling.

6. Willes and Richards, *Millennial Star* 15 (May 21, 1853): 333. In 1863, Matthew McCune, who had lived for twenty-two years in India and South Asia, wrote at length regarding the flora and fauna of India. He noted "huge elephants, wild and domesticated," the rhinoceros, the camel, the lion—mostly in the north, "the tiger abounds in every forest and jungle throughout the country," leopards, ounces, panthers, antelopes, wild deer, bears, wild boars, "hyenas and jackals go in packs of many hundreds," wolves, foxes, hares, squirrels, porcupines, hedgehogs, monkeys "of every description, from the large man-monkey, or orangutan, down to little creatures no larger than a common rat," and buffalo, both wild and tame. He also mentions some varieties of birds and snakes. Matthew McCune, "Chapters on Asia," *Millennial Star* 25 (June 6, 1863): 358.

7. "Dhoti: The loin-cloth worn by all the respectable Hindu castes of Upper India, wrapt round the body, the end being then passed between the legs and tucked in at the waist, so that a festoon of calico hangs down to either knee." Henry Yule and A. C. Burnell, *Hobson-Jobson: The Anglo-Indian Dictionary* (1886; reprinted; Hertfordshire: Wordsworth Editions, Ltd., 1996).

8. Willes and Richards, *Millennial Star* 15 (May 21, 1853): 333.

9. Fotheringham, "Travels in India," *Juvenile Instructor* 12 (July 15, 1877): 159.

10. Willes and Richards, *Millennial Star* 15 (May 21, 1853): 333.

11. Ibid., 333–34.

12. Fotheringham, "Travels in India," *Juvenile Instructor* 12 (November 1, 1877): 244. See also Carter, "Incidents," 4:213–14.

13. Willes, Journal and Reminiscences, 1851–1885. This passage was written in 1884 or 1885.

14. Willes and Richards, *Millennial Star* 15 (May 21, 1853): 334.

15. Nathaniel V. Jones, "Hindostanee Mission, Letter No. 5," *Deseret News* 6 (April 16, 1856): 42.

16. Ibid.

17. Nathaniel V. Jones, "Hindostanee Mission, Letter No. 2," *Deseret News* 5 (December 26, 1855): 334.

18. Carter, "Incidents," 4:210.

19. Ibid.

20. Fotheringham, "Travels in India," *Juvenile Instructor* 12 (September 1, 1877): 196.

21. Carter, "Incidents," 4:216.

22. Fotheringham, "Travels in India," *Juvenile Instructor* 12 (September 1, 1877): 196.

23. Carter, "Incidents," 4:213.

24. Fotheringham, "Travels in India," *Juvenile Instructor* 12 (October 15, 1877): 235.

25. Ibid., *Juvenile Instructor* 12 (November 15, 1877): 255.

26. Carter, "Incidents," 4:215.

27. Musser, Journals, 2:72.

28. Carter, "Incidents," 4:216–17.

5

TRAVELS TO DELHI AND BEYOND CONTINUE

While Carter and Fotheringham were attempting to gain a foothold at Dinapore, Chunar, and Mirzapore (May 16 to June 25, 1853), Elder Willes continued his efforts to spread the Gospel in the cities and towns from Agra north to Simla [Shimla], in the lower mountains of the Himalayas. In May 1853, he wrote to headquarters in Calcutta regarding some of the adversities he had endured; but a month later, June 28th, he thought it worthwhile to have other elders join him. President Jones had asked Elders Fotheringham and Woolley to go to Willes's assistance at Delhi. Delhi, with a population of around six hundred thousand, was the capital of the waning Mughal dynasty.

After Elder Richards left Willes, but before Fotheringham and Woolley arrived in the vicinity of Delhi, Elder Willes traveled alone from city to city and from cantonment to cantonment. By late June he was back in Delhi, having spent time in Kurnaul [Karnal], Umballa [Ambala], Calka [Kalka], Kussowlie [Kasauli], Sabbattoo [Sabathu], Dugshai [Dagshai], and Simla. The latter place is a so-called hill station, where British officers and civil servants retreated during the hot season. The scene was somewhat incongruent. Along the spine of mountaintops were government-built, British-style mansions beside shale-roofed dwellings of the local poor.

The rains were so heavy in the mountains that Willes soon made his way back to Delhi, where he believed the weather would

Governor's mansion at Simla

be more comfortable during the coming monsoon season. His only real success in the north was the baptism at Dugshai of Lance Corporal Edward Jones, whom I mentioned before. Jones was the friend of Private Thomas Metcalf, who died before he met a missionary of the Church. Jones was generous with Willes. He sold his watch to provide money for Willes when he had no money whatsoever. He also did all he could to bear witness regarding the Restored Gospel.[1]

In late June at Delhi, Willes was still encouraged and asked for help. A month later he wrote from Kurnaul. Now he was discouraged. I, Elder Musser, recorded:

> August 4. We just received a letter from Bro. Wm. Willes. His prospects are not very flattering. The objections his hearers bring up for not joining our Church [are] as follows. "You allow polygamy! If we went to the Valley we would have to dress our own food and work for a living. We would have to dispense with our servants; while remaining here we can have them." The above are some of the many objections that are brot up by those who live for this world and its comforts. How true the saying "not many rich, great, noble, or wise, will be saved."[2]

But discouraged or not, on August 10th, the brethren in Calcutta received from Willes a *hoondy* (a post office money order) for twenty-five rupees to help pay the cost of travel for someone to come to Delhi.[3]

FOTHERINGHAM AND WOOLLEY CONTINUE THE WORK IN THE UPPER PROVINCES

Between the time when Elder Fotheringham arrived back in Calcutta from Dinapore and when he and Elder Woolley departed for Delhi, Fotheringham spent two weeks in bed with chills and a fever. I noticed in reviewing my journals that there was seldom a day without a reference to someone being sick. Fevers and chills predominated. Malaria was endemic in every region in which we labored. Whether that was our common ailment I do not know.

Samuel Amos Woolley

Considering we drank water from almost any source, including the Ganges and many other rivers, from village tanks,[4] wells, and so on, it is a wonder that we all did not die of dysentery. We did suffer from frequent intestinal infections and bowel discomfort.

Elder William Fotheringham, age twenty-seven and single, and Elder Samuel Amos Woolley, almost age twenty-eight with a wife and three children at home, left Calcutta by government bullock train on August 28, 1853. They paid nineteen rupees each, roughly ten dollars in 1853 money. The entire trip required a month of days and nights on or near the bullock wagons to reach Secundrabad [Sikandarabad] near Delhi.[5] The elders found their

> journey to be tedious and fatiguing. Our condition in the gharry [cart, carriage, or wagon] was almost intolerable, having to sleep on the edges of boxes, except when, for a change, we would lean our backs up against the posts which supported the roof, or reverse our position, and place our feet against the posts and our backs on the boxes. The inside of the gharry was like an

oven. The sheet iron roof sometimes becoming so hot that we could not even bear our hands to come in contact with it. When we got out of the wagons, as we had to do often, to roll the wheels and help the poor brutes through the newly macadamized roads, we found the reflected rays of the sun, quivering and dancing close to the surface of the earth, almost unbearable.[6]

"We daily met vast numbers of travelers," Fotheringham wrote, "male and female, the most of whom were returning from Benares and Allahabad, whither they had been on pylgrimages. The men were generally armed with swords and shields to protect themselves against the Thugs, who are not uncommon in these parts, notwithstanding the exertions on the part of the government to exterminate them."[7]

At Secundrabad, they found Elder Willes waiting for them at the government bungalow. Although they had not previously met, they "hailed each other as servants of the Lord and representatives of the same great cause, and felt as though we had had a long acquaintance."[8] Willes was staying five or six miles away at Belaspoor with Mr. Thomas Skinner, a wealthy Anglo-Indian. Skinner kindly hosted the new arrivals for nine days, sufficient time for them to recover from the fatiguing effects of the trip. At that time, in early October, the three elders parted company at Secundrabad. Elder Willes took a place on the bullock train bound for Calcutta by way of Agra—he arrived in Calcutta almost two months later, on December 1, 1853[9]—and Elders Fotheringham and Woolley traveled to Meerut, approximately forty miles northeast of Delhi.

PURSUING EVERY MEANS TO ESTABLISH THE RESTORED GOSPEL AT MEERUT

Meerut is best known in history because the Sepoy Mutiny began there in 1857. It was home to one of the largest cantonments in Upper India (two or three regiments) and one of the largest

Anglo-Indian communities in that region (250 civilians). Elders Fotheringham and Woolley went there because they thought the large European populace would provide interested hearers of their message. For five weeks, they pursued every lead and possibility for gaining a foothold. But for five weeks, they were rebuffed and rejected at every corner they turned.

They did make some friends, however. A Mr. Kelly and his family hosted them for the period of time they stayed at Meerut. Mr. Courtney, manager of the Meerut Hotel, offered the use of his large dining hall for lectures. And Mr. Hayes invited them to use a large room in his home for meetings. But military officers forbade any and all missionary activity within the bounds of the canton-ment, including at the hotel, and Mrs. Hayes made it clear that they were not to preach in her house. In her note to the elders, she said: "I am sorry I cannot accommodate you with the house. My minister would be displeased with me, if I were to do so. I have no objections in the least to your enlightening the world with your new doctrines; and if you truly are the followers of Jesus Christ, as you profess to be, you can instruct the people out-doors, as the Savior did."[10]

The elders knew they could not preach inside the cantonment without permission from the commanding officer, in this instance, Brigadier Scott. When they met with him on October 17th, he denied permission, saying: "I would not consider it doing our ministers justice to allow you to preach here, for they are paid by government to preach in this station." Scott told the elders he had been asked by the Anglican bishop in Calcutta not to permit any Mormons to preach in the various cantonments.[11]

In a letter to me, Elder Musser, that was similar to the letter cited above, Elder Fotheringham wrote:

> We then asked him [Scott] if we could lodge in the can-tonments. He replied not without his permission and if he granted us two weeks stay in this place, as soon as the time was expired, we would be under necessity of having it renewed again and many other restrictions he laid upon us which would

be too numerous to mention. Amongst some of the restrictions was if we should get a place outside of the boundary lines to preach in we were not allowed to send a circular amongst the soldiers to notify our meetings. If we did we should be marched out of the cantonments without a moment's notice. Or if we should be found preaching to the soldiers on the streets we should be marched out. This is like tying a man's hands and feet and throwing him into a river and making him swim.[12]

Of course, they visited with the local ministers of religion, and although they were treated somewhat respectfully by two, the third and highest ranking minister, the Reverend Mr. Tuson, was almost violent as he yelled his insistence that they not preach to his people and that they not bother him. As they had done many times before, they testified that they knew Joseph Smith personally and "knew him to be a man of God."

Failing at holding lectures and bearing a spoken witness of the Restoration, they arranged to have one thousand copies printed of *The Only Way to Be Saved* by Lorenzo Snow. Woolley had to part with his watch to pay the expense. They hired an Indian to assist in the distribution of the pamphlets; doing such work in the heat of the sun was too dangerous for Europeans. But "out of five hundred bungalows there were only about ninety who would have them as a gift." Elder Woolley believed some of the citizens of Meerut "would obey the Gospel [only] if they could go to Heaven on 'flowery beds of ease.'"[13]

Elders Fortheringham and Woolley were disappointed in not finding a single person who was willing to study the Gospel seriously and prayerfully. Although they were treated unkindly by some men of the cloth, they were cheered that others contributed rupees to their cause, although not as Christians but as fellow Anglo-Saxons. They prayed for God's blessings to be upon those who made their burdens lighter and who contributed food, shelter, and money to pay for travel.

View of Delhi from the Palace Gate, c. 1845

Chandi Chowk, Delhi. A very busy area of the city

TO DELHI, KURNAUL, AGRA, AND TOWARD CALCUTTA

Fotheringham and Woolley left Meerut by bullock train on November 10, 1853, and arrived at Delhi thirty-eight hours later. They remained there until December 7th, or just under four weeks. Elder Fotheringham has left an engaging description of the city:

> The far-famed city of Delhi . . . is situated on the right bank of the river, Jumna [Yamuna], nine hundred miles, via the Grand Trunk Road, northwest of Calcutta. In approaching the city, the only buildings to be seen towering above the massive walls which surround it are the Jumma Musjid, with its superb domes and tall minarets, the towering battlements of the palace of the Moguls, and a few other public buildings.

Delhi . . . is not unlike other oriental cities in many particulars. The tall date trees, interspersed with the slim, bending acacias, waving over the many ancient tombs and city walls, enhanced by the beauty of the shadowy foliage growing on the gently-sloping parapet grounds, all combine to form a pleasing picture. . . .

Delhi is seven miles in circumference, and is surrounded by a lofty indented or crenellated wall, in the shape of a horse shoe. . . . The crowning splendors of Delhi are the great mosque and magnificent palace of the Moguls. The Jumma Musjid, or chief mosque, is situated in the center of the city. . . . [W]e were permitted to ascend to the top of the minaret, which was over two hundred feet in hight. It was ascended by a spiral stair, inside. From the upper balcony we obtained a magnificent view of the city and its surroundings.[14]

As interesting as Delhi was, their experience there was exasperating. They received the runaround from several persons who might have provided assistance but were fortunate to obtain help from a few. One man, Mr. Nixon, rented a room for them in an old dilapidated college, extremely humble, rat-infested quarters, that had not been used for years. Another, Mr. McNally, provided meals twice a day and some friendship. He also introduced them to some of his friends. The elders found the English population to be "very gay and frivolous, giving themselves little concern about their eternal salvation. After tea, they spent their time in singing, card-playing and throwing dice."[15] Yet another man, who had been unkind and somewhat insulting to the elders, rented a hall in a different part of town from that where they were staying, at which they held a short series of lectures, with attendance of eleven, ten, five, four, and finally, one person. They decided to fix up their quarters at the college by spending a few cents for matting on the floor. They then held an equally unsuccessful series of lectures at that place. Following an attempt to sell and distribute their books and pamphlets that accomplished little, they decided to move on to Kurnaul.

It was at Delhi that Elder Fotheringham felt most strongly that "God would shortly humble the pride of the people of Upper

The Jama Masjid, the great Muslim mosque of Delhi

India, for they were scornfully proud." Many years later, Fotheringham reported that he and Elder Woolley "often felt impressed" this way. Fotheringham wrote:

> While in Delhi, we occasionally accompanied Mr. McNally and others to the parade ground to witness the military maneuvers of the Sepoy[16] soldiers. . . . On one occasion Mr. McNally and others were admiring the fine physical forms, and military bearing of the native troops, remarking that they were a strong bulwark to the British power in India. We replied that the day would come when the Sepoy troops would bayonet the whites to the heart, with the queen's bayonets. But they did not believe a word of it.[17]

Hardly three years passed before Fotheringham's words came to pass. A number of the people the elders conversed with in Delhi died at the hands of the sepoy rebels.

Fotheringham made another perceptive observation regarding relations between the British overlords and their Indian subjects. In 1879 he penned:

> England has done much for India by establishing schools throughout the country to educate the natives, as well as in building roads, bridges, railroads and telegraph lines. She gave peace to a distracted country; for the people of India, previous to the English rule were in a continual state of anarchy. The inhabitants . . . have a sullen hatred towards their benefactors, whom they call "eringhees." Nothing but the presence of a powerful military force keeps the native population in subjection.[18]

The trip from Delhi to Kurnaul was only seventy-three miles north. Elders Fotheringham and Woolley left Delhi by bullock train on December 7th and arrived at Kurnaul thirty-eight hours later. Very few European people were there to teach and fewer at Umballa, the place they intended to visit next. The cantonment was largely abandoned, "without tenants, dilapidated and crumbling down." Woolley complained: "Our work will be short, to all appearance, in Upper India, for we now start down, and will call at all the stations, and try to get a chance to preach. It seems as if the people are not worthy of the Gospel."[19] Fortunately, Mr. Maddock, the postmaster, had acted the part of friend and host. He was also in charge of the bullock train station and gave the elders free fare to Agra.

From Kurnaul, they traveled through Delhi (where they stopped briefly to answer an attack that had appeared in a newspaper, the *Delhi Gazette*) to Agra. They were refused hospitality at the cantonment but were allowed to attempt to hold meetings outside the camp boundaries. They rented halls in two different parts of town, announced their intended lectures but were disappointed with the results.

At Agra, the power of Indian religious tradition closed in most heavily, although they did not consider Agra any worse a place than others. Fotheringham recalled:

> There seemed to be a heavy curtain of spiritual darkness that enveloped the land, which was hard to penetrate. . . . The powers of darkness, superstition, ignorance and priestcraft, with all its train of evils, had existed for ages. The spirit and influence of these gross superstitions which had been nursed from time immemorial could be palpably felt, and every intelligence in the land, Christian or pagan, was more or less affected by it.[20]

In mid-January 1854, they visited the old Moghul fortress called Agra Fort. Aside from the Taj Mahal, it was the most important historic structure in the area. Akbar, generally accepted as one of India's two greatest emperors, used the fort as his capital between 1556 and 1605. From the fortress walls, the elders viewed the Taj Mahal. "The crowning glory of Agra," wrote Fotheringham, "and the pride of the Mohammedan [Muslim] population, is the Taj Mahal. . . . This magnificent and beautiful tomb was built by the emperor, Shah Jehan, for himself and his favorite wife, Mumtaz Mahal. It took 20,000 men twenty-two years to build this mausoleum."[21]

After spending four weeks in Agra, they sought donations to pay their fare back toward Calcutta and raised enough to ride the bullock train. Every postmaster along the way treated them kindly

Agra Fort is one of the most imposing remnants of Moghul architecture

and generously. At many stops of the wagon train, the postmasters gave them food and clean water, offered them protection from the heavy rains or the blistering sun, provided other necessities, and often listened with honest interest to their missionary message. In several instances, they rearranged the freight so the elders would be more comfortable, and in one or two instances, including the Agra-to-Cawnpore trip, they even had native passengers wait for the next bullock train so as to make more room for the elders.

Although their discouragement and disappointment were evident—"It makes me almost sick at heart to read of the Elders in other countries doing such great works, and for me to be tied hand and foot, as it were, and told to swim"—these elders held their heads up and remembered whom they served. They were also grateful that their God had sustained them and never let them

Constructed in the 1600s, the Taj Mahal is one of the architectural wonders of the world

down. "We feel truly thankful to our Heavenly Father," recorded Elder Woolley, "for the blessings which He has bestowed upon us, for although the people are so bitter against us, and will not hear our doctrine, yet He has influenced men to give us all things necessary to our wants."[22]

The bullock wagon train from Agra to Cawnpore trudged through some of the worst weather the elders encountered. First, a "continuous wind storm, which stirred up the hot dust, filling the air and making it intolerable." And then, on the fifth day out from Agra, a rainstorm so violent that everything they owned was drenched. They could hardly see their way. Eventually, they got out of the wagon, guided the *gharrewans* (the teamsters), rolled the wheels, and selected "the best part of the road in order to make the best time possible."[23]

They lectured once in Cawnpore but were closed out after only eight days. Both men were sick at that time, Woolley being the weaker. Fotheringham administered to him in the name of the Lord, and he was soon healed of lung fever. Fortunately, a gentleman named Gee offered them a ride by coach to Allahabad, 126 miles distance. In their weakened condition, they were grateful not to ride the fifty hours in cramped conditions in the bullock train.

Once they were in Allahabad, they were on their own again. After being rebuffed by a man to whom they had been sent with a letter of introduction, they trudged around town in the hot sun for most of the day trying to find someone who would put them up for a few days. J. Booth and J. S. Collis, indigo planters, came to their aid. They stayed with them in Allahabad and at their plantations for two weeks, but were unable to accomplish anything. Elder Fotheringham summarized the situation in this way:

> We found the people in this station more hateful towards us than in any of the other places we had visited. This was principally brought about through the agency of the pulpit and the press, as both were arrayed against us, to prejudice our cause in the minds of the people. The result was that, excepting the kindness of Messrs. Booth and Collis, we had a

cold reception. The people were aristocratic and haughty, and surrounded with all the temporal comforts of life.[24]

They left Allahabad on February 21, 1854, having been supplied by Booth and Collis with twenty rupees to help with their journey. These friends also purchased books and copies of the standard works for fifteen rupees. The elders traveled through Benares and on east along the Grand Trunk Road on their way back to Calcutta. They arrived there on March 6th, feeling almost completely worn out.

After a month of recuperation, Woolley received word from President Jones that he was free to return home, if he wished to do so. In his honesty, Woolley said he did not want to be the "first to leave the country," preferring to stay until fall, "at least."[25]

Upon their arrival back in Calcutta, Elders Fotheringham and Woolley completed one of the greatest missionary journeys in the history of the Church. It had its beginning in November 1852, when Elders Willes and Richards departed Calcutta for Upper India. Willes and Richards walked to Cawnpore before taking places on the bullock train. Willes traveled as far north as Simla, in the foothills of the Himalayas. Fotheringham and Woolley, who replaced him and Richards, continued the work in Upper India and traveled almost as far together, reaching Kurnaul, north of Delhi. Willes and Richards baptized seventeen or eighteen souls; Fotheringham and Woolley baptized none.

NOTES

1. William Willes, "The East India Mission: Success of Elder William Willes in Delhi and Various Towns in the Himmalehs—Hospitality of the People" [Willes to Samuel W. Richards, June 29, 1853, Delhi], *Millennial Star* 15 (October 15, 1853): 686.

2. Musser, Journals, 3:14–15.

3. Fotheringham, "Travels in India," *Juvenile Instructor* 12 (November 15, 1877): 255.

4. Elder Fotheringham wrote: "Every village has its tank, or tanks, according to the wants of the inhabitants. These native village tanks are merely large excavations in the ground, the soil taken out forming the bank or bund, which, from the lapse of time, becomes sodded over. During the rainy season the average fall of rain is from sixty to seventy inches. These tanks are then filled to that depth from the clouds, which is all the supply the interior villages, that are not immediately situated on rivers, have until the return of the rainy season." Fotheringham, "Travels in India," *Juvenile Instructor* 12 (December 1, 1877): 267.

5. Elder Fotheringham detailed this journey in his "Travels in India" account in the *Juvenile Instructor,* which has been cited above. Only a few of his most colorful descriptions have been included in the body of this history.

6. Fotheringham, "Travels in India," *Juvenile Instructor* 12 (December 15, 1877): 280.

7. Ibid., 281. Fotheringham defined a *thug* in these words: "'Thug' is from the Hindustani word 'thaga,' which means a cheat, or deceiver. It is also the name of a religious society in India the members of which, in honor of the goddess Kali, the wife of Shiva, murder [by strangulation] their fellow [travelers] and live upon the booty obtained from their victims."

8. Fotheringham, "Travels in India," *Juvenile Instructor* 13 (April 15, 1878): 94. Woolley's record differs somewhat regarding the exact place where the three elders met. He says they met at Belaspoor, five or six miles away from Secundrabad. See Samuel A. Woolley, "The East India Mission: Travels of Elders Woolley and Fotheringham from Calcutta to Secundrabad, Belaspoor, Marat, Delhi, and Kurnaul. . ." [Woolley to Samuel W. Richards, December 9, 1853, Kurnaul], *Millennial Star* 16 (February 25, 1854): 124.

9. Jenson, *Church Chronology,* 49.

10. Fotheringham, "Travels in India," *Juvenile Instructor* 13 (September 1, 1878): 200.

11. Woolley, *Millennial Star* 16 (February 25, 1854): 125.

12. William Fotheringham to Amos Milton Musser, October 19, 1853. See Ralph Lanier Britsch, "A History of the Missionary Activities of The Church of Jesus Christ of Latter-day Saints in India, 1849–1856 (master's thesis, Brigham Young University, 1964), 53.

13. Woolley, *Millennial Star* 16 (February 25, 1854): 126; and Fotheringham, "Travels in India," *Juvenile Instructor* 13 (September 15, 1878): 206. Musser also notes these events in Journal, 3:106.

14. Fotheringham, "Travels in India," *Juvenile Instructor* 13 (November 15, 1878): 255–56.

15. Fotheringham, "Travels in India," *Juvenile Instructor* 13 (October 1, 1878): 218; and 13 (October 15, 1878): 233.

16. Yule and Burnell, Hobson-Jobson: *The Anglo-Indian Dictionary,* describe *sepoy:* "In Anglo-Indian use a native soldier, disciplined and dressed in European style."

17. Fotheringham, "Travels in India," *Juvenile Instructor* 13 (October 15, 1878): 233.

18. Ibid., *Juvenile Instructor* 14 (January 1, 1879): 9. The word that Fotheringham spelled as *eringhees* is usually spelled *feringhees*. From a Persian root, *feringhees* was used in the nineteenth century by the Indians for "European"; it implied "something of hostility or disparagement" (Yule and Burnell, *Hobson-Jobson: The Anglo-Indian Dictionary,* 352). Fotheringham's views on the relationship of the British military to the native Indian population were borne out by the rise of the Indian Nationalist Movement in the 1880s and the decades of events leading to independence in 1947.

19. Woolley, *Millennial Star* 16 (February 25, 1854): 126.

20. Fotheringham, "Travels in India," *Juvenile Instructor* 14 (March 1, 1879): 51.

21. Ibid., *Juvenile Instructor* 14 (April 1, 1879): 77.

22. Samuel A. Woolley, "The East India Mission: Continued Opposition by the Military Authorities—Lectures in Agra" [Woolley to Samuel W. Richards, January 18, 1854, Agra], *Millennial Star* 16 (March 25, 1854): 189–90.

23. Fotheringham, "Travels in India," *Juvenile Instructor* 14 (June 1, 1879): 123–24.

24. Ibid., *Juvenile Instructor* 15 (February 1, 1880): 29.

25. Ibid., *Juvenile Instructor* 15 (May 1, 1880): 99; and Samuel A. Woolley, "The East India Mission: Travels from Agra to Cawnpore, Allahabad, Calcutta. . ." [Woolley to Samuel W. Richards, June 27, 1854, Chinsura], *Millennial Star* 16 (September 9, 1854): 573.

6

STRIVING TO REACH SIAM

On May 15, 1853, Elders Chauncey Walker West and Benjamin F. Dewey sailed for Ceylon. A day later, Elders Carter and Fotheringham sailed by river steamer for Dinapore (a story we have already told). A month later, on June 15th, Elders Levi Savage and Elam Luddington took passage on the steamer *Fire Queen*, bound for Burma, from which place they intended to go on to Siam [Thailand] when the way opened. And five days after that, Elders Richard Ballantyne and Robert Skelton sailed for Madras on the ship *John Brightman*.

Three of the four pairs of elders experienced passages that involved great danger. West and Dewey found themselves on a ship infected with cholera. Twenty-nine people died before they docked at Madras and three more the first day in port. The ship Ballantyne and Skelton took to Madras almost collided with another of greater size on the Hoogly River before gaining the open sea and then they encountered a terrible storm. But the story of Luddington and Savage was most frightening. In the same great storm in the Bay of Bengal, the *Fire Queen* was forced to turn back. Just after the event, I recorded in my journal the following:

> While at dinner Brother Luddington came in, in an awful

predicament, close dirty, hat reduced to 2/3 the size, etc., etc. The ship they started to Rangoon in, three days after they left here she sprung a leak and they have been bailing and pumping water night and day ever since. They throwed all their cargo overboard and gave themselves up for a watery grave. They throwed all of the stores overboard, but the Lord delivered them safe. This trial came in exact fulfillment of what Brother [Wilford] Woodruff told us before we left home in the mountains. He said the spirit whispered to him that some of us would have great trials at sea, etc., etc.[1]

Luddington and Savage were quite sick for two weeks, but they were still determined to reach Siam.

Now that the other elders had gone to their fields of labor (or home in the case of Elder Carter), President Jones, Elder Owens, and I settled into a routine that included holding lectures, visiting homes in an effort to distribute books, tracts, and pamphlets (we had established what we called the "Calcutta Book Agency"), reading and studying, and working on various publishing projects.[2] Jones was particularly diligent answering an anti-Mormon publication titled *Mormonism Unvailed*. We had plenty to do because the local newspapers were filled with trash about the Latter-day Saints and plural marriage. (I must mention that the editors of the *Citizen* were more liberal and evenhanded than most.) President Jones stood toe-to-toe with detractors and was unabashed in his defense of the truth. He said he might have been more timid, but he and the rest of us had faced mobs in Missouri and Illinois and would not be intimidated in Calcutta. We followed this pattern until late September, when the monsoon rains dwindled. In my journal, I noted that between the early part of June and mid-September there were only two or three days that did not have fairly heavy rainfall.

Our daily pattern was interrupted when Carter and Fotheringham returned to Calcutta on June 25th. Carter's health was broken, and he sailed for home shortly thereafter. Fotheringham, too, was stricken for a time with ill health prior to leaving for upper India with Elder Woolley in August.

Elder Jones continued his work on what we came to call the *Reply*. On August 4th, *Reply to Mormonism Unveiled*, a one-hundred-twenty-page booklet, was off the press. We published two hundred copies.[3] Our expectation was that matters would improve; that is, that honest men and women would read our material and become interested in our message. Our arguments were soundly based on biblical scriptures, true principles, and quotations from the leading Brethren. In the long run, however, our publication efforts did not make much difference.

In August, our Calcutta contingent enjoyed some success. Charles Booth, with whom we had labored for some time, was baptized on the 14th. His wife was not ready then, but she later joined the Church.

Such was the situation at our Calcutta headquarters by late August 1853. It is well to note that from May 15th, when Elders West and Dewey sailed for Ceylon, the missionaries of the Hindostan or East India Mission (we called it by both names) never gathered as a body again. In effect, the mission became several missions: Calcutta, Siam, Madras, Burma, Bombay, and Sind [southern Pakistan], including Karachi and Hyderabad. When the work ran its course in each locality, the elders found their own way home, either in pairs or alone.

WEST'S AND DEWEY'S EFFORTS TO REACH SIAM

When the Siam-bound elders discovered they could not reach Siam by an overland route because of the Anglo-Burmese War, they concluded that two of their number, Elders Luddington and Savage, should go to Rangoon for a time to assist Brother McCune, who was attempting to establish the work there while serving in the army. The other two, Elders West and Dewey, should go to Ceylon [Sri Lanka] with the intention of establishing the Church there. Both companionships intended to go to Bangkok, Siam, when conditions changed, and the way was open. Of the four elders, only Elder Luddington finally reached Siam. Events preventing the others from reaching their assigned mission field were long, demanding, and trying.

Elders West and Dewey sailed from Calcutta on May 15, 1853, landed at Madras for a day or so, then sailed on for what was then called Point de Galle [now Galle], where they landed on May 26th. Ceylon, like most of India, was under British control. Portuguese and then Dutch colonists had occupied the island until 1796, when the British drove them out. Western influences were quite common by the 1850s. A small minority of Singhalese had been converted to Roman Catholicism and Protestantism, although the British had not encouraged missionary activity. Ceylon was a stronghold of conservative Theravada Buddhism. But Buddhists were not a problem for West and Dewey.

Almost immediately, they encountered antagonistic resistance from Protestants. Upon learning of their role as Mormon missionaries, two men with whom they conversed told them they would meet with "great opposition." Aside from Captain Carmel, a fellow passenger whom they had befriended on board ship and who had provided a carriage for them while in Madras, they had no friends in Ceylon. Carmel had lost his ship and was returning home to England. He believed their message and enjoyed their company. But everyone else, with one exception in Colombo, rejected the elders and even refused to offer them anything to eat.[4]

While in Ceylon, they attempted to find a place to preach in Galle, and then in Colombo, seventy miles away. They walked that distance in the searing sun and slept on the ground. Their food was primarily coconuts and rice. At no village were they welcomed or fed.

Anti-Mormon tracts and pamphlets from England had preceded their arrival. The day after they landed, an article in a newspaper warned the people that if they received Elder West and Elder Dewey "they would be partakers of our evil deeds."

The Reverend Mr. Ripen of the Presbyterian Church mistook them for new comrades in that work and invited them to his home.

On the Road from Galle to Colombo

Benjamin F. Dewey

On finding that they were the dreaded Mormons, he told them they could not expect any favors or help from him. He claimed to have read some Latter-day Saint works and "considered our doctrines absurd and unscriptural." West challenged Ripen on that point and asked for examples of LDS doctrine that did not agree with the word of God. After failing to sustain through the Bible his belief that baptism was unnecessary for salvation, he "flew into a passion, and requested we should work a miracle. . . . [W]e told him if he could find an account within the Bible where a servant of God ever did a miracle, when called upon by the people in order to make them believe, we would do one for him."

The Reverend Mr. Ripen then commenced to rail against polygamy. The elders affirmed their belief in that principle, stating their faith that the practice had been revealed through a true prophet. They told Mr. Ripen they "believed that one glimpse thro' the vail would teach a man more about the things of God, then the reading of volumes." They used father Abraham and his descendants as a prime example of God's acceptance of those who

Chauncey W. West

practiced polygamy. West quoted Matthew chapter 8, verse 11, wherein Jesus affirmed that the righteous would come from the east and west and sit down in the kingdom of God with Abraham, Isaac, and Jacob, "the greatest Polygamists of whom we read." He concluded:

> And moreover, in John's revelations there is an account of him having seen the Great City—New Jerusalem descending from God out of heaven, having its twelve gates on which were inscribed the names of the twelve Patriarchs, the sons of the great Polygamist, Jacob; and John says, "Blessed are they that do his commandments, that they may have a right to the tree of life, and may enter in thro' the gates of the city." Now sir, said we, if ever you get into that city, you will have to make friends with Polygamists.[5]

Not surprisingly, the Reverend Mr. Ripen was not convinced. And neither was anyone else in Ceylon. West and Dewey decided to seek a ship for Singapore, but failing that, they settled for one going to Bombay. Their thinking was that they would help Elder Hugh Findlay at Bombay and Poona until a way opened to go to Siam. Fortunately, the large Irish ship *Penola* came in for water, and Captain Rany welcomed them as passengers to Bombay. The voyage was rough. The day before they reached Bombay,

> while sailing along the coast about ten miles from shore, the ship ran aground; the wind was blowing very hard, and the waves were running very high, and when the waves struck the ship they would raise her up, and then she would come down with a tremendous crash, as if she must come to pieces in a very few minutes; and to all human appearance we must be lost in the great deep; as the small boats were so placed that it would take some time to get them overboard, and when they did it was doubtful whether they would ride the sea.
>
> Elder B. F. Dewy and myself [Chauncey West] went to our room and asked the Lord that the winds would cease blowing, and that He would save us from the fury of the elements. About this time they launched a boat and it filled [with water] in a minute; a few minutes after, they put over another boat, and in a few minutes more it was almost a calm.
>
> As we were about to leave the ship, Captain Rany discovered that she was afloat; he called to the carpenter to sound the pumps; he found three feet of water in her hold. The Captain then said he would try and take her into Bombay. He put some of the hands to the pumps and some to hoist the sails, and the next morning, the 25th of July, we landed in Bombay.[6]

Through the kindness of our Heavenly Father, the elders and all on board were saved "from the fury of the elements."

Elder Findlay, who had been ill for the previous two months, was happy to see Elders West and Dewey. He thought it best for West to remain in Bombay, where there were twenty members of the Church, and for Dewey to accompany him to Poona, where there were a similar number of Saints.

They remained with Elder Findlay and his brother, Allan, who arrived fresh from England on September 7, 1853, for more than five months, until January 1854. During that period, they maintained a watch for ships going to Siam or Singapore. Few, with the exception of the mail and other steamers, were sailing that course, and they were too expensive. Most captains who were bound for China avoided Singapore and the contrary monsoon winds of that region and charted a course south of the Dutch East Indies [Indonesian] island of Sumatra and through the Sunda Strait between Sumatra and Java. On hearing that there was a lively trade between Batavia [Jakarta] on Java, and Singapore, the elders concluded that shipping to Batavia and thence to Singapore on a different ship would bring them closer to their destination in Siam.[7]

They were refused passage by fourteen captains before Captain J. Bell of the 673-ton, three-masted *Cressy* consented to let them work their passage to Batavia.[8] They parted with the members in Bombay and took ship January 9, 1854. The voyage was uneventful until they arrived in Batavia on February 26th. They soon learned that with the exception of some Malay junks, which they did not dare take, there were no ships bound for Singapore. To make matters worse, Dutch law in Batavia required strangers to prove their ability to pay for their lodging or to ship out on the next vessel. The elders had no money. When Captain Bell offered to take them on to China with him, they concluded that they would have to pursue their quest to reach Siam from Hong Kong or some other Chinese port.

The voyage was complicated by the decision of Captain Bell and Captain Gamble, in whose ship's company the *Cressy* was sailing in tandem, to sail a course that, according to West, had not been followed for thirty years. It led around the eastern coast of the island of Borneo, a course filled with treacherous reefs and shoals, sand bars, small islands, vigorous tides and currents, and other impediments. The captains thought they would save time. In this, they were woefully mistaken.

What was normally a reasonably short voyage lasted from March 1st to May 2d, more than two months.[9] Almost every problem a ship could encounter, short of sinking, challenged the *Cressy* before it docked at Macao. West wrote, "There was scarcely a day during the passage along the coast of Borneo but what we saw reefs or shoals, consequently we had to keep a boat ahead sounding; we sailed nearly three thousand miles in an open boat steering, rowing or throwing the lead, and the sun hot enough to bake one's brains." They ran aground several times, nearly exhausted their water supply, were chased by hundreds of Borneo natives in canoes who wished to take over the ships, beat against strong tides for days before rounding certain points, and then, when finally past Borneo and into open sea, they suffered a typhoon in the South China Sea that took many other ships to the bottom. "It appeared truly miraculous to all on board that she ever rode the storm," wrote West. "A number of vessels were lost in that sea during the same gale, but through the distinguished favor of our heavenly Father, on the 30th April we beheld the coast of China." Three days later they dropped anchor off Macao, near Hong Kong.

The *Cressy* stood at anchor for only a day before a Chinese pilot guided her toward Wampoa in the mouth of the Pearl River leading to Canton, a voyage of four slow days. At that point, two of the ship's crew confessed their conversion to Mormonism and their intention to be baptized in England when they were released from service on the ship. Elders West and Dewey had their greatest missionary success on board various ships. Perhaps this was because they had time on board to get acquainted with the people they were traveling with and more moments when they could explain their message in a quiet uninterrupted manner.[10]

West reported that Dewey was in poor health, as was Captain Bell. Both men were suffering from the effects of the great heat of the sun while at sea. Bell's condition continued to worsen until he was transported to a hospital in Hong Kong, where he died. Dewey, fortunately, did not meet a similar fate, although his health remained frail for some time.

Elder West found Chinese culture interesting. He commented on local customs, such as setting off firecrackers to frighten away evil spirits and to ensure good luck at sea, burning candles and incense to ward off the *josh*, evil and devilish forces, and similar practices. They also visited the town of Wampoa and concluded

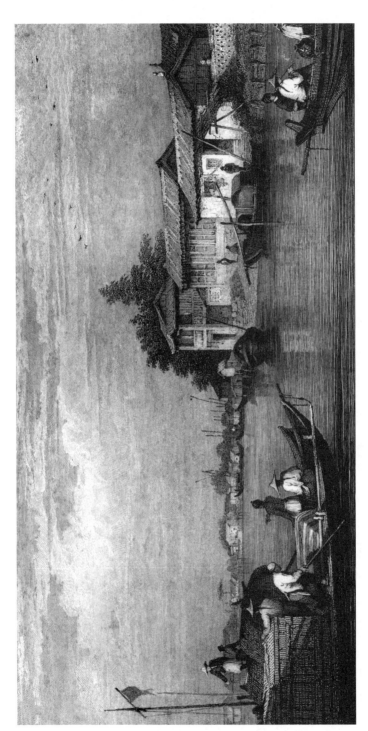

View on the River Near Canton, *by S. Prout, 1834*

that its citizens were morally degraded. The parts of life that were in plain view were obviously shocking to missionary eyes.

On May 10th, they sailed on the bark *Hiageer* for Hong Kong, a short journey of two days. "We came to anchor opposite the city," remembered West, " which is situated at the base of an almost barren mountain. It presented a beautiful appearance from the sea, but when close by it appears more obscure and irregular." While there, they looked for Elders Stout, Lewis, and Duncan, with whom they had traveled from Salt Lake City to San Francisco but found that they had already returned to America.[11]

As long as they remained on the *Cressy*, they had food and a place to sleep. Now, at Hong Kong, the elders were again destitute, and a heavy rainstorm was dousing the area. Dewey's health worsened, so in desperation, they returned to the *Hiageer*, where Captain Dibble kindly accepted them for two more nights. When the rains stopped, they found a cheap, Chinese boarding house where they stayed a few days and then were invited by a Chinese man named James Young to reside at his boarding house free until they could arrange passage to Siam.

While in Hong Kong, Elder West had three experiences of note. First, a friend invited him to go to Canton free of cost. The trip gave West the opportunity to see a thriving and historically important part of China. Canton was the site of the Opium War of 1839–1842. It was also the main location of the infamous opium trade. Canton was China's principal entrepôt. On the riversides, beautiful gardens, rice fields, fruit trees, pagodas, fortresses, and historic sites marked the way. Thousands of boats, large and small, crowded the estuaries below and above Canton. The city itself was packed with busy people, "nearly all of whom were carrying something from silk and satins to wood, vegetables, fruit, brick and mortar."[12]

West and his host, Mr. Elister, found the city to be filled with great excitement and anxiety. The Tai Ping rebels were approaching and might attack that night or the next morning. West and Elister did not wait to see if the attack came. By evening, they were back to Wampoa, where West spent the night on the *Cressy*. The next day, he sailed to Hong Kong with his friends and there found Elder Dewey about the same, but his fever and chills were somewhat broken. Mr. Young had been kind to him.

The second noteworthy experience related to Young's boarding house. Soon after returning from Canton, West visited Captain Miller, who replaced Captain Bell on the *Cressy*. He invited West and Dewey to stay on the ship until it sailed. On returning to Young's place, West and Dewey "agreed to go on board the next morning." When they informed Mr. Young of their plan, he encouraged them to remain over the weekend and leave on Monday. Elder West described the rest of the story in these words:

> The next day (Sunday) passed very dull, and about 4 P.M. we concluded to leave our trunks, go out to the vessel and have a little chat with Capt. Miller. We informed Mr. Young of our intentions, but he said we had better remain until after supper, which would be ready in the course of an hour, still we felt impressed upon to go. On reaching the vessel we found Capt. Miller and had a pleasant interview. [They remained on board overnight.]
>
> The next morning we were informed that Mr. Young's house had fallen down, and on going ashore for our trunks (which we found among the ruins) we learned that in about one hour after we left, while all were at supper, a large rock broke loose from the hill above the house, rolled down and struck the lower story, bringing it down with a crash and covering the inmates in ruins; some were killed and all more or less injured.[13]

They were, of course, distressed by the losses caused to their kind host but thanked the Lord for His watchful care over His servants.

Through all this, Elder West and Elder Dewey had continued their hope to fulfill their call to Siam. They watched for ships that were sailing to Singapore or directly to Siam. On June 25th, a ship came in that was going to Singapore, but they were unable to arrange passage. "The ship we were then stopping in," penned Elder West, "was about ready for sea and Elder Dewey's health was still failing, and as we both thought he would not regain his health in a tropical clime, after fasting and prayer to know the will of the Lord, we felt that the Spirit dictated that it was our duty to return to America."[14]

With that decision made, they began looking for a ship bound for San Francisco. And in the looking, the third notable experience occurred. Captain Dibble and the bark *Hiageer* were leaving soon for San Francisco with a load of Chinese passengers. He agreed to take the elders for one hundred dollars each, payable in San Francisco, a savings of at least half fare each. They moved their trunks on board and waited for the day appointed for sailing. But, "the second night on board I [West] dreamed that the vessel was wrecked, and that I saw the crew and passengers in great distress." The dream was repeated the next night, and Dewey then had the same dream three times. Leaving the ship at that point was awkward, but they did so. Early in July, they arranged with Captain Duncan McDonald of the British ship *John Gray* for cabin passage at one hundred fifty dollars each, to be paid in San Francisco. The *John Gray* was a 578-ton, three-masted square-rigger built in Scotland.[15] A few days later, they learned through Hong Kong newspapers that Captain Dibble and the *Hiageer* had wrecked at sea seven days out from Hong Kong. One fourth of the passengers had been lost, and the balance suffered severely before being rescued by a United States frigate.

On July 15, 1854, the *John Gray* lifted anchor and sailed into the China Sea. Fifty-four days later, it arrived at San Francisco. By that time, Elder Dewey was in moderately good health. Being out of the tropics seemed to have been the cure. The Asian part of their mission was over. Now all they had to do was pay Captain McDonald the fare of one hundred fifty dollars each and make their way back home to Salt Lake City.

Brother John M. Horner lent them the money, but then they had to repay him. Dewey saw an old friend, Q. S. Sparks, who offered to pay Elder Dewey's share if he would come to San Bernardino and do carpenter work for the winter. Within two weeks, Dewey was off to San Bernardino. West took work at Salmon Falls, near Sacramento, repairing Brother Ebenezer Hanks's millrace and mining. By December, West had repaid Brother Horner. After that, he traveled the area visiting friends and preaching to various groups and branches. He also did some mining until April, when he and others began making preparations to return home to Salt Lake City. By mid-May, he and his long-time friend and traveling companion, Nathan Tanner, were in San Bernardino. West found his "old, tired friend Elder Dewey" there in good health.

West and Tanner "rigged out three six-mule teams," loaded freight, and on June 7th, set out for the Valley. Elder Dewey remained behind at San Bernardino for a time.[16] West and Tanner arrived in Great Salt Lake City on July 15, 1855. West wrote: "Found my family all well and blessed with the comforts of life." He had left behind his wife, Mary, and three children.

Chauncey W. West's appraisal of their mission was honest and touching. He wrote:

> I cannot say that we have done any great things during our mission, but this much I can say, we have done the best that we knew how. I feel that we can say in truth that we have kept br. Amasa Lyman's counsel to the missionaries as we were on our way out; he said, "if you can do no more, mind and save one each, that is yourselves."
>
> I feel grateful to my Father in Heaven that my life has been spared to mingle again with the saints in these peaceful valleys, and I now report myself on hand for duty whenever the servants of God call, for the Priesthood is my law.[17]

ELDER LUDDINGTON'S SINGULAR ATTEMPT TO REACH BANGKOK

Two other elders, Luddington and Savage, were called to Siam [Thailand]. Savage spent most of his mission in Burma and never attempted to go to Siam (his story is told later). But Luddington maintained his determination to reach Siam, even though he, too, spent some time in Burma.

Their first attempt to go to Rangoon, Burma, nearly ended in disaster when the *Fire Queen* developed a leak and almost sank. But after a little more than a month in dry dock, the steamer was ready to return to service, and the elders sailed safely to Rangoon on July 29, 1853.

Luddington became involved in the mission work at Rangoon. He served for a period as branch president in Rangoon. But in January 1854, he considered it time to continue on to Bangkok and started searching in earnest for a ship headed on a route that could lead to Siam. He sailed from Rangoon on February 3d and again found himself on a sinking ship. For twenty-one days, the ship struggled, finally finding port at Penang Island in the Straits of Malacca in late February. Not one to let the opportunity pass by, Luddington spent his five days on Penang preaching from house to house. He found the island beautiful.

A brief and safe trip by mail steamer took Luddington on to Singapore. But he was without money and had no friends. Finally, to his aid came a Scottish church minister named Keeslerry, who boarded him and gave him a place to sleep for three weeks. He preached the Gospel from door to door for the duration of his stay but found no hearers.

Singapore, however, was but a stopping place; Bangkok was his assigned destination. Luddington became acquainted with Captain James Trail, of mixed Dutch and Indonesian parentage from Batavia, who had sailed the Gulf of Siam for fourteen years. He offered Elder Luddington free passage on his bark *Serious*. After a thirteen-day passage, they arrived at Bangkok on April 6, 1854. The next 127 days were generally difficult, but he had a moment of satisfaction when Captain Trail and his wife joined the Church on April 9th. Captain Trail was something of a philanthropist and much liked "by all classes." He could speak several languages. They were his only converts.

In 1854, Siam was in the third year of the reign of King

Mongkut, or Rama IV (ruled 1851–1868). Prior to becoming king, Mongkut had devoted twenty-five years to serious study and meditation as a Theravada Buddhist monk. He was completely dedicated to Buddhism and provided leadership for a reformation of Buddhism within his country. He was also a wise and strong monarch. Through careful negotiations and alliances, he and his son, King Chulalongkorn (ruled 1868–1910), successfully avoided foreign colonization and domination.

Luddington lectured every Sunday and devoted considerable time to meeting individuals of high position, such as Chao Phraya Thiphakorawong, the minister of foreign affairs, and various persons of the royalty. He also attempted to teach the nine Protestant ministers and eight Roman Catholic priests in Bangkok, but they banded together to make his life and work miserable. An interview with the famous American missionary "Mo" Dan B. Bradley, who had been in Siam since 1835, did not produce anything but animosity.[18] Other Christian missionaries had achieved almost no conversions among the Buddhists of Siam.

On June 1, 1854, Elder Luddington sent a descriptive letter explaining elements of Siamese culture. He was amazed with the power of the king, whom he described as an absolute monarch. He was also surprised that Siamese subjects were required to approach royalty in abject humility, bowing or crawling before his majesty. Seventy days of work each year were required of all peasants, usually referred to as *corvee* labor. Bangkok was a floating city, most business being done on the water. It has been called the Venice of the East. He mentioned the high place an albino elephant held in Buddhist tradition: "the natives believe that their former king has transmigrated into the white elephant."

In the same letter, he said he was trying to learn the Siamese language, a task he estimated would take a year or two. But he also acknowledged his willingness to give up and return home. "I will keep digging till you all say enough, and then if you see fit to call me home, I shall be truly in heaven and happy in the extreme," but he expressed his willingness to go on if that was Heavenly Father's will.[19]

As had occurred in every other place that our missionary band introduced the Gospel, anti-Mormon tracts and pamphlets appeared, and distorted and consciously malicious articles were published in the local press. It is not clear exactly what finally happened, but Luddington said he was "stoned, mobbed, and rejected" in Bangkok. He "fled" to Singapore but found the same problems there.

While Luddington was again in Singapore, Elder William Willes passed through that city on his way to England (a story whose major parts are presented elsewhere). He spent four days with Elder Luddington, "which was like balm to a wounded spirit, or water to a thirsty man."[20] They comforted one another, shared Chinese food, and endured the stares of passersby as they sat on the ground because they had nowhere else to go. They parted when Willes sailed on October 14th for Liverpool on the clipper ship *Gazelle*, under Captain George Leslie. Luddington found passage on the clipper ship *Prince Woronzoff*, mastered by Captain Harris, that shipped out of Singapore on October 27th, bound for Shanghai. His voyage was dangerous and nearly required his life. Because his description is so interesting, it is included in its entirety:

> I arrived in this place [Hong Kong] on the morning of the first instant, after a long and sickening voyage of 35 days from the Straits of Malacca, or Singapore. We put in here in distress. I was a passenger on board the *Prince Woronzoff* from Edinburgh, Scotland, Captain Harris. This unfortunate brig is three years old, clipper built, and as fine a vessel as sails the ocean.
>
> On the ninth day out, 15 miles to the westward of Paliwon [Palawan] Island . . . just before dawn of day, on Saturday the 4th of November, in a heavy fog and rain, our clipper struck with great violence on a coral reef, or sunken rock. The captain ordered port helm, and all on board was a silent as the charnel house of death. We struck three or four times on those rough and pointed rocks, and our hopes were almost gone, and death

stared us in the face; but thank the Lord, He sent to our relief an unusually large wave, which carried us over the rock into deep water. We manned the pumps, and sounded the water in the hold, and found that the vessel made one inch of water every three minutes, or 20 inches per hour. Our spirits groaned within us. It was a time of deepest distress. I felt that my mission had been according to the will of heaven, and I could not but ask, "Father, must I leave my body here?" But I felt, "Thy will, O Lord, be done."

I had a little hope that we might save ourselves in our boats, but to our terror the captain informed us that the inhabitants of Paliwon Island were all cannibals. The island is not far from Borneo, where live probably the most cruel race of beings on the earth, being both land and sea pirates.

Our gallant brig was bound for Shanghai, and the captain was determined to run her into that port, if possible to save expense, otherwise we might have put into Manilla, which would have been far better.

Here commenced *the epoch*—trouble, sorrow, sickness, pain, vituperation, and abuse. I was sick and had to stand in the water at the brake of the pump morning and night, to keep us afloat, and save our lives, with however little hopes. We were for 15 days in a gale of wind, almost a tiffon. Our sails were torn to ribands and new ones bent. Our yards were carried away, the rigging was chafed and much injured, and we were in momentary expectation of seeing the masts go by the board. Ringbolts were torn from the decks, and spars, boats, and lumber were adrift, being torn from their fastenings. Sometimes we carried on mountain waves, and then again thrust down into the great abyss of waters, in the troughs of the sea, expecting at times to be buried, as the vessel often shipped seas which swept the decks fore and aft. I was sick, and my body was borne down with pain from costiveness and the general disorganized state of my system.

All this was but trifling. Said the captain, "Ah! you are the Judas, your religion is of the devil, you ought to be put to death, and if Jesus was now on the earth, you would put him to death."

"No," I replied, "we are his friends, and not his enemies." The persecution came hotter and hotter. After reading Elder Spencer's letters, the captain said that he was a liar, for he condemned everybody and everything but his own order. I told the captain that the man, kingdom, or nation that fought against the Saints of Latter-days, should go backward and not forward, should sink and not swim.

We passed Formosa [Taiwan] Island two days out in the Pacific Ocean. The leak increased, and caused alarm, and we turned our course and stood for Amoy. The storm came on again, accompanied with thunder and lightening, the clouds gathered blackness, the elements became furious, and the seas again swept over our decks; we then put into Hong Kong. After running within three days' sail of Shanghai, we were driven back 700 miles to the very place where I wanted to land 35 days before.[21]

Elder Luddington arrived at Hong Kong on December 1, 1854. Ten days later, when he wrote the letter above, he had arranged passage to San Francisco on the ship *Lucas*, that was expected to sail about December 20th. I do not know exactly when he reached San Francisco, but it was probably in January or February 1855. He returned to the Great Salt Lake Valley in time for October Conference that year. Luddington had traveled more than thirty thousand miles since leaving home three years before.

Thus concluded our efforts to establish the Church in Siam. The efforts of Elders West, Dewey, and Luddington to reach that land and fulfill the Lord's command to take the Gospel to every nation could not have been more determined or courageous.

NOTES

1. Musser, Journals, 2:71.

2. The missionary methods employed in India were similar to those used in England. The elders preferred to lecture in halls to large groups when possible; only failing this did they turn to smaller settings. They announced their meetings and lectures with handbills and flyers and by direct contact on the streets and in homes. See Jan G. Harris, "Mormons in Victorian Manchester," *BYU Studies* 27 (Winter 1987): 52–53.

3. Musser, Journals, 3:14.

4. Chauncey Walker West to Samuel W. Richards, "Letter" [July 29, 1853], *Deseret News* 3 (December 15, 1853): 1; West, "The Siam Mission" [West to S. W. Richards, August 10, 1853, Bombay], *Millennial Star* 15 (October 29, 1853): 714–16; and West, "The India Mission: Sketch of the Travels of Elders Chauncey W. West and Benjamin F. Dewey in Hindostan, Islands of Ceylon, Java, Borneo, Banga, and China" [August 11, 1855], *Deseret News* 5 (September 5, 1855): 198. The last item is the first of a six-part series that West wrote following his return to Utah.

5. West, "India Mission" [August 11, 1855], *Deseret News* 5 (September 5, 1855): 198.

6. Chauncey W. West, "The India Mission: Ceylon, Bombay, Poona, Arabia," *Deseret News* 5 (September 5, 1855): 206.

7. Ibid.

8. Sonne, *Ships, Saints, and Mariners*, 56.

9. Full details of this distressing voyage are found in West's letter number 3. See Chauncey W. West, "The India Mission: Sailing Along the Malabar Coast, Island of Java, Borneo, Banga, Arrival in China," *Deseret News* 5 (September 26, 1855): 230.

10. Chauncey W. West, "The India Mission: Macao, Wampoa, Bamboo, Preaching on Board Mail Steamer, Wampoa," *Deseret News* 5 (October 25, 1855): 264.

11. R. Lanier Britsch, "Church Beginnings in China," *BYU Studies* 10 (1970): 161–72.

12. Chauncey W. West, "The India Mission: Visit Canton, Return to Wampoa, Elder Dewey Still Sick, July 15, Sail for San Francisco and Arrive There in 54 Days, Arrived in G. S. L. City, July 15, 1855," *Deseret News* 5 (October 24, 1855): 264. West's descriptions match closely those of visitors to China in the late twentieth century. Consider West's words: "At nearly every shop we were importuned to go in and look at their goods, and a dozen or more followed us during our walk trying to get into our good graces by running down other traders, and telling how good and cheap their articles were."

13. Ibid.

14. Ibid.

15. Sonne, *Ships, Saints, and Mariners*, 120.

16. I have not found sources to establish the date of B. F. Dewey's return to Salt Lake City.

17. West, *Deseret News* 5 (October 24, 1855): 264.

18. Elam Luddington, "The Siam Mission: Voyage of Elder Luddington from Burmah to Prince of Wales Island, Singapore, and Bankok, Baptisms, the Success of American Missionaries" [Luddington to Franklin D. Richards, May 1, 1854, Bangkok], *Millennial Star* 16 (August 26, 1854): 540–41.

19. Elam Luddington, "Siam" [Luddington to George B. Wallace, June 1, 1854, Bangkok], *Deseret News* 4 (November 16, 1854): 4.

20. Elam Luddington, "India—China: Perilous Voyage from Singapore to Hong Kong—Departure of Elder Willes for Liverpool" [Luddington to Franklin D. Richards, December 10, 1854, Hong Kong], *Millennial Star* 17 (March 3, 1855): 140–42.

21. Ibid., 140–41.

7

TO THE MADRAS PRESIDENCY

British administration of India in the 1850s prior to 1858 was divided primarily among three presidencies, or geographical areas: Bengal Presidency was governed from Calcutta, with penultimate authority for all of India; Madras Presidency, in the south; and Bombay Presidency, on the western side of the subcontinent. Each presidency had a governor, originally a president, but the governor, at Calcutta was supreme over the other two. It made sense that the Latter-day Saint mission to India was divided along somewhat the same lines. Elder Richard Ballantyne was appointed president of the Madras mission, but he was under the direction of President N. V. Jones in Calcutta. Hugh Findlay in Bombay arrived in the country before the Utah elders and was president of the Bombay mission, but after the Utah elders arrived President Jones directed him, too.

ELDERS BALLANTYNE AND SKELTON
SAIL TO MADRAS

Following their arrival in Calcutta, Elders Ballantyne and Skelton traveled to their various geographical fields of labor. With the monsoon coming, fewer and fewer ships, especially those dependent on sails, were heading south into the Bay of Bengal.

From the time they received their assignment to go to Madras, Elders Ballantyne and Skelton, and sometimes Elder Owens, went to the docks seeking a ship that was headed there. Most of the captains were abrupt and discourteous and refused to even consider taking two or three ministers who had such limited funds. Their reputation as purveyors of a religion that practiced polygamy— Gross sensualists! Blasphemers! Deluded ignoramuses! they cried. —made them unacceptable company for ladies and even gentlemen. As the days and weeks passed, the number of ships in port diminished to only two. The captain of the British mail steamer absolutely refused them passage, so they were left with only one choice, the *John Brightman*, under Captain Thomas D. Scott. The ship was relatively small, a 404-ton, three-masted square-rigger. Scott was part owner of the craft.[1]

Scott was no friendlier than other captains had been and initially refused to take them at any price, even at 350 rupees each. For five mornings in a row, Captain Scott turned down their request for passage. Then, on the sixth morning, Ballantyne faced the matter with even more prayerful resolve. He would approach the captain in the name of the Lord. Following fervent prayer, he and Elder Skelton again visited Captain Scott and found him in conversation with a Parsee merchant. Following introductions, the merchant began asking questions regarding the Church and its doctrines, especially plural marriage. The conversation became extended, with Scott becoming interested in what the elders were saying.

After the merchant left, the elders again broached the question of passage to Madras. They had very little to offer, only eighty-five rupees each, but they promised Captain Scott a safe voyage. He finally gave in and told them to be on board in a week.[2]

Considerable sickness was plaguing the Utah missionaries at this time. Skelton had been so sick he could not stand. Jones and Ballantyne were likewise very ill. Owens was so weakened when it came time to embark that he stayed behind in Calcutta. The day before sailing, Ballantyne was helped on board and went directly to his bunk, only to get sicker and return to Sister McCune's house overnight for better care.[3]

The *John Brightman* hoisted anchor on June 20th and drifted downstream with the tide. Elders Ballantyne and Skelton were on board. It didn't take too long before Ballantyne was feeling better. With no tugboat to pull the ship, the voyage down the Hoogly was slow. When they passed Acra Farm, Sister Meik "suspended a white flag from an upper window, as a token of regard for our welfare," wrote Skelton.

Five days into the voyage, the *John Brightman* had a near wreck that riveted the attention of everyone on deck. "We were getting over the most dangerous part of the river Hoogley," wrote Ballantyne, when

> a very singular occurrence transpired. While there were evident signs of danger, by reason of the contrary and precarious winds, the Captain came to me and said, "You promised me a safe voyage." "Yes," I replied, "and you shall have it." In a few minutes after I had given him this assurance, another ship that was beating down with us in the narrow channel tacked suddenly round, and, either to run into our vessel, or drift on to the quicksand bank seemed the only alternative. Captain Scott, of our vessel, being much alarmed, exclaimed "It's impossible to avoid a collision." But the hand of the Lord was over us, and just as it was expected that a fearful collision would take place, and the broadside of our vessel be run into, the other ship was suddenly controlled and turned round, so that she passed the side of the *John Brightman*, within a few paces, to the no small joy of the Captain and those on board.[4]

Ballantyne remembered "a few paces," but Skelton said the ships "were within arms reach of each other." Skelton continued, "This was a striking incident of God's favor to us manifested in the eyes of the captain, who was much impressed with what Bro. Ballantyne told him."[5]

The remainder of the voyage was occasionally comfortable but mostly miserable. Storms battered the craft, keeping everything and everyone wet and ajar. Sometimes the winds came at gale or

Madras Waterfront, by William Simpson, 1867

hurricane speeds for days on end. "Our passage, altogether," recorded Skelton, "has been a very rough one. Scarcely a day passes but some sail or another is carried off or torn to shreds by the violent wind accompanied by almost certain rain."[6] But after thirty-six days of storm and struggle, they made it safely through. By the time they reached Madras roads and dropped anchor at that busy international port on July 24, 1853, the captain and his first and second mates were believers, all three speaking of baptism. Unfortunately, these were baptisms that never happened. Through long discussions with the elders and reading of Church literature, the worldly Captain Scott had experienced a near complete, though temporary, change of attitude and heart. He became their patron and benefactor for the time he was in port.

Although they said little of the cultural and geographical change they had made by moving to Madras, the elders found themselves in a different environment than that of Calcutta. Rather than Bengali, the people of South India spoke Tamil, a completely unrelated language. The complexion of the Tamil people was somewhat darker than the Indo-Aryan Bengalis. Temperatures in Madras were a few degrees hotter, although the sea breezes softened the effect, and the landscape was more tropical. Madras was already an old city. The original name of Madras was Madraspatnam. The first Britishers settled there in 1639, when Francis Day of the East India Company received the right to establish what became a factory (storehouses, mess halls, and barracks) and fort. This happened fifty years before the East India Company settled what became Calcutta. By the 1850s, the population was estimated to be around eight hundred thousand, making it one of India's three largest cities. The vast majority of these people were Hindus, but there were also small, well-established communities of Muslims and Christians.

By the 1850s, the British had a firm establishment there. Buildings in the city and at Fort Saint George were large, permanent, and boasted the British style. The barracks inside that fort were two stories high and a hundred yards long. Saint Mary's

Anglican Church inside the walls of the fort would have been at home in England. A large number of troops, both European and sepoys, defended the East India Company and other British interests. There were several cantonments in the region.

Late in the nineteenth century, the British constructed a fine harbor, but before then the large amount of international trade carried on was done under difficult and somewhat dangerous conditions. Ships of any size were forced to remain at anchor a considerable distance from the shore. During the monsoon season with its high seas, most captains avoided Madras if possible. Freight and passengers were ferried ashore through the rolling, churning surf on a variety of small boats, often at considerable risk. So it was with Elders Ballantyne and Skelton as they came ashore with Captain Scott.

THE FIRST FEW DAYS AND WEEKS IN MADRAS

The elders first set foot in Madras on the morning of July 25, 1853. Captain Scott, who knew Madras well, took them directly to the "Madras Home," a hotel for soldiers and sailors. He paid for first class accommodations for them and headed off into the city to take care of business. Before leaving the ship's cabin, Scott had given Ballantyne a pair of new shoes and a purse holding fifty rupees. He promised to see them soon, which he did. The elders found the city much less congested than Calcutta and initially liked it, believing it to be healthier than Bengal.

Most of the British were settled in or near Fort Saint George, but some were located near Saint Thomas Mount, about nine miles away. Madras itself was divided into blocks—Brahmins, Muslims, and Christians, with lower castes living on the outside perimeters. The elders were initially housed in the Madras Home, the best hotel in the city, but their stay there was short-lived. Only a few days passed before they received "a polite note from the secretary of the institution" asking them to leave. They were told only soldiers and sailors were allowed; however, they knew anti-Mormons were at the base of their removal. Elder Ballantyne, especially, had tangled with a scripture reader and others regarding the literal meaning of various scriptures. From there, they went to the Temperance Hall, but their few rupees were quickly expended, and they needed someone to provide a roof and food. A number of generous persons cared for them for a few days or for longer periods of time, but the elders complained that "penuriousness" was too common. For a large part of the next year, they subsisted on bread and water or a little milk if they could obtain it.

Their presence in Madras created quite a stir. Ballantyne wrote: "I hear of no important public news. 'Mormonism' seems to be the engrossing question here." The local press had already been actively informing the public regarding the "blasphemous delusion" of polygamy.[7] Elder Ballantyne immediately answered a bitter attack in a Roman Catholic paper.[8]

Getting literature into the hands of potential converts was a high priority for Elder Ballantyne. He knew that publications were only part of a successful missionary approach, but he considered them very important. Later, he said that he wrote materials regarding the faith for "two purposes—the vindication of the cause, and a public proclamation of the Gospel."[9] While on board the *John Brightman*, the elders had shared Lorenzo Snow's pamphlet *The Only Way to Be Saved* and Parley P. Pratt's booklet *The Voice of Warning* with Captain Scott. The message of these publications resounded favorably with his thinking. When they reached Madras, Scott shared their desire to get some pamphlets into print. He paid for the reprinting of the first publications in Madras, *The Only Way to Be Saved* and an extract of Parley P. Pratt's *Proclamation of the Gospel*. Ballantyne made arrangements with Mr. Bowie of the Oriental Printing Office for one thousand copies of each.[10] *The Only Way to Be Saved* was off the press on July 30th, and *Proclamation* followed on August 5th. They immediately began distributing the two pamphlets, "taking the streets in turn . . . in a systematic

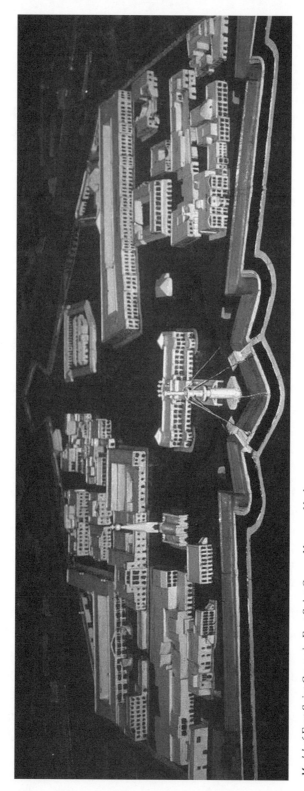

Model of Fort Saint George in Fort Saint George Museum, Madras

order," placing more of the former than the latter. All this was done in their first ten days in Madras.[11]

At the beginning of their second week in Madras, the elders were visited by John Charles, a Church member from the cantonment at Saint Thomas Mount. Matthew McCune had baptized Charles while on military duty in Burma. McCune had enough confidence in him to ordain him an elder. Now, in Madras, he seemed happy to once again be united with brothers in the faith. Initially, Elders Ballantyne and Skelton felt the same about him, but time proved Charles to be a weak soul.

Charles invited the elders to visit him and his wife at Saint Thomas Mount. He promised to rent a "suitable place" to hold public meetings in that town. About ten days later, they accepted his offer and traveled out to his home. By then, they were almost destitute and were grateful to have promise of a roof and sustenance. But when they arrived at the Charleses' home, they found him gone into Madras, which they considered peculiar. Why had he not called on them? they wondered. "We soon began to feel something [was] very much out of place," wrote Skelton. Mrs. Charles received them cordially but gave them "to understand that her husband was not the steadiest of men." Soon Charles "came home beastly drunk; swearing profanely using the Lord's name reproachfully." This grieved the elders considerably. Desiring solace, they left and found a place to pray for the welfare of their mission. On returning to the house, they were given a "miserable room, loathsome with filth," in which they spent "an excessively hot" night.[12]

When morning finally came, the elders reasoned with Charles regarding the ill effects of his drinking but also regarding his blaspheming the name of deity. He appeared sorrowful. The elders rebaptized him the following day.

A few days later, on August 8th, the three members of the Church in Madras Presidency (Ballantyne, a high priest, Skelton, a seventy, and Charles, an elder) formally organized the Church in that area. They covenanted with one another and with the Lord to

View of Saint Thomas Mount, *by James Hunter, c.1790. Elder Skelton sometimes climbed to the hilltop to refresh himself and meditate*

sustain each other and to do what they could to build up the Church in that place. After instructing one another regarding the doctrines of the kingdom, they sang "Now Let Us Rejoice in the Day of Salvation," prayed and adjourned the conference.[13]

About a week later, after some encouragement from the elders, Brother Charles rented a large house for them to live and preach in. By this time, the elders had met with Brigadier Winyalt at Saint Thomas Mount cantonment headquarters seeking permission to preach there. After taking the question to a council of chaplains and ministers, the brigadier reported back that the elders could not hold meetings in the cantonment, nor could they live there. But by a stroke of geographical good fortune, the town was situated around the base of Saint Thomas Mount, and the cantonment formed most of a circle beyond it. The house Charles rented was conveniently located "right in town" at the "heart of the

Cantonement" within easy access by military personnel. Further, it was situated directly across the road from the Baptist chapel and near two Roman Catholic cathedrals.[14]

They soon gave out handbills announcing their meeting and lecture schedule. The first few lectures were fairly well attended. Ballantyne did most of the preaching. Skelton gladly bowed to his greater years and experience. He obviously admired Elder Ballantyne, whom he said was "an exceedingly zealous man for the conversion of mankind." Skelton said he liked to "observe the manner, the weapons he uses to slay the arguments of men. . . ."[15] But he, too, participated by bearing his testimony and adding his witness to the truth of their message.

Not surprisingly, the local Roman Catholic and Protestant clergymen feared losing part of their flocks. European Christians had not been hard won, but Indians had been difficult to convert in the Madras area. Indeed, their Hindu neighbors had cruelly persecuted most native Christian converts. Soon the ministers and fathers threatened members of their congregations with loss of their jobs if they persisted in attending the Mormon meetings. The churches employed some of the Indian Christians in Madras in a way similar to that used in Calcutta and elsewhere. Regarding the effects of this circumstance, Ballantyne reported:

> A great number of catechists have come to inquire concerning our doctrines, and, should we judge from appearance, many of them are believing, but it is to be feared that among this people there are many of that class who hear the word joyfully, but not having root in themselves, when persecution arises because of the word, bye and bye they are offended. This would not be the case, so much, were the natives free from European and priestly influence. But as all the lucrative offices in Church and State, are at the disposal of the Anglo-Saxon race, the people are not free; and, in carrying out their convictions, are intimidated by the consequences of losing office and salary.[16]

DOING THE WORK DAY BY DAY

Around August 20th, Elder Ballantyne suggested that Elder Skelton continue working at Saint Thomas Mount and at Palaveram, another military station about three miles farther south, and he would move back into Madras. Skelton remained in the rented house and spent his days going from door to door talking with people and placing tracts and pamphlets. It was not long before he had talked with everyone who would listen to him or attend his preaching meetings.

So he moved on to Palaveram, where the government had situated a number of invalids from the army and civil services. Palaveram was on a flat plain where the air was fresher and more pleasant. The air may have been more pleasant but his reception was not. Although the officer in charge allowed him to distribute literature from home to home, Skelton was not allowed to preach in the cantonment. Most people treated him with contempt. After Skelton advertised his meetings there, no one came. "I find the people are swayed by their priests who intimidate them," wrote Skelton, "threatening to withdraw the small pittance which many are allowed for petty offices which helps them in obtaining the means of subsistence. A few out of the many will read our tracts but eternally object to the first initiating ordinances, Viz Baptism, Laying on of hands for the Gift of the Holy Ghost, gathering of Israel, divine authority of Joseph the Prophet, but especially Polygamy."[17]

He, like Ballantyne, was living on little but bread and water. Several compassionate ladies, wives or widows of pensioners, occasionally checked on him or sent their servants to see if he had food to eat. Even though a Mrs. Taylor, who had initially attended their meetings, lost the Spirit when her friends began to persecute her, she continued to send food for Skelton to eat. He believed the Lord had moved upon these people to take care of his needs.

With little or nothing happening in his district, Skelton frequently walked the fatiguing nine and one half miles into Madras

Robert Skelton

to work with Elder Ballantyne. In September, Elder Skelton entirely gave up on Saint Thomas Mount and Palaveram and decided to move back to Madras. Settling the rent proved to be the final incident in his relationship with John Charles. Although Charles had arranged for the house, he now refused to pay the rent. Not only that but he denied the faith. The Reverend Mr. T. Richards had convinced him the Church was a "humbug." Elders Ballantyne and Skelton subsequently had to excommunicate him.[18] Mr. Ben, a friend with limited resources, came forward and paid the rent in installments. He had no interest in the Church, but he had mercy on a fellow human being.

Elder Skelton's journal reveals his feelings on leaving Saint Thomas Mount. Indian Christian tradition holds that the Apostle Thomas Didymus taught the Gospel in India and was martyred on or near the mount that bears his name.[19] "I often take a walk up to the top," penned Skelton, "in order to get a fresh breeze and to

Richard Ballantyne

meditate upon the objects around me. It is equally a place of retreat for me when I am bow'd down to the earth by the enemies of truth, and am glad to retire from the spirits of contention and seek the solitude of the Apostle's Mount in order to relieve my burthened soul in supplicating our Father who is in Heaven."[20]

Keeping control of their emotions was sometimes an arduous task. People who came to their house in Madras or who listened elsewhere frequently became infuriated when the elders brought up substantial scriptural justification for Mormon practices and beliefs. They tried to maintain "a continual guard over [their] passions, not suffering [themselves] to get in possession of the same contentious spirit."

Elder Ballantyne rented a large house on Anderson Street. The elders lived there and taught the Gospel. Interested callers often came by to ask questions. More East Indians[21] and natives than Europeans were among those who came by and who attended their meetings. The interests of these people, however, seemed to be more curiosity regarding how much the elders were paid and how they lived than in the principles of the Gospel. As was the pattern in other parts of the mission, they held three to five lecture meetings a week, in addition to Sabbath services. For the first month or two, these meetings were quite well attended but few were regular attendees.

One Protestant missionary, a City Missionary named Collet, was especially determined to disturb their meetings. Three times he attended and interrupted the speaker and raised questions unrelated to the lecture. Finally, Elder Ballantyne "sharply reproved him, and forbad him to speak." Skelton said Ballantyne "told him he was not a gentleman or he would not come here to make disturbances." This had the desired effect. Collet remained silent and did not return.[22] But Collet's non-attendance at meetings did not indicate that he and the opposition had retreated. The local English language press was quite united against the Mormons. There was much more to come.

Late in September, considering the number of native Indians they were working with, Elder Ballantyne encouraged Elder Skelton to learn the Tamil language. Skelton did not immediately make much progress because he could not find a regular teacher. He also castigated himself for being unable to learn quickly. But by early in 1854, he had found a qualified teacher, and he was making progress in the language. Ballantyne, too, wanted to learn Tamil, and even expended some effort on the undertaking, but was too busy teaching and writing to make much headway.[23]

On October 4th, Ballantyne wrote about a meaningful meeting and interview a few days before with eight or nine Indian gentlemen, "well dressed and intelligent." Ballantyne said:

> The oldest was a gentleman about fifty years old, full grown, plump, and somewhat dark coloured. He had formerly been a Roman Catholic priest. He said—Thirty years ago I was dissatisfied with our religion. Have not found peace since. My bosom has found a lack—we need a physician, we are sick, we

need the Holy Spirit, and if you can tell us what to do, we will do it. I said—If you believe in the Lord Jesus Christ, with all your heart, will repent of all your sins, and be baptized by immersion, for the remission of your sins, in the name of the Father, Son, and Holy Ghost, you shall receive the Holy Spirit, by the laying on of hands; then shall you have joy, then shall you have peace, then shall your hearts be filled.

I preached to them some time, and so did Elder Skelton. They said—We will come to get instruction. The old man shed some tears, and so did one of his sons.[24]

During the next three weeks, the elders continued to teach the Gospel to this man and his son. Then, on October 23d, they baptized the son, the first baptism at Madras. The father seemed to believe, "but has not stamina enough [to] forsake the old systems of men, and embrace the truth." The baptismal service created considerable interest among their friends. The elders chose the water's edge at Vepery, in the northern part of Madras, to perform the ordinance. Elder Ballantyne taught the group regarding the principle of baptism for the remission of sins. After the baptism, they returned to the home of Mr. Brown, where Ballantyne was now spending much of his time, and confirmed the lad a member of the Church. Ballantyne and Skelton spoke and bore testimony to the group again at Brown's house.[25]

By early November, it was clear that not enough people were attending their meetings to justify renting a large house. Their inability to pay caused the elders to decide not to rent any more houses. Elder Skelton blamed the people, saying, "if the people will not furnish suitable places for preaching in," they would "leave them, and go where they will do it." Unfortunately, the number of friends and options available were few. Ballantyne moved to Mr. Brown's house in Vepery. Against his wife's will, Brown gave him a "half finished" room, furnished his verandah with chairs and lights, and welcomed tolerable numbers of hearers to Ballantyne's lectures. He also occasionally provided food for the elders. Skelton asked an East Indian named Caldonie to put him up. His home was on Harbor Street in the middle of the Muslim section. This was a good place for Skelton to "devote [his] attention wholly to the study of Tamil." A native catechist most frequently provided his food.[26]

By November, Elder Ballantyne and Elder Skelton had established a pattern in their work that was to continue with not many variations for a number of months. Their lives were thrown somewhat out of regularity, however, when Elder Robert Owens arrived from Calcutta on January 2, 1854. They initially rejoiced to have another worker in their field, but not many weeks passed before problems emerged. One historian summarized the difficulties with Owens this way:

> He was in constant trouble with his fellow workers in India. He was "tried" and his missionary license taken from him on 29 May 1853 for his "abuse to the Council, false teachings, revengeful spirit, etc." Owens was restored to fellowship on 13 June but was again in trouble by 26 June 1853. . . . Owens remained in [the] Calcutta area until December 1853, when he was again assigned to Madras. He remained in this general area until he left to eventually return to the United States via Australia. He was a constant problem to Ballantyne, a situation that grew worse as time passed. It eventually separated the two men and was quite disruptive to the unity of the missionaries in Madras. Owens's behavior reached very serious proportions by April 1854, when his rather lewd conduct seriously undermined Ballantyne's work with several potential converts.[27]

When Owens arrived in Madras, Elder Ballantyne, who presided over that part of the mission, assigned him to Chengalpattu [Chingleput], a few miles south of Madras. Owens was eager to get to work, but, according to Skelton, "on finding the rebellious dispositions of the people, became disheartened and desired to leave for some more favorable place." He attempted to enlist Skelton in this notion, but Skelton and Ballantyne stood firm in their desire to create a branch of the Church in Madras. Owens expressed harsh words to Ballantyne and wounded his feelings "very much."[28]

On April 23d, Mr. Brown's servants accused Owens of inappropriate behavior. They said, "We will not call him Padre [priest or minister] any more, 'But *Sailor.*'" Ballantyne wrote to President Jones in Calcutta for counsel, but by the time the letters made the round trip, Owens was set on leaving for Australia. In the meantime, he left the other elders and went to work at Vigapatam, another town near Madras.[29]

In early May, Elder Ballantyne became ill. He had been very sick twice before during his mission, first with smallpox and later with what might have been malaria. This time his disease was debilitating. Elder Skelton had to take over preaching at their regular lecture meetings. Ballantyne was so sick, however, that Skelton spent most of his time caring for him. "Being much reduced," wrote Elder Skelton, "I have to brace him up, wash and handle him the same as I would a child." Elder Skelton felt strongly that he had been set apart to take care of his companions. In his journal, he wrote: "Alth'o my brethren have been much afflicted, I have been greatly preserved from sickness, and am made to rejoice on doing good for them, even as Bro Woodruff predicted upon my head before leaving home—'You shall be a comfort to your brethren in that far off land.'" For a day or two Skelton despaired for Ballantyne's life. Three weeks passed while he "could not speak above his breath."[30] Several times, Skelton called it a liver attack, but he also spoke of problems in Ballantyne's kidneys, of congested lungs, muscular aches, and fever. It is not clear exactly what was plaguing him, but it may have been malaria again.

While Ballantyne was sick, Skelton wrote to President Jones in Calcutta for directions. On June 25th, a letter arrived counseling Elder Ballantyne to "'*go home*' seeing there are no prospects of doing any good among the inhabitants of India." They searched for a couple weeks and found Captain Robert Wright of the *Royal Thistle*, who agreed to provide Ballantyne free cabin passage but asked him to provide his own food. For a week or two before he sailed, the Church members gathered clothing for Ballantyne and gifts for Sister Ballantyne and her little ones. Mrs. Caffarly "supplied him with a sufficient supply of bread for the voyage."[31] Fortunately, once at sea Captain Wright regularly invited Ballantyne to dine at his table.

On sailing day, after a secret prayer in which they dedicated themselves to the Lord, the companions went to the beach. Skelton said Ballantyne "took boat in company with the Captain whom we found ready waiting." A friend accompanied Skelton to the bay, and they "both waited until the Ship weighed anchor and put out to sea. After which I returned very sorrowful indeed." Ballantyne sailed from Madras for London on the brig *Royal Thistle* on July 25, 1854, one year to the day after his arrival in that city.[32]

The small (only 259 tons), two-masted *Royal Thistle* docked at London on December 6, 1854, after an extremely long voyage of 134 days.[33] When he arrived in England, Ballantyne felt better physically, and he felt more content with his mission. His months on board the ship had given him time to reflect on India and his struggles there. His mind was at ease regarding his efforts. He had done his best. And he had taught the Gospel regularly while on board, and a number of those whom he instructed, mostly sailors, expressed their belief in his message and the will to submit to baptism.

Regarding his work in Madras, Ballantyne wrote:

> I have nothing special to write you by way of news. When I left Madras we had baptized 12 persons; ordained one Elder; preached the Gospel in almost every nook and corner of that large city, and several of the adjacent villages and cantonments; established a monthly paper of 8 pages; printed 1000 numbers of the "Only Way to be Saved;" 1000 of the "Proclamation of the Gospel;" 400 of a "First," and the same number of a "Second Reply" to the Rev. T. Richards, of the English Church; 400 numbers of a "Dialogue on Polygamy;" several letters in the Newspapers; and a regular issue, monthly, of 300 copies of the little periodical already alluded to.[34]

The "little periodical already alluded to" was the *Latter-day Saints Millennial Star and Monthly Visitor,* first published on April 6,

1854. It was modeled after the *Millennial Star* from Liverpool, England, although more modest in size. Ballantyne published four numbers and then Skelton added three more after Ballantyne's departure.

Obviously, the man was overly modest. His defense of and imparting of Mormonism through publications was prodigious. Elder Skelton believed Ballantyne lost his health through too much exertion in defending the truth, "having [written] most assiduously in vindicating the truth . . . having out done himself his constitution being but weak at the best."[35] All this he accomplished among a people whom Skelton labeled "penurious," that is, miserly and cheap.

After visiting some of London's most famous sites (among others, Saint Paul's Cathedral and the Crystal Palace) Ballantyne was on board the train, his first ever, to Liverpool. He went directly to 107 Finch Street, the mission office, to report to Elder Franklin D. Richards, president of the British Mission. His intention was to ask for an assignment as a missionary in the British Isles for the next two years. To his surprise, President Richards asked him to lead a company of 403 LDS emigrants to America. The company had been delayed when their original ship, the *Helios*, sprang a leak while at anchor. The Saints left that ship, and before long, arrangements were made for their passage on the *Charles Buck*, under Captain W. Smalley. Some of the emigrants endured uncomfortable conditions while waiting for the second ship. Because provisions were moved from one ship to the other, insufficient quantities of some foods were stocked on the *Charles Buck*. In combination with an unusually long voyage, these factors strained the resources of the company. Nevertheless, hardly two weeks passed after Ballantyne arrived in England before he embarked for New Orleans. The *Charles Buck*, an American ship, was large by the standards of the time—1424 tons. As was true with many other LDS emigrant companies, the group was divided into wards with a president over each. Generally good conditions prevailed during the voyage. The *Charles Buck* arrived at New Orleans on March 17, 1855.[36]

From New Orleans, the company traveled up the Mississippi River to St. Louis. Ballantyne was relieved of his duties there, only to be assigned as leader of a wagon company of similar size that he led to Utah. That company started on July 24th and arrived in the Salt Lake Valley on September 25, 1855. Elder Richard Ballantyne's mission to India was completed almost three years after its commencement in October 1852. In addition to everything else he had done, he had circumnavigated the earth "without purse or scrip." His wife, Huldah, had heard of the company's imminent arrival and traveled out to meet Ballantyne in President Brigham Young's carriage. At her side was their eldest son, Richard Alondo. Their reunion was joyous.[37]

SKELTON'S SERVICE ALONE IN MADRAS

Robert Owens, that enigmatic figure, had not had much to do with Ballantyne and Skelton for several months. Sometime before Ballantyne sailed for England, Owens had made his way back to Calcutta. He embarked from there for Australia on July 24, 1854.[38] So, from the end of July 1854 until he closed the mission in Madras in December, Elder Skelton served without a missionary companion. Skelton seldom had a companion for long until he closed the entire mission in 1856. Fortunately, he was not without friends and fellow workers. In his journal, he mentions the names of several people who came to his aid from time to time. He also speaks with respect and admiration of John McCarthy, who joined the Church before Ballantyne left and whom the missionaries ordained an elder in the priesthood on June 25, 1854. Another friend was an elderly woman named Mrs. Caffarly. In late April 1854, she allowed Skelton to live in part of her house. She deeply respected Elder Ballantyne and wept bitterly when he left, knowing she would not see him again in this life. And there were others who helped.

From April 1854 on, Elder Skelton focused his efforts on Fort

Barracks at Fort Saint George, where Elders Skelton and Ballantyne met with interested soldiers

Saint George, the cantonment in Madras. Built along the waterfront, Fort Saint George was the main center of the East India Company and other British operations in Madras Presidency. Of course, Skelton's hope was to find a few honest soldiers who would listen to his message. He regularly entered the fort in the evening to talk with soldiers when they were off duty. Several times, he was marched out of the fort by an armed guard, but because he had not been explicitly told not to enter again, he walked around to another entrance and in again. Eventually, he was told not to return to the barracks, even though everyone was supposed to be free to enter the public areas.

Ballantyne and Skelton had achieved nothing by seeking permission from authorities to preach in the cantonments, but Skelton decided to try again. For two weeks, he attempted to see the commanding officer at the fort but failed. Finally, he agreed to an interview with a lesser officer but was ultimately rebuffed.

He continued his attempts to teach the soldiers at Fort Saint George until he sailed from Madras. There were a few honest, interested men who cared for his message and who seemed to desire membership in the Church but who lacked the fortitude to withstand the persecution that was hurled at all Mormons. On one occasion Skelton pressed a few, saying in effect, Why don't we go now, at this moment, to the water to perform the baptismal ordinance? A small group followed him to the water's edge, but most of the men, fearing the persecution that would surely follow baptism, literally ran away. Skelton understood their fear. He was verbally abused with the most foul and blasphemous language and taunting whenever he went to the fort. Most of the soldiers mocked him and persecuted anyone who expressed sympathy with the Mormon cause. "I never go among them without receiving indignities from them," wrote Elder Skelton.[39]

A case in point was the abuse Thomas Peirpoint received from his sergeant and others over him. In April or May 1854, Peirpoint had made it known to Ballantyne and Skelton that he had joined the Church in England before joining the army and shipping out to India. He confessed his weaknesses but also his love for and belief in the Restored Church. Skelton re-baptized him and enjoyed his fellowship and support, financial and moral. Over the following months, however, Peirpoint's sergeant and colonel calculatingly made life miserable for him. On unfair charges, he was not allowed to have a pass; then he was charged with insubordination and placed in jail. There he became very sick and was sent to the hospital, where he continued to receive harsh treatment. Peirpoint and Skelton were convinced that such persecutions were directly related to his attempts to live the life of a good Latter-day Saint.

Skelton, himself, showed remarkable courage by going into the fort regularly to hold meetings and distribute tracts to the small band of interested hearers. The buildings within the walls of the fort were large but fairly close together. There was no opportunity for anonymity for Skelton or for interested hearers. He could have been arrested and jailed, but he pressed forward, ever seeking one more soul who would submit to the demands of the Gospel. He produced a new tract every month. Ultimately, he was not successful at the fort, but he stressed in his journal that he was doing his duty in warning everyone he could so that each of his or her sins would not be on his head.

Elder Skelton did not list the names of everyone he baptized. It is not clear how many souls he brought into the kingdom, but he mentioned a few. James Mills and his wife were especially fine people. Mills started attending preaching meetings early in 1854 and before long began defending the Mormon position among his Protestant associates. He showed unusual courage, for he was superintendent of the Religious Tract Society Depository. Formerly a Baptist minister, Mills was still involved in missionary work. In mid-May, Mills received a short letter from a committee of Baptist clergy, saying: "We do not consider it right to have you remain any longer in our employment, believing and preaching Mormonism as you do."[40] Actually, they were right. His loyalties had shifted, and he no longer represented their position. His break with the Baptists, however, did not come immediately. Elder Skelton baptized Mills and his wife about September 1st. This act, of course, finally cost him his job. He immediately signed on as doctor[41] on a ship of emigrants bound for Sydney, Australia. Skelton ordained Mills an elder and encouraged him to act as a missionary among those on the ship. Incidentally, Mills doubled his income by making this move.[42]

Through September, October, and November, Skelton continued holding meetings three or four nights a weeks, plus two meetings at the fort, as well as sacrament meeting with his little flock every Sunday. Although the numbers who joined the Church were few, he reported tolerably good attendance at his services. Some friends were especially faithful, Mrs. Caffarly and her daughter, Miss Stevenson, Dr. and Mrs. Geils, and a few others, and supported Skelton at meetings, provided him food and housing, and gave him money to pay for his printing projects. Geils opened his home for preaching whenever Skelton desired, and John McCarthy moved his own residence to a place on Anderson Street, near where Ballantyne had rented a house for a time, so he and Skelton would have a good public location for their meetings. Incidentally, Elder Skelton devoted much time to carefully teaching Dr. Geils one principle of the Gospel after another. He deeply admired Geils's logical and organized way of thinking. Skelton also liked meeting with their family and teaching the children the "songs of Zion."

CLOSING THE MISSION IN MADRAS PRESIDENCY

On November 19, 1854, Elder Skelton received a letter from President Jones asking him to leave Brother McCarthy in charge of the Madras Saints and come to Calcutta to take leadership of the mission. Jones had decided he could do nothing more for India and was going home. By that date, President Brigham Young had given a general release to all the missionaries to stay or return as they thought best.[43]

Skelton seemed to have mixed feelings toward the reaction of the Madras Saints. Being complimented, yet needing to go to Calcutta, he wrote: "The brethren being loathe to part with me make no effort to get me away." Before long, however, Dr. Geils arranged for Skelton's passage on the ship *Affaghan*, under Captain Isaac Colebank. It was scheduled to depart in late December. Fare was seventy rupees, to be paid in installments by Geils and the members of the branch.

Leaving his friends and fellow members in Madras was a deeply emotional matter. Mrs. Caffarly considered him one of her family, and others loved him as sincerely. A day or two before Christmas, Skelton preached his farewell sermon, joined the congregation in singing "Adieu to the City Where Long I Have Wandered," "which melted Mrs. Caffarly down to tears," and closed with "When Shall We All Meet Again."

The remaining day or two, Skelton visited the homes of the members and Dr. and Mrs. Geils, counseled them all to be faithful (including Brother Peirpoint in the army, to whom he gave a special blessing), received gifts: a silver purse from Mrs. Caffarly "intended when you return," an exquisitely carved sandalwood fan from Miss Stevenson, and a silk handkerchief with some coins tied in the corner from Dr. Geils—"He has been in the habit of doing this all along." Mrs. Geils and her maid asked to be baptized at this late moment. Because Elder McCarthy was now in charge, Skelton asked him to do the ordinances at some convenient time. Many tears were shed, but Skelton's were mostly tears of sorrow that his beloved friends and fellow Saints would be left to the evils of the world.[44]

In the evening of December 27th, Dr. Geils and his little girls and Brother McCarthy accompanied Elder Skelton to the beach. There they met Captain Colebank. After some delays, during which Elder Skelton sat and sang the songs of Zion with the children, he then took his leave, his "soul yearning within [him] for their deliverance from the corruptions of Great Babylon." Skelton wrote: "At day break on the 28th inst we put out to sea, soon losing sight of Madras."[45]

ANOTHER VOYAGE TO CALCUTTA

Captain Colebank was a good and humble man. He allowed Elder Skelton to teach the Gospel freely and helped prepare his cabin for Sabbath meetings. Skelton penned: "I had the spirit of my office and calling to rest upon me whilst preaching and indeed during the whole voyage a peaceable good spirit has prevailed for which I feel to praise the Lord. For by its peaceable influence, many on board are convinced of the truth."[46]

The *Affaghan* traveled the 1,404 miles from Madras to the Sand Heads in fourteen days. Another three days were required to reach anchor at Calcutta. On January 17, 1855, Elder Skelton found his way to Number 58 Lower Circular Road, where Brother Meik and his family were now living. "When I entered the gate," wrote Skelton, "the dogs made a great disturbance and the brethren being engaged at this moment in family prayer, Bro. Jones, . . . arose upon his feet and told the family that it was brother Skelton that had come; Alth'o no one had neither seen nor received any tidings from me: yet sure enough he was right. And he came running down stairs saying 'God bless you bro Skelton.'"[47]

NOTES

1. Sonne, *Ships, Saints, and Mariners*, 117–18.

2. Sonne, *Knight of the Kingdom*, 112–13. Sonne published a second edition in 1989. His book is somewhat frustrating because he provides no notes and because he sometimes novelizes and presents the reader with dialogue in quotation marks and at other times seems to be actually quoting Ballantyne's journals. It is difficult to discern what is quoted and what is imagined.

3. Skelton, Journal, 86–87 (typescript, 57–58).

4. Richard Ballantyne, "The East India Mission: Arrival of the Elders at Madras—The Captain and Two Mates of the Vessel Favourable to the Work—The Elders Introduced to the 'Plymouth Brethren'—Publication of Two Thousand Pamphlets—Opening of a Room for Preaching" [Ballantyne to Samuel W. Richards, August 3, 1853, Madras], *Millennial Star*

15 (October 22, 1853): 700. Ballantyne retold this story in an article that was published posthumously; see "A Promise Fulfilled," *Improvement Era* 6 (June 1903): 590–93.

5. Skelton, Journal, 88 (typescript, 59).

6. Ibid., 90 (typescript, 60); some grammar and syntax standardized.

7. Ballantyne, *Millennial Star* 15 (October 22, 1853): 701.

8. David J. Whittaker, "Richard Ballantyne and the Defense of Mormonism in India in the 1850s," in Donald Q. Cannon and David J. Whittaker, *Supporting Saints: Life Stories of Nineteenth-Century Mormons* (Provo, Utah: Brigham Young University Religious Studies Center, 1985), 184. Whittaker's study is derived from his doctoral dissertation, "Early Mormon Pamphleteering," (BYU, 1982): 243–64 and notes 41–119 on pages 289–305. Whittaker provides two appendixes in his dissertation that are useful for study of the India mission. Appendix D, "Selected Letters and Related Printed Matter of Mormon Missionaries Serving in India in the 1850s," provides a nearly complete catalog of India missionary correspondence through the *Millennial Star, Deseret News,* and several other Church periodicals. Whittaker has arranged these items chronologically by author. Appendix E, "Chronological Listing of Major LDS Works Published in India in the 1850s," is self-explanatory. Whittaker's thorough notes in the published article (and the dissertation) are useful for scholarly research regarding Ballantyne and the India mission.

9. Richard Ballantyne, "The Madras Mission: Opposition by Europeans—Interest of the Natives in the Work—Publication of 400 Tracts" [Ballantyne to Samuel W. Richards, October 4, 1853, Madras], *Millennial Star* 15 (December 3, 1853): 797.

10. Ballantyne, *Millennial Star* 15 (October 22, 1853): 701. See also Whittaker, "Richard Ballantyne and the Defense," 183.

11. Ibid., Ballantyne. See also Skelton, Journal, 99 (typescript, 66) .

12. Skelton, Journal, 101–2 (typescript, 67–68).

13. Ballantyne, *Millennial Star* 15 (October 22, 1853): 702.

14. Skelton, Journal, 104–5 (typescript, 69–71). Skelton may have been mistaken about there being a Baptist chapel. There seems to have been only an Anglican chapel near a Roman Catholic church.

15. Ibid., 132 (typescript, 85–86).

16. Ballantyne, *Millennial Star* 15 (December 3, 1853): 797.

17. Skelton, Journal, 119 (typescript, 78).

18. Ibid., 126–27 (typescript, 82).

19. For more information on the Apostle Thomas in India see Stephen Neill, *The History of Christianity in India, The Beginnings to 1707* (Cambridge, England: Cambridge University Press, 1984), "Christianity Comes to India," 26–49; and Samuel Hugh Moffett, *A History of Christianity in Asia, Beginnings to 1500, Vol. 1* (San Francisco: Harper, 1992), "The First Missions to India," 24–44.

20. Skelton, Journal, 128–29 (typescript, 83).

21. Terms used to denote individuals of European ancestry, individuals of mixed European and Indian ancestry, and individuals of native Indian ancestry are often confusing. Uses changed during the nineteenth century. I have found useful and followed the guidelines created by Andrew Ward in his book *Our Bones Are Scattered: The Cawnpore Massacre and the Indian Mutiny of 1857* (New York: Henry Holt and Company, 1996), xx. He writes: "*Indian* and *native* refer to all non-European inhabitants of the Indian subcontinent; *Anglo-India* to British persons born, raised, or living for much of their lives in India; *Eurasian* to people of mixed Indian and European ancestry (especially since many were part Irish, Dutch, French, or Portuguese)." My difficulty is in discerning uses such as *East Indian* that do not make clear which of these uses Skelton or another missionary is using. I presume Skelton is using *East Indian* to refer to Eurasians. His use of *native* seems to refer to people of non-European Indian ancestry.

22. Skelton, Journal, 134 (typescript, 86–87); Ballantyne, *Millennial Star* 15 (December 3, 1853): 797.

23. Sketon, Journal, 136 (typescript, 88); and Richard Ballantyne, "The Madras Mission: Baptisms—Opposition—Anti-Mormon Tracts from England" [Ballantyne to Samuel W. Richards, February 6, 1854, Madras], *Millennial Star* 16 (April 15, 1854): 239.

24. Ballantyne, *Millennial Star* 15 (December 3, 1853): 798.

25. Skelton, Journal, 139 (typescript, 89).

26. Ibid., 140–42 (typescript, 89–91).

27. Whittaker, "Richard Ballantyne and the Defense," n. 35, 201–2. Whittaker includes a number of references for those who wish to follow this matter further.

Although a hardworking missionary, Owens had been a problem to the American missionaries from the time they reached San Francisco and maybe before. He accused the others of treating him unfairly and unkindly. On the voyage to India he was very cool toward the brethren and uncooperative. See Musser, Journals, 2:38.

28. Skelton, Journal, 159–60 (typescript, 100–101).

29. Ibid., 175–76 (typescript, 107–8).

30. Ibid., 190 (typescript, 114).

31. Ibid., 203–4 (typescript, 120–21).

32. Ibid., 205 (typescript, 122). In his journal, Skelton wrote a stirring tribute to his missionary companion: "My feelings on this occasion were of no ordinary kind, having to part with my beloved brother and fellow laborer—even a worthy servant of God who has ever sought the interests of His kingdom and magnified his office with honour and dignity. And, from whom I have at all times received the best counsel and advice in all things relative to my ministry in this far off land. His amiable examples and many virtues in serving not only God but his brethren also, I shall always cherish with peculiar satisfaction. . . . He is a man that is endowed with good attainments, possessing a great degree of faith and who diligently seeks the Lord upon all matters connected with His kingdom. Striving for the spirit of revelation, which he has richly enjoyed in all his moments, and especially those of a public nature. In defending the *Gospel* he has been signally blessed and endowed with the spirit of his office and calling, in refuting the many rebellious statements relative to our doctrines and people located in Utah. He has gone enjoying the utmost confidence of the Saints who deeply regret his departure." Skelton, 205–7 (typescript, 122–23; punctuation and syntax standardized).

33. Sonne, *Ships, Saints, and Mariners*, 172–73.

34. Richard Ballantyne, "Madras: Labours of the Elders—Prospects of the Work" [Ballantyne to Franklin D. Richards, December 13, 1854, London], *Millennial Star* 17 (January 13, 1855): 28.

Elder Ballantyne's reference to his pamphlet *Dialogue on Polygamy* deserves further comment. The full title of the pamphlet was *Dialogue between A. and B. on Polygamy*. It was published in Madras in March, 1854. According to John S. Tanner, the tract contains "the earliest published Latter-day Saint reference to [John] Milton's views on polygamy." Tanner further states, "Ballantyne's eight-page tract includes . . . the first two paragraphs from Milton's discussion of polygamy in the *Christian Doctrine*, entitled 'Milton on Polygamy.' Within two years after Ballantyne cited Milton in Madras, Mormon publications in Liverpool, Salt Lake City, St. Louis, Sydney, Copenhagen, Lausanne, and Calcutta all printed excerpts from the *Christian Doctrine*, usually complete transcriptions of Milton's defense of polygamy" (John S. Tanner, "Milton and the Early Mormon Defense of Polygamy," *Milton Quarterly* 21 [May 1987]: 42).

35. Skelton, Journal, 189 (typescript, 113–14).

36. See Sonne, *Knight of the Kingdom*, 157–64; Conway B. Sonne, *Saints on the Seas: A Maritime History of Mormon Migration, 1830–1890* (Salt Lake City: University of Utah Press, 1983), appendix 1, 151; and Richard Ballantyne, "Mississippi: Voyage of the Charles Buck—

The Passengers Taken on to St. Louis" [Ballantyne to Franklin D. Richards, March 5, 12, 1855, Caribbean], *Millennial Star* 17 (May 12, 1855): 300–303. I must here insert a personal note. While writing this chapter I made the connection that my great-great-grandparents, John Sutherland Cairns Todd and May Orr, as yet not married, were part of Ballantyne's emigrant company on the *Charles Buck*.

37. Sonne, *Knight of the Kingdom*, 164–70.

38. Nathaniel V. Jones, "Hindostan: Baptisms—Indifference of the People—Departure of Elder Owens for the Valley" [Jones to Franklin D. Richards, August 2, 1854, Calcutta], *Millennial Star* 16 (October 14, 1854): 651. Jones's report to England simply stated: "Brother Robert Owens, who was appointed to Madras, has shipped for Australia, on his return to the Valley. He shipped on the 24th of July, at this place." "At this place" meant Calcutta, from which place Jones was writing.

39. Skelton, Journal, 236 (typescript, 135); spelling standardized.

40. Ibid., 181 (typescript, 110).

41. It is not clear whether Mills was a doctor or an apothecary, that is, a pharmacist. In a letter published in the *Millennial Star*, Skelton refers to Mills as a doctor. In his journal, however, Skelton refers to him as an apothecary. At the time the distinctions may not have been so clear as they have since become.

42. Skelton, Journal, 226 (typescript, 131); and Robert Skelton, "Hindostan: Lectures—Baptisms—Opposition of the Military, &c." [Skelton to Franklin D. Richards, November 8, 1854, Madras], *Millennial Star* 17 (January 20, 1855): 45.

43. Skelton, Journal, 241 (typescript, 138).

44. Ibid., 247–50 (typescript, 141–43).

45. Ibid., 251–52 (typescript, 143–44); spelling standardized.

46. Ibid., 254 (typescript, 145); spelling and punctuation standardized.

47. Ibid., 255–57 (typescript, 145–48); spelling and punctuation standardized.

8

FIRST FRUITS IN BURMA

Burma is inhabited by a number of tribes: the Karens, near Rangoon and bordering Siam east of Moulmein; the Shans, in the northeastern part of the country; the Kachins, in the far north; the Chins, on the west bordering Assam, India; and so forth. Like Siam, which is dominated by one group, the Thais, the Burmese tribe dominate Burma. As in Siam and Ceylon, most people in Burma, whether tribal or not, believe in Theravada Buddhism, the School of the Elders, mixed with a good deal of spirit worship and superstitions of various sorts. Temples, pagodas, and *poongee* (or *phoongy*)[1] houses (monks' dwellings) are everywhere. Unlike India where caste dominates social, occupational, and religious matters, when our missionaries were there, the Burmese were far more open in their social and religious interactions. Matthew McCune described the Burmese as being "of a cheerful, happy disposition, faithful and affectionate in their family circles, and though the laziest of all people, yet, with a perfect independence to many, except for the indulgence at drinks, devotedly sincere in their religion, and personally make sacrifices, in order to be able to present a valuable offering at their gods, of gold, silver, wood and stone or to their priesthood."[2] But elements of Indian art, music, and mythology created an underlay for the Burmese way of life.

SGT. MATTHEW McCUNE INTRODUCES
THE GOSPEL IN BURMA

Brother Matthew McCune, a staff sergeant in the arsenal department of the East India Company's Bengal Artillery, was assigned to Burma in July 1852, after war broke out in April between the British and that country. Twenty-five years before, in 1824, hostilities had erupted along the Indo-Burmese border. At that war's conclusion in 1826, the British exacted an indemnity of ten million rupees, control of the Arakan and Tenasserim coasts (leaving a gap where the mouths of the Irrawaddy River reach the Bay of Bengal), and some loss of sovereignty. The Burmese kings had chafed under the terms of the Treaty of Yandabo and as years passed made conditions disagreeable for British traders in Burma. In early 1852, Commodore Lambert, whom Governor-General Lord Dalhousie deputed to Burma to improve relations, followed his own inclinations toward gunboat diplomacy and provoked a war. The British were successful but decided not to pursue their interests very far north. At the conclusion of hostilities, Dalhousie annexed Lower Burma to British India.[3] Matthew McCune and other Church members were involved in this short war.

When we missionaries from Utah arrived in Calcutta, McCune was already in Burma. His wife, Sarah, hosted us on our arrival and continued to support the Church despite her misgivings regarding the doctrine of plural marriage.[4] Matthew, who had been ordained an elder by William Willes and James Patrick Meik on April 11, 1852,[5] was much more interested in preaching the Restored Gospel as a part-time missionary than fighting a war with the Burmese as an artillery sergeant. He considered the war to be unnecessary, if not unjust. When he arrived in New York with his family in March 1857 on his way to join the Saints in the Salt Lake Valley, he submitted a letter to *The Mormon*, a Church-sponsored newspaper in New York City, stating the portion of Burma that was "appropriated by the ruling powers in India" was taken "on the principle, I suppose, of might making right, telling his majesty [the Burmese

Matthew McCune

king], who naturally felt dissatisfied at such a procedure, that, if he would keep quiet, they would allow him to keep the remainder of his province, but, if not, they would take the balance from him also."[6] Subsequently, in 1886, the British annexed the remainder of Burma into India, anyway.

Nevertheless, McCune was obligated to follow his vocation and prepared to move with his outfit against the Burmese enemy. On July 14, 1852, he baptized his wife, Sarah Elizabeth, and his eldest living son, Henry, in the tank at Acra Farm.[7] He gave his farewell address to the members of the Calcutta Branch on July 25th and left the next day for Rangoon. After an unusually long period at sea, waiting eleven days for a fair wind to complete the voyage, Matthew arrived at Rangoon on August 17th,[8] and joined his friend and fellow convert, Sergeant William Adams, a teacher in the Aaronic Priesthood, who had been sent there earlier. Of McCune and Adams's presence in Burma, William Willes wrote:

"We have opened Birmah."[9] Willes, as presiding elder in Calcutta, sent McCune with authority to teach the Gospel and organize the Church.

Teach they did, and organize, too, to some extent. Together, they held the first sacrament meeting in Burma in an empty poongee house on August 22d. The next day, having advertised a public lecture with handwritten handbills, McCune delivered his first address to an audience of twenty people. He notified the public, mostly British military men, that lectures on the Restored Gospel would be given every Thursday and Sunday evening "unless engaged with the enemy."[10] A number of meetings that followed were held in a poongee house that McCune and Adams took over. McCune reported "crowded audiences."

Almost from the beginning, opponents of the Church brought anti-Mormon threats and claims against McCune, Adams, and others who joined them. But a few brave souls came forward and asked for baptism. Between mid-October and January 11th, McCune baptized eight men, "a bombardier and two gunners, of the Madras Horse Artillery; a sergeant, and one private of the 1st Bengal Fusiliers; an officer of the 1st Madras Fusiliers, and two privates of Her Majesty's 80th Regiment."[11] Although McCune had baptized only Europeans, he was learning Burmese and hoped to introduce the Gospel to them and the Karen people, a hope that never came to fruition.

They were all in the midst of a war, and troop transfers required adjustments. For example, Captain George Markham Carter of the 1st Madras Fusiliers was sent to Prome, so McCune ordained him an elder and told him to establish the Church there. McCune himself was ordered to Moulmein and Martaban. Prior to his transfer, he ordained John Charles of the Madras Horse Artillery an elder and left him in charge at Rangoon. Others were ordained to other callings in the priesthood. By January 1853, there were four elders, two teachers, one deacon, and three members in Burma—a total of ten Latter-day Saints.

McCune's assignment took him to Martaban on January 3,

1853, and then north up the Sittang River Valley to Bilin, Shwegyin, and Toungoo, and a number of small villages along the way, all being strongholds of the Burmese forces. By late 1852, British military supremacy was shown and that part of the country was annexed into British India, but battles continued while McCune and his colleagues marched through various jungles, rice fields, and villages. They passed hundreds of houses built on piles,[12] to stay above water during the rainy season. Their marches varied in length: four miles one day, eleven the next, seven the day following, and so on. Matthew recorded several encounters with the Burmese enemy. On January 16th, his unit received fire. "Returned with interest by our guns; killing a number of them." Three days later his unit killed "upwards of a hundred." Fortunately, there were not many such incidents. McCune taught the Gospel regularly in each place and baptized one man on the march and two others at Shwegyin. He spent two months at Shwegyin, where he was in charge of an artillery park, a place for storing military equipment. Along the way and while there, he and the other members suffered almost continuous persecution. There were "repeated attempts to interrupt . . . by cutting ropes of the tent during meeting, throwing stones, etc."[13] and "many threats . . . to burn the house down, to shoot us, &c."[14] Two times McCune established himself in poongee houses, and on March 27th, he moved into a Buddhist image house where he began holding meetings. Three times hostile officers under one pretext or another forced him out. This is how he described his third ejection:

> I now took possession of an Image-house near a Pagoda, and through the kindness of the Engineer Officer got it walled in and floored, and again commenced preaching. The Burmese Gods in this house were from 12 to 14 feet high, built of bricks and mortar, and gilt over with gold-leaf; the effect when lighted was very fine, as the images reflected the light in the most brilliant manner and appeared to be looking down upon our proceedings in their sanctuary with wonder and astonishment. I had not been long in possession before the authorities discovered that they required to run a wall through the back part of

this, my new chapel, to enclose a powder magazine, which had been erected for my ammunition. I was again warned to turn out, and they unroofed the house sufficiently to render it uninhabitable, and then left off.[15]

On April 6th, he moved into a tent, feeling discouraged and sensing his work at Shwegyin to be done. Two weeks later, McCune was ordered back to Rangoon. He was relieved to return there but disappointed that John Charles, whom he had ordained an elder and left in charge, had been so severely persecuted that he had stopped holding meeting and preaching the Gospel. The Rangoon Branch had been temporarily shut down.

It was about this time that we Utah missionaries arrived in Calcutta. Word of the doctrine of plural marriage had arrived before we did. Brother McCune reacted to this news the same way his wife did, with shock and questions. On April 19th, he penned: "Received a letter informing me that polygamy was a doctrine held and practiced by the Saints, and quoting a revelation given through the prophet Joseph—It has quite upset the church in Calcutta, and my own mind is much disturbed about it."[16] He said he was "astounded and much grieved, though I could not doubt for a moment that this was the Church of Christ." He had "esteemed this [plural marriage] as sin, which would be followed by chastisement if not repented of."[17] But he retained an open mind and wrote to Calcutta for more information. While waiting for a reply from us in Calcutta, to his great joy, Elders Luddington and Savage arrived in Rangoon. McCune was soon convinced that the doctrine of plural marriage was of God. He wrote: "I can now contend with all confidence for the above doctrine, as revealed by the Lord, for the exaltation of His Saints in the world to come."[18] McCune's testimony was incredibly strong. He had withstood great persecution before learning of the doctrine of plural marriage. To have endured all that and then accepted this difficult doctrine proved the strength of the man's dedication to the Church. The Rangoon Branch house, which had been closed for several months, was

Levi Savage, Jr.

immediately opened, and the Gospel was again preached in that city.

By that time, August 1853, Elder McCune was looking forward to the expiration of his obligation to the government with the hope of emigrating to Zion. He was also grateful to have two full-time missionaries to share the burden of preaching the restored Gospel.

LUDDINGTON AND SAVAGE ARRIVE

Getting to Rangoon had been a harrowing experience for Luddington and Savage. I briefly described their attempted voyage in an earlier chapter, but Savage added fascinating details in his journal account. He wrote:

> June 15, 1853, Wednesday. Brother Ludington and I went on board of the Fire Queen, a government steamship to sail for Rangoon in Burma. We took deck passage and boarded ourselves. The deck was crowded with coops filled with chickens,

geese, ducks, pigs, and sheep; some of the sheep and goats running loose. There were over a hundred natives as deck passengers and a few whites besides ourselves and some cabin passengers all on board amounting to 240 souls. We sailed the 16th.

June 18, 1853, Saturday. The wind had increased, the weather thickened and some rain, the sea quite rough and all had the appearance of a severe storm. At about 12 o'clock at night we discovered the ship had 18 inches of water in her hold. The pumps were tried and found them choked so they would not work, so we went to hoisting the water out with buckets which was a very slow process. We concluded to about ship and turn back to Calcutta.

June 19, 1853, night. The storm had increased to a perfect gale and all hands were engaged in throwing over cargo and to pumping and bailing water for they had gotten two of the pumps so they would work a little by this time.

June 22, 1853. We came in sight of the mail steamer, we hoisted a signal of distress and she came to our assistance, but said she could do nothing but get us a pilot, which she did and which we needed as we had now arrived at sand heads. The storm still continued frightful. About 9 o'clock at night we anchored at a lighthouse one mile from shore with eight feet of water in the hold. The officers made arrangements for the hands and passengers to bail the water out and then with as much liquor as they could carry went to bed. They all worked for awhile and then some were drunk and said they were going to rest and so went to bed. But, a few continued to work. The native passengers would not do anything, only as they were compelled, because they said they would lose their religious caste. The wind had lulled a little but now began again to blow a gale and I expected the ship would sink with all in bed. I was determined to save myself if I could, so I cut the lashings of one of the boats that was on the wheel house, so when the ship sunk the boat would swim and I would get on. But thank the Lord the ship by its power was kept alive and all came safely into Calcutta the next day, the 23rd. [19]

They tried unsuccessfully to find another ship to take to Burma, and after repairs were made on the *Fire Queen*, they finally took passage on her and embarked again on July 30th, arriving at Rangoon on August 10th, almost a year after McCune. They reported to President Jones in Calcutta that the Church in Burma had only ten members, including the three of them. John Charles had been transferred back to Madras, and other members had also been moved or had fallen away. Eleven days after their arrival, Elder Luddington was elected presiding elder over the Church in Rangoon.

For all his strengths, it must be remembered that Elder McCune had little experience in Church government and administration. His journal reveals a number of excommunications and disfellowshipments. There were also a number of re-baptisms, a practice that was fairly common in the Church at that time. Perhaps his military training and strict adherence to rules and discipline brought about these strict actions, but he was a demanding leader. A number of new converts fell away because of persecution, demands of membership, and doctrinal disagreements. But McCune even cut off from the Church his good friend William Adams for drinking. And after McCune's wife arrived in Rangoon, he even briefly cut her off from membership. He himself recorded on October 16th, the year before: "About this date I left off the use of tea and all hot drinks, in obedience to the Word of Wisdom." His full compliance with the expectations of the Church was still young but very earnest. Evidently, he expected as much from everyone else as he himself gave. McCune was willing to forgive but held a high standard, sometimes acting to cut people off before they had been sufficiently labored with. Fortunately, Adams was re-baptized by Elder Luddington on August 22, 1853. He remained faithful and desired to emigrate to Utah but died in Calcutta two years later.

Elder Savage and Elder McCune had strong and conflicting personalities. Both were men of character and will, but their differences of opinion resulted in Savage exiling himself to Moulmein not long after arriving at Rangoon. Their differences centered on Savage believing McCune had "grossly insulted" him. The alleged insults were actually trivial matters: a contradiction in a conversation, supposedly evasive answers to Savage's questions, and

Savage's feeling that McCune believed himself to be better educated. Perhaps McCune did come across that way. Savage also
believed that McCune had received a letter from his wife in
Calcutta that prejudiced him against Savage. Although they "ami-
cably settled by shaking hands and forgiving each other" the day
the problems flared into the open, the matter still festered in
Savage's mind. Several days later, Savage again made angry accusations, and again they forgave one another. But McCune and
Adams were "totally disgusted with bro, S's conduct."[20]

There must have been behind-the-scenes discussion of the
matter and considerable tension among the small group of members. Savage explained to me, Elder Musser, his view of what happened next. He said he tried to get along with Brother McCune,
but that everything he did seemed to make matters worse. Elder
Luddington took McCune's side and before long suggested that
Elder Savage should not partake of the sacrament with the rest of
the branch. Then, on Sunday, September 25th, Elder Luddington
arose and said (according to my journal—I had received a letter
from Savage) that it was his painful duty to propose that

> Bro. Savage should be cut off from the Rangoon Branch, which
> was seconded by Bro. McCune, and carried unanimous, with-
> out ever asking me to say a single word in any way. A singular
> move tho't I, as there had not been any trial, not even a
> charge.[21]

Of course, Savage was correct that standard Church procedure
had been abridged, but there was little he could do. He felt ostra-
cized from his brethren, and with donations from McCune and
Adams, three days later he bought passage on the steamer
Tenasserim and sailed across the Gulf of Martaban for Moulmein,
where he worked alone for almost a year.

Stitching the Burma mission story together over the next year
is more like making a quilt than a blanket. A number of pieces
must be joined together, but some are missing. After Elder Savage
moved to Moulmein, Elders Luddington and McCune pursued

the building of the kingdom in Rangoon. They were blessed with a number of baptisms, perhaps ten, two of whom later apostatized, but at least one family, the John Hefferans, later emigrated to Utah. McCune considered Hefferan a learned man. He was born in India of mixed parentage. By profession, he was an apothecary (pharmacist) who worked at the military hospital in Rangoon.

On January 1, 1854, a month before Elder Luddington left Rangoon in his effort to reach Bangkok, Siam, he reported the Church's progress in Burma to Samuel W. Richards in England. He and McCune were preaching three times a week near the great Shwe Dagon Pagoda. At that moment, their meetings were well attended. Luddington was quite excited about one of their preaching experiences. He wrote:

> A few Sabbaths ago, I preached on the government wharf to a company representing most of the nations and peoples under heaven—Birmese, Bengalese, Malays, Brahmins of different castes, Mussulmen, Armenians, Jews, and Gentiles. I spoke at the top of my voice, so that all should hear.[22]

Luddington was particularly hopeful regarding the Armenians, although little seems to have come of his interactions with them.

In mid-January 1854, Matthew McCune was delighted to have his wife, Sarah Elizabeth, and children join him and add to the Rangoon Branch. Henry, age fourteen, enlisted in the navy and served in Burma for a time. The family strengthened the branch, but Sister McCune continued having reservations regarding doctrinal matters.

At the end of that month, Elder Luddington sustained Matthew as presiding elder preparatory to his own departure for Siam on February 6th on the *Fazil Carreem*. The Rangoon Branch contributed eighty rupees toward Luddington's transportation costs. Luddington was still determined to reach his assigned mission field.

Only five weeks passed following Luddington's departure before the Rangoon Branch received Elder William Willes from

Calcutta on March 12th. He had been in India since Christmas day 1851 and had traveled a major part of northern India. President Jones gave him his freedom to return to England or go to the Valley, but McCune and other members in Rangoon begged him to join them for a time. Brothers McCune and Adams, who had associated with Willes in Calcutta, each contributed fifteen rupees to pay his fare from Calcutta to Rangoon.[23] He stayed in Burma for about six months and saw "nearly twenty added to the Church." This brought the number of baptisms in Burma to more than thirty. Next to Bombay and Poona, it was probably the most productive of baptisms of any part of the East India Mission. Willes, an educated man, also opened a school for teaching the English language. He charged a modest tuition which, when added to contributions from the Burma members, paid his passage home to England.[24]

Willes, like the other elders who served in Burma, appreciated the Burmese people. "In Burmah," he wrote, "the natives follow the patriarchal order of plurality [of wives], and until they were corrupted by *Christians*, licentiousness was almost unknown among the female sex. . . . The Burmese are a jocular, sociable kind of people but live in a primitive sort of style, although weaving and some few simple and ornamental arts are in vogue." Willes said the Buddhist priests were highly respected, even venerated. "They act in the capacity of teachers to the male population, all of whom, I believe, are able to read, write, and cipher." He found it amusing but sad that Burmese children frequently took up cigar smoking almost as soon as they were weaned—"it is quite general to see little ones of a year old, puffing away with the greatest zest imaginable."[25]

One of Willes's reasons for going to Burma was to investigate the Karen tribe as possible recipients of the Gospel message. He soon concluded that their beliefs did not match well with those of Mormonism and reported this to President Jones in Calcutta. But Jones was "sick of trying to do anything with the people of India" and "gladly sought an opportunity to try another [field]." Burma provided "an ample pretext for so doing." So he went to Burma to do his own investigation and to help strengthen the branch there. Following a quick, six-day steamer voyage, Jones arrived at Rangoon on August 25th.

He was pleased with the condition of the branch. After giving a few lectures and working with the members in Rangoon, on September 16th he sailed on to Moulmein to check up on Elder Savage. Savage was pleased to see him for he had been almost a year "without the society of any one belonging to the Church."[26]

A few days before Elder Jones joined Elder Savage on September 11, 1854, Elder Willes embarked on the Siamese bark *Velocity*, under Captain Powell, for Penang Island, en route to America or Liverpool. His hope was to go directly to San Francisco because that would have been the quickest way to the Valley. His wife and family had emigrated to Great Salt Lake City while he was in India and Burma.[27] He stayed at Penang Island for only four days, but he used his time well teaching the Gospel, distributing tracts, and bearing his testimony. He also tried to find a ship that would take him to America. In this he failed, even with the sincere efforts of the American consul. So he decided to sail on to Singapore, where he hoped to find a greater number of ships that might transport him to San Francisco. A captain offered to take him to Singapore gratis. Considering the captain a generous man, Willes accepted the offer, only to discover after being on board, "that he had offered me the passage that I might assist him and his crew in defending them from the piratical Malays, who infest the Straits of Malacca." Fortunately, the voyage proceeded without incident, and in six days he was in Singapore.[28]

At Singapore, Willes found Elder Luddington who had been to Bangkok and was on his way home. They spent four days together and then parted. Willes took passage on the small, three-masted bark *Gazelle*, under Captain George Leslie, and sailed on October 14, 1854. The voyage home to England from Singapore took four and a half months, but Captain Leslie "behaved with much kindness, and permitted" Willes to teach the Gospel while on board. He even took him ashore at Saint Helena Island west of Africa and helped him arrange to deliver a sermon there. Ever a missionary, Willes left copies of the Book of Mormon and other Church literature with businessmen at that place. Perhaps he was the first witness of the restored Gospel in that small East India Company outpost in the Atlantic Ocean. After an absence of almost four years, Elder William Willes arrived home in Liverpool, England, on March 1, 1855. But he considered his trip only partly complete; he was bound for Zion to embrace his family as soon as he could make arrangements.[29]

Elder Willes spent less than two months in England before joining a Mormon emigrant company headed for the United States. Around April 23d, he embarked with 577 other Latter-day Saints on the large, American square-rigger, the *S. Curling*, under Captain Saunders Curling. Willes served as secretary to the company and played an active role in the organization and administration of the Church on board. The company was presided over by a president and two counselors, plus seven presidents of wards. Although the passage was unusually rough, everything went well. Aside from seasickness and the birth of two healthy babies, there were no medical problems. The captain provided full support for the Saints. He said, "You are Saints, for you have acted like such in every way, and, of all passengers I never saw such, for you have been no trouble to me at all; more of a pleasure than a trouble." The *S. Curling*, the first Mormon immigrant ship to arrive at New York since the early 1840s, docked on May 22, 1855.[30] Elder John Taylor met the ship. By steamer, railroad, and wagon, the company made its way to Garden Grove. After waiting there for ten weeks for wagons and provisions, the company made its way on to Utah, arriving in Salt Lake City on October 20, 1855. When his wife took him home to see their children, they did not recognize him. He had been away from his family for four years and two months.

SAVAGE TRIES TO LEARN BURMESE AND TO TEACH THE GOSPEL IN MOULMEIN

We left Elder Savage with Elder N. V. Jones at Moulmein, Burma, in mid-September 1854. We are not privy to their conversations when they got together, but they must have talked long about their separate experiences in Calcutta and Moulmein. Elder Savage had willingly gone among the native people of Burma because he believed the Gospel needed to be taken among all people. He had occupied himself in the serious study of the Burmese language from the time of his arrival in Burma. After seeing him in action, Jones reported that Savage spoke the language "well." Savage did not give himself such high marks. He was fortunate to find Burmese friends, such as Mouny Shwagoon, who shared their knowledge freely. He had also visited among the people to "acquaint [him]self with their ways." More than once, he traveled to villages outside Moulmein to survey life as it was.

Savage also visited with American Baptist ministers in that area. One told him that "any man that went around teaching the doctrine of Joe Smith—deceiving the people, ought to be put in jail." And another, the Reverend Mr. Bigby, said he did not consider Savage "a Christian and that he would do all he could to prevent [his] success." Elder Savage's experience with the cantonment commander was the same as elsewhere in the mission. Colonel Johnston threatened to report him to the guard if he entered the cantonment. In all, few people came to his assistance. B. George Jefferson, an Englishman who operated a small hotel, hosted him for his entire stay, free of charge. Savage and the Jeffersons became good friends. "I have been as kindly treated by all in the house as though I were a member of the family," remembered Savage. He even had his own room where he could put on the robes of the priesthood and offer his prayers of thanks to his Heavenly Father without fear of disturbance. Mr. Jefferson believed in Mormonism except the doctrine of plural wives. He read Savage's books and pamphlets and appreciated their contents.[31]

On August 1, 1854, Savage wrote: "The spirit has for a month past and does yet urge me very much to leave this place and unless prospects should appear more favorable I intend to leave on the next steamer, which is daily expected." Three days later, the steamer arrived with a letter from Elder Jones, expressing his interest in coming to Burma. Elder Savage returned a letter to Jones in which he described the Burmese and Karen people and invited him to come and see for himself. So Jones went to Burma.

JONES AND SAVAGE VISIT THE KAREN PEOPLE

Jones did not remain long at Moulmein. On September 20th, he and Savage said goodbye to the Jeffersons and embarked on the *Tenasserim* for Rangoon. Once there, they immediately began making preparations to visit the Karens. They first tried to go by land but soon learned that boats were the only means of transportation. Jones probably knew better, but he was still hoping to find a people who would accept their testimony. "The first night," wrote Jones, "set us far beyond the reach of the European population, in the midst of the swarming multitudes that inhabit this country. That night we stopped in a Karen village, which we reached sometime after nightfall, in not very agreeable condition, for I had the misfortune just before night to get an *overturn*, by which I was enabled to judge correctly the depth of the water, which I found to be several feet." Savage described the overturn this way: "About sunset I was assisting to push the boat and uncautiously stepped over to the side of the boat where Brother Jones was sitting on his trunk, that caused the boat to tip until it nearly dipped water, pitching Brother Jones head first out of the boat. It was with some difficulty that he crawled back into the boat, dripping from head to foot."[32]

Jones went on:

But with the day light came a strange and magic view, to American eyes—a whole community of villages upon posts from six to ten feet above the water. They looked like the inhabitants of Neptune, that had just emerged from the watery element. An old adage came to mind with much force, which was, that "one half of the world do not know how the other half live." This is literally true.

The whole country, for miles around, is submerged in water from two to five feet in depth, though at a superficial view it presents quite a different appearance. Here is a kind of coarse cane grass and water weed, that grow up from the earth, and float upon the surface of the water until they have formed a body, in some places a foot in thickness. Upon this is a kind of short grass growing, which gives it the appearance of one continuous plain. All through this are channels in which the people travel with their boats. These channels are to the Karens what public high roads are to us—a thoroughfare of business, boats going to and from market.

This district of country is settled principally by Karens, who have come down from the hills for the purpose of raising rice, to which it is peculiarly adapted. . . . Every few miles are villages, with from fifteen to thirty houses in each, and with sometimes two and three families in a house, besides hogs, dogs, and fowls, living upon the same platform.[33]

But although Jones's ethnographic observations were interesting, he was disappointed in the Karens' religious views. "They do not worship the 'Great Spirit,' as the [Protestant] missionaries have stated." He had in mind the "Great Spirit" worshiped by the American Indians in Utah, whom he believed to be closer to the truth. He found the Karens to be either Buddhists or non-believers who did not worship anything. When Savage attempted to introduce the ideas of Mormonism, the people did not understand at all. Jones found the raw material too basic to work with. They "traveled from village to village for some days, and what we learned in the first we learned in the last—they were all alike."[34] They were all alike in one other way: They were friendly and generous. Every night the elders stayed in a Karen home and shared their rice, fish, and eggs. Never would they take money for their generosity. The mosquitoes were less liberal. They exacted their fee. Savage complained, "This morning when I awoke I could only find a part of myself for during the night the mosquitos had carried away a large portion by piecemeals." The entire Karen adventure lasted only three and a half days. By midday of September 27th, they were back at Brother McCune's house.

MISSIONARY WORK CONTINUES IN RANGOON

President Jones remained in Rangoon until October 9th, but the day before he sailed for Calcutta, he formally organized the Rangoon Branch. The formal organization made little actual difference in the way affairs were carried out. Jones called Matthew McCune as president of the branch, and McCune called Savage as his first counselor and John Hefferan as second. Hefferan was also asked to serve as secretary to the branch. Savage considered himself to be a lone missionary again, but he had the support of several dedicated members of the Church—McCune, Hefferan, William J. Thompson, and a few others.[35]

The branch met regularly on Sundays, and Savage, McCune and others held preaching meetings during the week. Until January 1855, Savage lived with the McCunes and spent considerable time helping Matthew build a house. The government had turned out McCune for preaching.

Ironically, on December 10th, the Sunday when the branch met in the new McCune house for the first time, First Counselor Savage and Branch President McCune had another disagreement. Matters were so strained that three weeks later, McCune suspended Brothers Hefferan and Thompson "for refusing to do their duty in bro. Savages case and refusing to submit to the authority of their brethren in disfellowshiping bro. S." Hefferan also refused to turn over the branch records to McCune when he demanded them. Savage and Hefferan sent President Jones their version of the difficulty and waited for a reply. The problem was officially resolved when McCune received a letter from Jones on February 19th. McCune wrote as follows:

> Communications having been received from bro. N. V. Jones, Calcutta, giving the description of a council of Elders upon the existing difficulty between bros. L. Savage & M. McCune, Consisting of N. V. Jones, William Fotheringham & Robert Skelton[,] a meeting was appointed for the purpose of reading the decision on the 20th. The decision was condemnatory of Elder McCune in the difficulty and justificatory of Elder L. Savage and appointing the latter to preside instead of the former.[36]

Savage said little of this in his journal. He noted only his time spent building McCune's house. McCune, however, proved his mettle by accepting the decision of the elders' council with complete humility. A month later, Savage re-baptized McCune. Elder Hefferan joined Savage in re-confirming him and re-ordaining him an elder. McCune willingly served as Savage's first counselor in the branch presidency until Savage left for Calcutta on June 16, 1855. Before leaving, Savage once again sustained McCune as branch president. Elder Savage, a seventy in the Melchizedek Priesthood, was far more schooled in the ways of priesthood administration. McCune, on the other hand, was the ballast for the branch in Burma. Both men served well; they simply had different personalities and varied experience in the Church.

While these internal problems were going on, Elder Savage continued his efforts to establish the Church among the Burmese. He moved into Moning Gallay's house on January 17, 1855. Gallay, a Burmese, welcomed him into his home and never charged him a cent until he left in June. Like so many of the Burmese, he was hospitable and kind. Savage worked on the Burmese language and became fairly competent in its use. "I set myself to obtain the Burmese language," he wrote, "with great faith that the Burmese would obey the Gospel when they understood it. I have spent the most of my time with and among them." In Burmese, he could explain "to some little extent" the First Vision, some ideas regarding prophets, the resurrection, and "point out to them their erroneous traditions, and absurd superstitious ideas of the deity, &c."[37]

He also made a concerted effort to get Joseph Smith's account of his first vision and other parts of the Pearl of Great Price translated. The translators found the words difficult. Savage said "in the piece that I had [given the translator] there were a few words that are very difficult to find the correct meaning in Burmese."[38] In May 1855, Savage wrote to Elder Franklin D. Richards in England regarding these efforts, saying that although he had been trying for a year to get these works translated, he had "failed in [his] every attempt."[39]

Savage, like Willes, opened a school for young Burmese to learn English. Although the fees were ultimately helpful, Savage's main purpose was finding an inroad among the Burmese people. The parents of his students became his good friends and even showed some interest in his Gospel message. Ultimately, however, all of his efforts in this area proved ineffectual. "I have not found one that has manifested the least interest in the things that I have told them," he wrote.

Elder Savage might have found his efforts completely depressing had he not baptized a few Europeans in Rangoon. On February 11, 1855, Savage wrote:

> Today I spent the day at Brother Hefferan's. Mr. John [D.] Rozarria . . . much unexpected by me, desired admittance into the Church by baptism. After noon we resorted to a beautiful lake about three-fourths of a mile from Brother Hefferan's and attended to the ordinance. Here I saw a dream literally fulfilled, which I had a short time past. For in the dream I saw myself standing in the waters of a beautiful lake about up to my hips, with a male person, whom I baptized, while two or three stood on the shores to witness. This was the exact occurrence of the above-mentioned baptism. Brothers Hefferan and Thompson and a Mr. Fuller were the witnesses. I confirmed him and then we returned to Brother Hefferan's, after which I returned to my Burma home.[40]

Brother Rozaria, a clerk by trade, was born in Madras. On September 15, 1855, he emigrated to Zion by way of Antwerp and Liverpool on the ship *Statesman*.

In February 1855, Savage received notice that Elders Jones and Fotheringham were preparing to go home. Then in April, Elder Skelton said he was ready to leave, even though he was not able to do so for a number of months. Elder Woolley had sailed the previous November. The mission was clearly coming to an end. Based on a letter from the First Presidency, President Jones had earlier told the elders to gather the few Saints who would go and head for the valleys of the mountains.[41]

Savage's hopes were fading, and his courage, too. "Ever since my arrival to this country," wrote Savage in his journal, "I have always had strong hopes and great faith that many of this people would obey the Gospel when they understood it. . . . [But] my faith in regard to their receiving the Gospel, has become much shaken and my hopes nearly blasted. When I think upon the untiring exertions and the long continued efforts to introduce the Gospel among them and without the least success or prospects of success, it is truly discouraging; and I feel the sooner I left this country, the better."[42]

In his May 30th letter to Elder Franklin D. Richards, Savage finally allowed himself to say publicly what he had been writing in his journal for some time: he was discouraged and ready to go home. He apologized to Richards for not writing sooner but said he had "nothing to write but the same that the Elders were frequently writing to you from all parts of India, namely, the ill success of the Gospel in these parts." He had found the way to Siam, his appointed mission field, "perfectly obstructed" and had remained in Burma for lack of a better place to serve. He found the Burmese to be "generally possessed of tolerably good principles," but "for any one to depart from their old traditions and national customs is so degrading in the eyes of their own community, that if they become convinced of a truth that comes in contact with their old traditions, they cannot muster courage sufficient to embrace it and withstand the scoffs and frowns that would be heaped upon them."[43]

At the end of May, Elder Savage received a request from Elder Skelton to come to Calcutta and watch over the members there for a time. Skelton was on his way to Cuttack to help Brother Meik with his timber cutting business. Savage hoped to gather a few Saints in Calcutta and migrate with them to America. On May 30th, he discontinued his school in the morning and in the evening told Brother McCune of his intentions. Savage spent the next two weeks saying his good-byes, reappointing McCune as branch president, gathering some donations to pay his way home, counseling the brethren to "endeavor to create union in their midst and gather up to Zion as soon as possible," and packing his things. On Saturday, June 16, 1855, Elder Savage bade farewell to Brothers McCune and Rozaria, "all in good spirits," and went on board the *Fire Queen*. She sailed "down the river, bound out to sea" between one and two o'clock in the afternoon.[44] The Rangoon Branch had contributed fifty rupees to help defray his fare. In the same collection, branch members set aside thirty rupees for the Perpetual Emigration Fund.

ELDER SAVAGE'S REMARKABLE TRAVELS HOME TO UTAH

When Levi Savage arrived in Calcutta on June 20th, he found that Elder Skelton had already gone to Cuttack. All of the other missionaries, with the exception of Elders Allan Findlay, Truman Leonard, and Amos M. Musser on the west coast, had left India. Savage was not surprised, for Skelton had warned him that he might be away. He found his way to the home of Sister McMahon (he spelled it McMayon) and her two daughters. They were stalwart members. Mr. McMahon, on the other hand, had apostatized over the doctrine of plural marriage. For the next four months Elder Savage spent most nights at Sister McMahon's home in Calcutta or at Mr. McMahon's place at Cosipore [Kesabpur], where he was a police administrator. In addition to the three McMahons, there were also a Brother Aratoon (an Armenian), one or two others, and "an old native woman" named Anna. She had remained somewhat faithful, the only Indian to do so. There were nine Saints in all.

Not long after Savage arrived in Calcutta, he began looking in earnest for a way to travel back to America. His journal details the pain and insults he endured from unkind captains who refused to consider taking him home because he was a Mormon. On July 20, 1855, he complained: "What to do, or where to go, I do not know for I have not the means for leaving this country, and there is not a place in all this country for an Elder of God to lay his head." He did not want to impose upon Richard Lewis, the American consul, but eventually did so. Lewis was the only American to provide any real help. Lewis not only asked American captains to contribute funds for Savage's passage but also finally provided financial help and arrangements with a captain for Savage's passage. Before this happened, Elder Savage wrote: "I returned in low spirits not knowing what to do. There is no opportunity of preaching the Gospel, and I have no way of obtaining means to pay my passage. I cannot render the very few poor Saints here the least assistance; and thus to remain here in idleness in this land of devils is something so repugnant to my feelings that I scarcely know how to contain myself. I must be patient and wait until the way opens."[45] In an effort not to waste time, Savage tried to find a job, attempted to get to America as a sailor but was not qualified, visited the small branch (eight members in two families) at Chinsura (he rode the new railroad), and ministered to the few members in Calcutta.

Finally, on August 29th, Consul Lewis told Savage that he would provide a way for him to sail to America. A month later, Lewis informed Savage that he would have "cabin passage and go like a gentleman." Savage blessed Lewis and praised the Lord for raising up a friend who would provide for his needs. Three days later, on September 27th, Elder Savage received a letter from Brother McCune in Rangoon. The letter contained "an order authorizing [Savage] to receive 200 Rupees and a silver watch from Mr. Cartland, his money agent here. Brothers Hefferan and Kelly gave 60 Rupees each. The remainder I do not know who gave it, but suppose is mostly, if not all, was given by Brother McCune. The watch is from Brother Kesseck."[46] Unbeknownst to Savage, Elders Skelton and Meik had written to Rangoon asking the branch to contribute the funds.

Before going on board the ship *Herbert*, Savage gave Mr. Lewis a package of books: a Book of Mormon, a Doctrine and Covenants, a *Government of God* by T. Taylor, one *Reply to Mormonism Unveiled* by N. V. Jones, a copy of *Patriarchal Order or Plurality of Wives* by Orson Spencer, and one *Pratt's Works*. Lewis said he would read them.

On October 12th, Savage embarked the *Herbert*, under Captain Done, at Garden Reach, three miles below Calcutta. The following day, they lifted anchor and started drifting down the Hoogly River with the tide. At the end of the day, he thankfully wrote, "I can only look upon my passage as a blessing direct from the Lord."

The voyage was long, one hundred forty days, from Calcutta to Boston. The *Herbert* endured an extremely vigorous and threatening storm rounding the Cape of Good Hope and then, because of the length of the voyage, almost ran out of water and food. The contrast between the heat of Calcutta and the ice and snow near Boston was shocking to Savage's system. But he was grateful to be back on American soil. The *Herbert* docked at Boston on February 28, 1856.

Savage had become close friends with his captain. Captain Done read Savage's Latter-day Saint books and pamphlets and seemed to embrace much of what they had to say. When they arrived at Boston, they went to dinner and took lodgings at Mr. Read's private boarding house, which was suggested by the captain.

Savage traveled among the Saints in the eastern states, visited with relatives in Ohio and Illinois, and eventually joined what he called the Camp of the Saints near Iowa City, Iowa, on July 10, 1856. Two days later, he was appointed "captain over the second hundred in Elder [James G.] Willie's [handcart] company." By August 11th, the company had moved to Florence, Nebraska, the starting point for the long journey to Utah, and final preparations were undertaken. Because the disaster of the Willie and Martin handcart companies is one of the best-known chapters in LDS history, I will not review the details of those sad events. Savage played a heroic role in the episodes that followed. He was opposed to leaving so late in the year and made his views clearly known. He wrote, "I myself am not in favor of, but much opposed to, taking women and children through when they are destitute of clothing, when we all know that we are bound to be caught in the snow and severe cold weather long before we reach the valley." At least one other experienced leader, Brother Atwood, agreed with him.

At a meeting held in the evening of August 13th, Brother Willie "exhorted the Saints to go forward regardless of suffering even to death." Savage then spoke his mind:

> I Said that we were liable to have to wade in snow up to our knees, and should at night rap ourselv[e]s in a thin blanket, and lye on the frozen Ground without a bed; that was not like having a wagon, that we could go into, and rap ourselves in as much as we liked and lye down. No, Said I, we are with out waggons, destitute of clothing, and could not cary it if we had it. We must go as we are. The handcart system I do not condem. I think it preferable to unbroken oxen and inexperienced teamsters. The lateness of the season was my only objection to leaving this point for the mountains at this time.[47]

But he was overruled. The company having voted to attempt the journey, three days later they moved forward five miles. The fatal error had been made.

Savage's response when the decision was made to go on was in character with the sacrifices he had made while a missionary in India and Burma. According to John Chislett, another leader in the ill-fated company, Savage said: "Brethren and Sisters, what I have said I know to be true; but, seeing you are to go forward, I will go with you; will help all I can; will work with you, will rest with you, will suffer with you, and, if necessary, will die with you. May God in his mercy bless and preserve us. Amen."[48] "Brother Savage was true to his word," wrote Chislett. "No man worked harder than he to alleviate the suffering which he had foreseen, when he had to endure it. Oh, had the judgment of this one clear-headed man been heeded, what scenes of suffering, wretchedness, and death would have been prevented."[49]

As the company moved along, Elder Savage documented struggles, sufferings, and too frequent deaths among the Willie Company. Of the five hundred emigrants in that body, mostly Britishers and Scandinavians, sixty-seven lost their lives along the way. It was truly a trail of sorrow. With the help of rescue parties sent to recover these Saints, the Willie Company entered Great Salt Lake City on November 9, 1856. After a mission of more than four years, Elder Levi Savage, Jr., was home. He had circumnavigated the globe without purse or scrip.

CLOSING DOWN CHURCH OPERATIONS IN BURMA

Elder Savage sailed from Rangoon in mid-June 1855. By that date, the McCunes and some other members were making definite plans to emigrate to Utah, but money and military obligations caused delays and were a problem for most of them. They worked individually and collectively to save money and find the means to emigrate.

Brother McCune cared deeply about his friend William Adams, who had become very ill with a "complication of diseases, the chief of which was the dysentery," while serving in the army at Bassein, directly west of Rangoon on the coast of the Bay of Bengal. Adams came to Rangoon on September 15th and was immediately hospitalized. A week later, McCune went to Bassein, presumably to cover for Adams while he was sick. He returned to Rangoon about a month later. Adams was not improving, and indeed this was his final illness. The military gave him his discharge and sent him to Calcutta in the hope that he would regain his strength there. At that place, the few Saints tried to minister to his needs but to no avail. I, Brother Musser, was there at the time and "made it my business to study his comfort and promote his wishes." I had the good fortune of finding in port Captain Zenos Winsor, who had conveyed us from San Francisco to Calcutta. He agreed to take the two of us to England for six hundred rupees, but before the time for sailing, Brother Adams, who was in the hospital in Calcutta, grew worse and "unexpectedly to us, his spirit left its earthly tenement." His wife and babe had died sometime before his demise. He died in February 1856. "Brother Adams was one of the *few* bright stars that shone with becoming brilliancy in the oriental constellation."[50]

Through all this, the little branch in Rangoon kept meeting and tried to prosper. After Savage's departure, there were at least two baptisms. On September 16, 1855, McCune baptized George Henry Booth, a medical doctor, whose mother, Hannah, and brother Charles had become members in Calcutta two years earlier; and McCune baptized his son George on December 30th. George Booth remained faithful and lived in India until 1884. In that year, he visited Salt Lake City and convinced the Brethren that a mission to India should be again attempted. He and three others, William Willes and Henry F. McCune among them, served a mission in India which began in 1884 but was soon aborted. In addition to the baptisms of Booth and young George McCune, three former members were re-baptized in November.[51]

Another important branch activity was the saving of money for the Perpetual Emigration Fund. These funds were intended to help the poor members in India and Burma emigrate but were ultimately used to help send Savage and Skelton home, two hundred rupees for Savage, and one hundred rupees to aid Skelton, in April 1856.[52]

The McCunes started toward the Valley on February 7, 1856, when Sister McCune and three of her children, George, Alfred, and Edward, boarded the steamer *Fire Queen*, bound for Calcutta.[53] Calcutta had been their principal home for many years; there were many things to be done there. Later that year, on November 23d, Matthew was pensioned off and, along with Henry, joined his family in Calcutta. The McCunes sailed for New York on the 1454-ton, full-rigged, three-masted *Escort,* under Captain Alfred E. Hussey, on December 10, 1856. The voyage lasted eighty-three days, the *Escort* putting in at New York Harbor on March 3, 1857. The McCunes crossed the plains with the Delaware Company and arrived in Great Salt Lake City on September 21, 1857.[54] On the date of Matthew's leaving Rangoon, the Rangoon Branch and all Church activities in Burma ended until 1884, when the Church briefly sent missionaries there.

NOTES

1. *Poongee* or *phoongy* is the name most commonly given by the British for the Buddhist religion in Burma. It signifies "great glory."

2. McCune, "Correspondence of Elder McCune," *The Mormon* 3 (April 11, 1857): 431.

3. Karl J. Schmidt, *An Atlas and Survey of South Asian History* (Armonk, New York: M. E. Sharpe, 1995), 68.

4. Sarah's reservations now seem moot. After emigrating to Utah, she accepted three other wives into the family.

5. McCune, Journal.

6. McCune, "Correspondence of Elder McCune," *The Mormon* 3 (April 11, 1857): 431.

7. McCune, Journal, July 14, 1852.

8. Ibid.

9. William Willes, "Introduction of the Gospel in the Birman Empire" [Willes to Samuel W. Richards, September 4, 1852, Calcutta], *Millennial Star* 14 (December 11, 1852): 670.

10. McCune, Journal, August 23, 1852.

11. Matthew McCune, "The Birman Mission: Baptisms—Spirit of Inquiry—Demand for Books" [McCune to Samuel W. Richards, January 11, 1853, Martaban, Burma], *Millennial Star* 15 (April 9, 1853): 236. In his journal McCune kept a good record of each baptism. He listed full names, place and date of birth, parentage ("mixed parentage," "European," and so on), occupational training ("cotton weaver," "apothecary," and so on), present rank and unit, if in the military, or other occupation, and a word about education ("reads and writes" or "learned," and so on). McCune was a good writer and appears from his comments to have been quite concerned with the intelligence and education of his converts.

A fusilier was originally an infantryman armed with a "fusil," a light flintlock musket. The name remained after the muskets were gone.

12. When Levi Savage arrived in Burma, he wrote the following description of Rangoon: "The buildings are very inferior, mostly built of bamboo mats fastened on posts set in the ground. This forms the outer wall, also the partitions (if they have any). The floor is composed of bamboo and is from three to four feet high from the ground; thus, the house has the appearance of standing on stilts but is much healthier and cooler than it would be if it were close to the ground. Their best houses are sided up with boards. The floor is made of boards and the roof is made of tile. The others are thatched with flag or grass. Their priests,

or men of note, generally occupy the wooden houses. A considerable part of the city has the appearance of standing in the woods, from the thickness of the trees and shrubbery." Savage, *Journal*, 19.

13. McCune, "Correspondence of Elder McCune," *The Mormon* 3 (April 11, 1857): 431.

14. Matthew McCune, "The Burman Mission: Baptisms—Persecutions—Plurality of Wives" [McCune to Samuel W. Richards, August 27, 1853, Rangoon], *Millennial Star* 15 (November 26, 1853): 782.

15. McCune, "Correspondence of Elder McCune," *The Mormon* 3 (April 11, 1857): 431; see also McCune, *Millennial Star* 15 (November 26, 1853): 782.

16. McCune, Journal, April 19, 1853.

17. McCune, *Millennial Star* 15 (November 26, 1853): 782.

18. Ibid.

19. Savage, *Journal*, 19.

20. McCune, Journal, September 8, 11, 1853.

21. Musser, Journals, 3:84.

22. Elam Luddington, "The Birman Mission: Baptisms and Ordinations—Interest in the Work" [Luddington to Samuel W. Richards, January 1, 1854, Rangoon], *Millennial Star* 16 (March 25, 1854): 190.

23. McCune, Journal, October 9, 1854.

24. William Willes, "East India Mission: Voyage from Calcutta to Rangoon . . . The Burmese—Labours Among Them" [Willes to Franklin D. Richards, March 3, 1855, Liverpool], *Millennial Star* 17 (March 24, 1855): 189. McCune noted that Willes had saved one hundred forty-nine rupees "by keeping school," and additional contributions of one hundred and eleven rupees from members of the Rangoon Branch. See McCune, Journal, October 9, 1854.

25. Ibid., 190–91.

26. Savage, *Journal*, 22.

27. McCune, Journal, October 9, 1854.

28. Willes, *Millennial Star* 17 (March 24, 1855): 189.

29. Ibid.

30. William Willes, "Voyage of the S. Curling" [Willes to Franklin D. Richards, May 20 and following, 1855, 300 miles from New York], *Millennial Star* 17 (July 7, 1855): 423–24. See also Sonne, *Ships, Saints, and Mariners*, 178–79.

31. Savage, *Journal*, 20–22.

32. Ibid., 23.

33. Nathaniel V. Jones, "Hindostan: Voyage of Elder Jones to Birmah—Lectures and Baptisms in Rangoon—Prospects Among the Birmese—Visit to the Karens—Departure of Elders Willes and Woolley for Zion" [Jones to Franklin D. Richards, November 7, 1854, Calcutta], *Millennial Star* 17 (February 10, 1855): 93.

34. Ibid.

35. Savage, *Journal*, 24–25; McCune, Journal, October 8, 1854.

36. McCune, Journal, February 19, 1855.

37. Levi Savage, Jr., "Burmah: Indifference of the People—Anticipated Emigration of the Saints" [Savage to Franklin D. Richards, May 30, 1855, Rangoon], *Millennial Star* 17 (September 8, 1855): 573.

38. Savage, *Journal*, 27.

39. Savage, *Millennial Star* 17 (September 8, 1855): 574.

40. Savage, *Journal*, 27.

41. On August 31, 1854, Brigham Young and his counselors sent a general letter "To the Missionaries from Utah." It was published in the *Deseret News* on that date and in the *Millennial Star* on November 18, 1854 (see *Millennial Star* 16 [November 18, 1854]: 721–22). The pertinent paragraph read: "The Elders from Utah now in Australia, Hindoostan, and

the Cape of Good Hope, are at full liberty, upon reception of this article, to tarry in their respective missionary fields, to extend their labours to new fields, or return home as the Holy Ghost may dictate in their councils, with reference to their respective joint or individual movements, and all will be right" (Clark, *Messages of the First Presidency*, 2:147–49). Exactly when this intelligence arrived in Calcutta is not known, but it was probably there within a month to six weeks after its date of publication. This would make its effective date in India about January 1, 1855.

42. Savage, *Journal*, 29–30.

43. Savage, *Millennial Star* 17 (September 8, 1855): 573–74.

44. Savage, *Journal*, 32–33.

45. Ibid., 39.

46. Ibid., 43–44.

47. Ibid., 65–66.

48. Joseph Fielding Smith, *Essentials in Church History*, 13th ed. (Salt Lake City: Deseret Book, 1953), 487. President Smith wrote: "These were noble sentiments worthy of the archives of time." The most thorough study of the disaster is Howard A. Christy, "Weather, Disaster, and Responsibility: An Essay on the Willie and Martin Handcart Story," *BYU Studies* 37, no. 1 (1997–98): 6–74. Another useful piece is Paul H. Peterson, "They Came by Handcart," *Ensign* 27 (August 1997): 30–37. There are also many older studies that might be consulted, such as LeRoy R. Hafen and Ann W. Hafen, *Handcarts to Zion: The Story of a Unique Western Migration, 1856–1860* (Glendale, Calif.: Arthur H. Clark Company, 1960; reprint, Lincoln: University of Nebraska Press, 1992); and Wallace Stegner, *The Gathering of Saints: The Story of the Mormon Trail,* The American Trail Series (New York: McGraw-Hill Book Co., 1964).

49. "Mr. [John] Chislett's Narrative," in pt. 1 of ch. 37, in T. B. H. Stenhouse, *The Rocky Mountain Saints: A Full and Complete History of the Mormons, from the First Vision of Joseph Smith to the Last Courtship of Brigham Young* (New York: D. Appleton, 1883), 317.

50. Amos Milton Musser, "Home Correspondence" [Musser to Orson Pratt, July 29, 1856, London], *Millennial Star* 18 (September 6, 1856): 569. Robert Skelton wrote the following tribute to Adams in the *Millennial Star:* "Brother Adams was among those who first received the Gospel in India, and has faithfully discharged his duties pertaining to his office, to the best of my knowledge. His name stands most prominent on the tithing list, and that of the P. E. Fund [Perpetual Emigration Fund], which is conclusive evidence of his strong faith in the work. He was exceedingly anxious to return to Scotland and take his mother to Zion. He would, I am informed by brother Musser, often exclaim, in a flood of tears, 'O that I may live to take her to the Valley!'" (Robert Skelton, "Hindostan," *Millennial Star* 18 [May 31, 1856]: 349).

51. McCune, Journal, by date.

52. Ibid. On April 2, 1856, Matthew McCune's journal ends.

53. Ibid.

54. Andrew Jenson, *LDS Biographical Encyclopedia*, 4 vols. (Salt Lake City: Arrow Press, 1920), 3:161. There are a number of errors in the account of McCune given in Jenson's work; however, it is the only source for a few factual items.

9

TO THE BOMBAY PRESIDENCY

Bombay Island has a long history dating back at least to the time of Christ. It has been known variously as Bom Bahia, Mumbai, or Mubadevi (officially it is known as Mumbai, after one of the names of the god Shiva's consort Parvati). The English acquired it in 1661, when it was ceded to Britain as part of a marriage arrangement between King Charles II and Catherine of Braganza, sister of the king of Portugal. Seven years later, in 1668, the island was given to the East India Company, which made it the headquarters for western India. The East India Company developed the area, and by the nineteenth century, there were more than fifty thousand inhabitants. Bombay became the capital of the Bombay Presidency. The geographical region beyond Bombay is known as Maharashtra, a territory once ruled by the great Hindu patriot Shivaji. Long known to be a safe harbor, Bombay was surprisingly underdeveloped when the British took over. But it soon became the most important port on the western side of India.

Bombay is situated on an island [now a peninsula, many of the former waterways and coastal areas having been reclaimed] along the narrow coastal plains below an abrupt escarpment known as the Western Ghats. The coastal plains vary in width but seldom exceed sixty miles. Bombay's weather is hot and muggy most of the year,

Street in Bombay

with highest temperatures during May and June and extremely heavy rainfall, twelve to twenty-four inches monthly, and intense humidity during June, July, and August, the first three months of the monsoon. During those months, Bombay citizens who were able retreated to Poona (Pune), ninety miles southeast, where the weather is drier and less humid. The governor of the Bombay Presidency annually moved his offices to Poona during the rainy season. Poona, incidentally, had served as Shivaji's capital during the 1600s. It is situated in the rolling tablelands of the Deccan Plateau.

At the time of Elder Hugh Findlay's arrival in Bombay, the city was large, but the European population was relatively small, so small that after he had labored there for two years, he was convinced that every European in the city knew his purposes. Most of Bombay's multicultural inhabitants were Indians. Almost all citizens of Bombay were and are immigrants from other parts of India. The dominant group speaks Marathi, but there are also Gujaratis from the region to the north, Goans from the south, and other peoples from points east. The Parsees, or Zoroastrians, also contributed to the cultural mix. The languages spoken in this part of India, although related to the Indo-Aryan Bengali, Hindi (Hindustani), and Urdu of the north and east, are virtually unintelligible to speakers of those languages.

In the 1850s, Bombay was a beautiful port city with palm, mango, tamarind, and banyan trees. To the north of the city on Salsette Island, wild animals still haunted the domain: tigers, leopards, jackals, and deer. But in the city, typical domesticated livestock roamed the streets: sacred cows, bullocks or zebu, sheep, goats, and dogs. In addition to smaller birds, there were ducks, vultures, pigeons, and cranes. But Elder Findlay did not devote much time to observing such things.

HUGH FINDLAY OPENS LATTER-DAY SAINT MISSIONARY WORK IN BOMBAY

Elder Hugh Findlay received first notice of his mission to Bombay in a letter from Elder Lorenzo Snow, dated September 1, 1851. He accepted the Lord's call to India and made rapid preparations to leave for his mission field. As matters worked out, he was given passage on a steamship at a much-reduced rate. The voyage that began on October 20th took only three weeks. Findlay's route was through the Mediterranean Sea to Egypt, then overland for 107 miles by way of the Isthmus of Suez, and on to Bombay by another steamer. The Suez route reduced his trip to India from England by thirty-five hundred miles and two or three months over the old standard voyage around Africa's Cape of Good Hope.

The written record of Elder Findlay's arrival and doings when first in Bombay is missing. The story begins in April 1852, with Findlay carrying on a no-holds-barred battle in the Bombay newspapers: the *Telegraph and Courier*, the *Bombay Gazette*, and the

Protestant missionary-sponsored *Bombay Guardian*. He had done enough proselytizing to gain the attention of all the editors in Bombay, as well as the military and ecclesiastical authorities. That he had gained interest and a little following is evident from the newspaper coverage of his actions. Not surprisingly, most of the coverage about him and the Church was negative. The *Bombay Guardian* published reports falsely telling of debauchery in Utah and especially regarding the practice of polygamy. Findlay, who had left England before hearing anything regarding the doctrine of plural marriage as practiced in Utah, adamantly denied that such a thing was taking place. He called the reports "slanderous and unfounded." A number of months passed before he learned that his denials were incorrect. An evenhanded editor asked if polygamy was practiced, whether or not Hugh Findlay thought so. Various articles cited American newspapers, such as the *Banner and Cross*, that averred, Utah "is the very plague spot of our country" and "licentiousness and vice, in the worst forms, prevail there to a shocking extent. Polygamy is in full vogue."[1]

To these accusations and other theological statements, as well as many untrue assertions regarding the Prophet Joseph Smith, President Brigham Young, the reported denials of the witnesses of the Book of Mormon, the supposed internal inconsistency of the Book of Doctrine and Covenants, and so on, Brother Findlay wrote extensive articles of clarification and correction. He elaborated on most doctrines relating to the Latter-day Saint understanding of Christ's mission and atonement, baptism by immersion, the salvation of little children, apostasy from and Restoration of priesthood authority, the nature of the Holy Trinity, the corporeal nature of God, the fallacy of a "hireling ministry," and so forth. His words were profuse and flowery and seemed a bit pretentious. First, the editors asked him to be briefer and more to the point. Then, they cut off debate and ended the discussion, saying the arguments were tedious to their readers. They may have been. Nevertheless, the editors did not cease to publish articles that were critical of Findlay's testimony and peculiar beliefs.

Elder Findlay was completely unafraid of direct confrontations and arguments based on scripture. He challenged the local religious establishment—chaplains and missionaries—to meet him on even ground at any time. His knowledge of the Bible, as well as Mormon scripture, was deep and broad. He was convinced that he could win any debate and seemed to relish the fight.

Findlay was particularly upset with the distribution of an anti-Mormon tract written by J. G. Deck titled *"The Mormons" or "Latter-day Saints."* He spent considerable time writing a reply to it that was published under the title, *"The Mormons" or "Latter-day Saints"; A reply by H. Findlay to a tract bearing the above title by J. G. Deck.* He also wrote lengthy rebuttals of the tract in various newspapers.

About the end of May or the first of June 1852, Elder Findlay learned through the newspapers that a local minister, the Reverend George Candy, pastor of Trinity Chapel, was commencing a series of lectures on the "delusion of Mormonism." After he read a copy of Candy's first lecture, Findlay immediately started writing rebuttals for the local papers. He and all of us missionaries were amazed at the meanness of the attacks on the Church and its leaders. We were also surprised that seemingly every criticism and lie told about the Church elsewhere in the world had found its way to distant India. Who would think that in India the Spaulding manuscript would be spoken of as the source of the Book of Mormon, but it was in every city where we worked.

Fortunately, several editors demanded that the antagonists of Mormonism play by fair rules. On June 3d, the editor of the *Bombay Gazette* chastened the Reverend Mr. Candy for being "unnecessarily severe" against Mormonism in a sermon prior to his series on the subject. The editor also challenged Candy and other ministers to take up Findlay's invitation for a public debate. He wrote: "The Christian public mind is much agitated at the circumstance of the ministers of our churches concealing themselves from Mr. Findlay." He then took the ministers to task for employing measures they had criticized among others. Said he:

They forcibly seize every Mormon tract seen in the hands of their flocks (like the Roman Catholic priests do the Protestant tracts). They fly to persons in authority, and bias their mind against Mr. Findlay, and prevent him from coming within certain limits of Upper Colaba [the cantonment]; and they also speak against the Mormon principles from their pulpit, instead of stepping forward boldly in the power of Jesus, like David, and slay the Mormon Philistine.

If this desirable measure be carried out at once, it will put to rest the minds of Christians in general and the taunting of the heathens, who say where are your able holy ministers who can only boast of their wisdom and religion before an ignorant population of heathens, and shrink before a single Mormonite?[2]

But when Candy took the pulpit to explain the fallacies of Mormonism, he did not accept the editor's counsel. He advised his congregation that they should rely on him and trust his studied judgment: "Be content that I should *show* you *from the word of God*, instead of you going through the laborious process of finding out for yourselves, for which *all* of you are not qualified." He cautioned against reading books that might cause them to question. Mormonism, said he, "is an awful and impious imposture."[3] His lectures went on, and Elder Findlay countered with lectures of his own. Ultimately, the people of Bombay seemed to call a stalemate.

The army regiment was garrisoned in a fairly large cantonment at Colaba on the southern part of the island. The buildings were permanent and of considerable size. It was to the enlisted men there that Findlay had first directed his attention. His efforts created interest among the ranks of the soldiers. This interest called forth the response of the ministers to have Findlay kept away from his soldier-investigators.

The matter came to a head when Elder Findlay applied to the town major, Lieutenant Colonel H. Lyons, to use a room in the town barracks that had been open to the public for meetings of many kinds. Findlay's application was received civilly, but the officer said that for the sake of formality, he would refer the matter to Lord Falkland, governor of Bombay Presidency and commandant of the Bombay garrison. "Instead of the permission being granted," wrote Mr. Jamison, the editor of the *Telegraph and Courier,* "down came a most peremptory order from his Lordship that on no account was Mr. Findlay to be allowed the use of *any* Government public room, and that the same Mormon Elder was not to be allowed within the precincts of the Barracks, either of the Highlanders or the Artillery, on any account whatever." After being summarily displaced from the garrison and also from use of a public hall for his meetings, Elder Findlay announced that he would hold his meetings out of doors on the rocks by the sea. Even this was prevented by the military police, the rocks being within the military boundaries. In concluding his article, Mr. Jamison wrote: "We declare it almost impossible to believe, that an English nobleman [Lord Falkland] would behave so utterly at variance with the spirit of the age."[4] But being "at variance with the spirit of the age" did not bother the military establishment in Bombay. Findlay was largely prevented from meeting with soldiers under any circumstances.[5] Editor Jamison said he was "not aware that the Governor of the Garrison had the power to interfere with the religious persuasions of the Soldiery."[6] Writing in September from Poona, Findlay complained: "When an English commanding officer told me in Bombay, that I should remember that I was not exactly under English law in India, I spurned the idea as a piece of petty tyranny: but we are always learning; *now I know it is so.*"[7] Protestations by Findlay and the editor notwithstanding, the situation with the military did not change. Although Elder Findlay had trouble maintaining his faith and confidence in his future success, he persisted and lectured in homes of friends, in open places, and wherever he could find a hearer.

On May 28, 1852, Elder Findlay baptized his first convert, Douglas W. Davies, in the clean waters at upper Colaba Beach, Bombay. Davies was of Eurasian birth and worked as a clerk in the government mint.[8] His wife, Helen, was not ready for baptism at that time, but she was baptized a few months later. Brother and Sister Davies were generous friends and faithful supporters of

Findlay's mission and of the Church. Elder Findlay relied on him to help as book agent, as his helper on the reply tract project, and in many other ways. Before leaving Bombay for Poona, Findlay baptized two other converts whose names have escaped the record.

The few loyal local Saints proved to be of inestimable help and support to the lone missionary. In late April, Brother Findlay received a letter from William Tait, who, with his wife and family, were living at Poona. Tait was a Church member, although his wife was not yet. He had been baptized into the Church and ordained an elder in Scotland, evidently by Elder Parley P. Pratt, but had joined the army and been transferred to India. His question—Had the Prophet Joseph Smith been shot?—revealed his long separation from the body of the Church. He encouraged Findlay to come to Poona, where he would find a home with the Taits.[9] Findlay did not immediately go to Poona, but he was grateful to have a place to go at the end of June when the monsoon rains came dark and heavy.

FINDLAY SHIFTS HIS EFFORTS TO POONA

The monsoon rains came crashing down on Bombay in mid-June, and Elder Findlay needed no further encouragement to move to higher ground: Poona. Brother Tait and his family came to Bombay and escorted Findlay across the large Bombay harbor on the east side of Bombay, across the flat plain, up the Western Ghats, and on to the tableland of Poona. They traveled by bullock wagon. Months later, in January 1853, Findlay shared his awe after traveling a second time over the Western Ghats:

> These Gatts are the greatest wonder I have yet beheld connected with the geological world; what throes of nature must have rent those majestic rocks and formed those deep caverns, casting mountains as it were, in mid-air and leaving ravines not to be approached by the foot of the traveler. It must have proved an almost impassable barrier to the first European

troops who traveled up the country previous to the road being constructed. The construction of which manifests no little talent in engineering.

The windings are most ingeniously cut. Sometimes the one almost perpendicular over the other; at three or four different corners, the traveler supposes he has attained the summit, but lo, when he rounds the corner he finds himself buried in rocks still. This height is supposed to be 5000 feet [actually closer to 3000] and the road ascending . . . 5 miles. It is still infested by the tiger.[10]

The entire trip took three days.

Findlay began this new phase of his mission on June 27, 1852. His success at Poona was immediately greater than it had been at Bombay. His problems with the military were similar, and his confrontations with the ecclesiastical establishment were ultimately the same, but he was able to organize a branch that prospered in a small but satisfying way.

Findlay's first task was to find a place to meet. He used a small room (he frequently noted that the benches were full) for three weeks, and when it was no longer available, he rented an empty Parsee chapel within the boundaries of the cantonment and moved in. Because the officer in charge thought Findlay was planning to remain in camp only until the rainy season ended, or more briefly, he gave permission for Findlay to live and preach there.[11]

Findlay's first two and one-half months at Poona were busy and fulfilling but also somewhat frustrating. He held three lecture meetings weekly, visited investigators regularly, maintained his little chapel, and defended himself and the Church against some strange attacks. For example, the rumor was spread that he had come to purchase the discharges of all soldiers who would join the Church and move to California. This caused a stir among the military officers as well as two hundred men who were ready to accept the offer.

After that rumor was shown to be a lie came the next problem. An LDS tract, Lorenzo Snow's *The Only Way to Be Saved*, was left on a table in the public library. It was reported to the chaplain, who reported it to his superior officer, who had the librarian arrested and imprisoned. Following the librarian's denials that he was a sympathizer with the Mormons, he was released—"no military law could be found to condemn him."[12] Findlay regularly spent time composing a reply to Deck's anti-Mormon tract, which he said "seems to be the only tool the priests have got here and which they are most diligently distributing."[13]

In addition to his persistent anti-Mormon battles, Findlay had some encouraging success. He performed his first baptism about a week after arriving at Poona. On August 8, he baptized four more converts, and on the 12th, another. Ten days later, he baptized yet another new member. The work seemed to be progressing. On Sunday, August 29th, Findlay blessed and named Brother and Mrs. Tait's two sons according to LDS procedure. Six days later, on September 4th, he baptized three additional souls.

The next day, Sunday, September 5, 1852, Findlay made this positive entry in his journal:

> This afternoon we organized the saints in Poona into a branch. By calling John Zecherias Hewett to the office of elder [he had been baptized on August 22] and Brother George Johnston to the office of teacher [he had been baptized on August 29]. To be called the Poona Branch of the Church of Jesus Christ of L.D.S. Composed of 12 members with prospects of a speedy increase.[14]

Findlay became branch president with Tait and Hewett as counselors.

Not long after the organization of the Poona Branch, several matters combined to create some new challenges for Elder Findlay. The first convert he baptized was a soldier named Thomas Brown. Even on the day of Brown's baptism, Findlay noted a feeling that the spirit was not right. On July 25th, Findlay learned that Brown had been imprisoned for insubordination. This was embarrassing to the Church members and to Findlay especially. But this problem was soon entangled with another. Brown insisted on his right to be marched to chapel as other soldiers were.

But he would not go to the Protestant church. He demanded the right to meet with the Mormons. At about the same time, Brother Tait requested permission to meet with the Mormons, but his request was turned down on the pretext that if he were allowed to meet with his church, Brown would have to be accorded the same privilege.

But the issue became more complicated. On September 13th, Findlay received an official letter from Captain T. R. Morse, superintendent of the bazaar and police, saying: "I am directed by the Brigadier Commanding the Station [Brigadier Trydell] to inform you that he withdraws the permission granted to you to reside in Cantonment, and desires that you will leave as soon as possible, and not enter it again." Although Elder Findlay had discussed that very day the possibility of building a place for meeting outside the cantonment, he had not expected to be evicted so soon nor in so peremptory a manner. He concluded that his banishment was related to Brown's imprisonment and subsequent request to meet with his church. Whether this was true is not clear from what followed. Findlay did not leave the cantonment without a verbal fight, but when the exchange of letters ended, he was required to leave the camp by October 1st.[15]

Findlay's disagreements with Lord Falkland in Bombay and Brigadier Trydell in Poona were saturated with considerable bias and bigotry on the part of the officers. That they were strongly prejudiced against the Church seems abundantly evident from many encounters throughout the country. But Elder Findlay, like all of us missionaries, saw the issue strictly in terms of religious liberty and freedom of conscience and the perceived abridgement of our rights as Christian missionaries to speak our minds wherever we desired. We saw no reason for boundaries between the rights of military people and civilians. Nevertheless, it is true that such rights have never been recognized among military people of any nation. Intruders on military bases have always been carefully restricted. On the officers' side, nothing takes priority over the strictest discipline. In war or at peace, discipline is everything in

Temple to the Hindu goddess Parvati, at Poona

the army. We were no doubt seen as an unnecessary disruption in the smooth operation of the military machine. Our views as missionaries and theirs as military officers allowed no compromise.

The Poona Branch continued to meet as usual until September 29th, when it held its last meeting in the cantonment. By then, Findlay, Tait, and others had found some empty ground only one hundred yards from the old meeting place but outside the camp boundaries on civil land. At the far corner of the ground stood a building that was formerly used for a currier's shop. Findlay moved into this humble dwelling. It served as meetinghouse and missionary quarters. Regarding his temporary quarters, Findlay wrote:

> This house is a little uncouth to the eye, bearing a resemblance to an English store-room, or a Bombay go-down, having a door, six feet by six feet, at each end, and two windows, four feet by six, on each side, with iron bars, and the light of day as an apology for glass; indeed, having such an edifice for bedroom, parlour, and sanctuary, it requires considerable faith to convince one's self that imprisonment is not added to banishment. But we "stoop to conquer," and are thankful to the Lord for it.[16]

His quarters were humble, but he had the hope of moving into something better in the near future. The branch had agreed to back the building project financially and to help in obtaining loans, but that proved to be the easiest part of the undertaking.

As soon as Findlay thought he had an agreement to lease the land for ten years, the old man who owned the property started negotiating with another party for use of part of it. Since the branch did not need all of the property anyway, Findlay eventually signed a seven-year lease for a smaller parcel of the land. Then the problem of getting the meetinghouse constructed became the concern. The whole process nearly drove Elder Findlay to desperate acts. A building large enough to hold 150 people was supposed to be ready for occupancy by the end of November, but by that date it was far from completed. The original *goundee* (builder) eventually disappeared and a second builder finished the job so the meeting-house could be occupied on January 23, 1853. The building cost two hundred rupees and eighty annas (an anna is 1/16 of a rupee). The branch still owed two hundred rupees on that date.[17] Findlay was delighted to move from his "prison."

Through the weeks and months, Elder Findlay continued teaching the Gospel in regular weekday and Sunday meetings. He also called regularly at the homes of individuals and families who showed interest in the Church. Civilians of various occupations and soldiers from various units attended his lecture meetings in satisfactory numbers, and eventually, a few were baptized. Unfortunately, he had to excommunicate two of his three fusiliers for failure to attend meetings and for backbiting and drinking. Among his most faithful converts were Elizabeth Exabia Tait, wife of Elder Tait, whom Tait baptized on October 23d, and Helen Davies, wife of Douglas W. Davies, whom Findlay baptized and confirmed in Bombay on Sunday, January 9, 1853. Findlay had resided with the Davies when he first arrived in Bombay. His love for this family was very deep.

In addition to maintaining his growing branch, supervising the building project, and fending off regular attacks from the Church's adversaries, Elder Findlay pursued other interests and concerns. He frequently noted in his journal his efforts to find a Marathi *moonshi* or teacher. He was eager to share the Gospel with the Indian people and made a steady study of the language. He also met regularly with the Young Men's Society, a group of college-aged Brahmins. This group made it a practice to study world philosophies and religions. They were eager to sponsor a debate between Findlay and a Protestant minister named James Michel. The negotiations among Findlay, the young Brahmins, and Michel's representatives went on for weeks before the first of only two meetings finally took place on January 25, 1853. One reason for the lengthy arrangements was the difficulty of finding a place (it was an old palace) other than their own homes because, according to their custom, the Brahmins' homes would have been defiled by the entry of a European. Of that meeting, Findlay wrote:

> I . . . listened to a harangue of the old stamp; nothing new and what the people did not want. The Spaulding tale, spiritual wifeism, Danites, witnesses for the Book of Mormon, Bad grammar of the Book, etc., etc., whilst the people were led to expect a test from the Bible whether he or we had the truth on our side.
>
> The few questions that I had time to put, put him in such a pickle and rage that he rather lost himself the meeting.[18]

Three days later, Findlay had his chance to lecture, but before he had proceeded far, the Reverend Mr. Michel's man interfered and said the lecture had to end because Findlay was not reading his paper word-for-word. This technicality destroyed the series. The Reverend Mr. Michel had found a reason for the process to be discontinued. It is hard to say who was most discouraged with the collapse of the series, Findlay or his young friends, but they were both sorely disappointed.

Over the next couple of months, Elder Findlay continued to labor in Poona. But his attention was divided. He maintained great concern for the little group of Saints in Bombay, which, incidentally, had grown some because of troop transfers and employment moves from Poona. He also relied on the Bombay group for financial support. In early March, he wrote to the Bombay members and asked for contributions to help pay for the Poona meetinghouse. He counseled them that they, too, would probably need a meeting place soon and then the Poona Saints would return the favor. He suggested that every member needed to pay a full tithing, which funds would be used for the debt. And furthermore, he asked, "if the Lord has taught you the secret of abstaining from Tea, Coffee, Tobacco, &c., &c., and you being happier and better men and women than when you used them, that the balance should go to the Lord's side?"[19] The Bombay members agreed to send a contribution every month.

Findlay was still at Poona when relationships in the Bombay

Branch began to unravel. On March 7, 1853, Elder Hewett posted a letter to Findlay that was as supportive and enthusiastic as one could expect. But two weeks later, Brother Davies wrote saying Brother Hewett "has fallen away sadly." Being low-spirited and depressed, Hewett told his employer at the newspaper that he had some questions about Latter-day Saint principles and doctrines; but his real problem was with Brother Brown, who had purportedly broken his marriage engagement with Hewett's sister-in-law, Jessy. Hewett wanted to bring a lawsuit against Brown. This problem terribly disrupted the little group. The upshot was an angry Brother Hewett who soon turned against the Church and used his influence as a newspaper reporter to supply negative information to his editor regarding the doings of the Mormons. He soon became a complete enemy to the Church. It was a sad outcome, indeed.

In late March or early April, Elder Findlay moved back to Bombay and in with the Davies again. By this time, he had been aware for several months that we missionaries from Utah were on our way and would be landing in Calcutta sometime soon. At least twice, he had asked Church leaders in England to send him help. On April 28th, two days after the Utah elders arrived in Calcutta, Findlay wrote Liverpool with a report he had gleaned from the newspapers, saying: "Only two days ago the shipping intelligence of Singapore showed the ship *Monsoon*, from America, passing there, with a hundred 'Mormons' on board for Calcutta, remarking that if the 'Mormons' could not convert India, they were determined to colonize it."[20] The editors of the *Millennial Star* caught the irony, but Findlay was not sure. He later asked President N. V. Jones if the missionaries were accompanied with colonists. Of course, only thirteen Mormon missionaries were on board.

Not hearing immediately from Jones in Calcutta, on May 27th, Findlay sent a welcoming letter to Calcutta. "Your arrival has to us appeared long! long!" he wrote. "For fourteen months I have laboured here alone, under opposition from all quarters, from the Governor down to the pettiest official. . . . I therefore pant for assistance." He explained the difficulty of keeping two stations going at once: "the one gets neglected whilst I attend to the other." Coming from the heart of the Church, the Utah elders' experience would truly be valued and used.[21]

Before Findlay's letter reached Calcutta, President Jones dispatched one to Bombay written by me, Brother Musser. My letter introduced the missionaries and explained where they had been assigned to serve. Of greatest interest to Findlay was the news that Elder Woolley and I had been appointed to Chinsura, but only until we learned whether Elder Findlay required our assistance. We were to go to his side of the country if we were needed. In my letter, I also asked, "I presume you have heard of the order of Celestial marriage in the Church." I told Findlay we had pamphlets about the subject. At President Jones's suggestion, I asked for a general report on Findlay's progress and quite presumptuously reminded him, saying, "As you know this Gospel of the Kingdom has got to be preached to all the world, that no one can have an excuse at the final consummation."[22] With the possible exception of Elders Willes and Richards, who were at that time in the vicinity of Delhi, no one in India had worked harder than Findlay to accomplish that requirement of the Lord.

Elder Findlay happily reported the work around Bombay. He had baptized twenty-eight at Poona, but because of two excommunications and some removals, there were now sixteen affiliated with the branch. "As to Bombay," he wrote, "through a courtship affair, in which they managed almost all to get entangled, I found them on arriving here all disaffected with one another, which breach is not yet healed, though I have hopes of saving the most of them."[23] There were fourteen members at Bombay at that time. Sadly, Findlay had heard about the large numbers Elder Willes had baptized around Calcutta early in his mission and was suffering with feelings of failure in comparison. He did not know that most of Willes's native converts had fallen away or that, in total, he, Findlay, had a greater number of active converts than existed in Bengal.

After Elder Findlay wrote to President Jones in late May, he heard news from President Samuel W. Richards in England that Richards had appointed his, Elder Findlay's, brother Allan as a missionary to Bombay. Ship passage being so expensive, it was not known how soon Allan could come to India. Despite this promised help, Elder Findlay asked President Jones to please send Elder Woolley and me to assist him.[24] Jones probably would have done so immediately, had not Elders West and Dewey gone to Bombay after failing to find a foothold in Ceylon. My trip to Bombay was delayed for a number of months, but when I did go, Elder Leonard was my companion, not Elder Woolley.

On July 12th, Elder Findlay organized the Bombay Branch with twenty members, five new people having recently joined the Church.[25] On June 17th, West and Dewey had written Findlay a letter informing him that they were on their way. They arrived at Bombay on July 25, 1853. Their intention was to remain in Bombay and Poona only until the monsoon winds shifted in the fall, and sailing would again commence toward China. In the meantime, Elder Findlay assigned Elder West to take charge in Bombay, and he took Elder Dewey to Poona with him. (Through May and June, Findlay had been very sick. He said he "fell victim to the intensity of the sultry months, in a complication of diseases, as if my system had become a general wreck, fever predominating.")

On September 7th, when Elder Allan Findlay arrived, Elder Hugh Findlay asked his brother to join him at Poona and to take charge there. In early October, Elder Hugh Findlay and Elder Dewey returned to Bombay. Elders West and Dewey devoted much of their time trying to secure passage to Siam via Singapore. But they also lectured three or four times a week, visited every home (which was many) in an effort to teach the Gospel, and even ventured into Fort George to leave their notices—from which place West was marched with a military guard.[26] After being refused passage by many captains, on January 9, 1854, they sailed from Bombay on the *Cressy*, Captain Bell, master.

During the last quarter of 1853, affairs in Bombay ground to a halt and began to decline. Membership stood between seventeen and twenty, but troop movements to Aden in Arabia greatly diminished (Elder Hugh Findlay said "wrecked") the size of the branch. The Mormon soldiers who were transferred to Aden were probably the first Latter-day Saints to practice their religion in that country, but that did not help the Bombay Branch. Amazingly, anti-Mormon articles continued in the Bombay press during all this time. Elder Hugh Findlay continued to defend the faith with rebuttals to the editors, but by October 1853, he was thinking of moving farther up the coast to Sind, the lower part of the Indus River basin.

Meanwhile, Elder Allan Findlay was trying to promote the work at Poona. He moved carefully back into the cantonment from which his brother had been expelled and preached in the open air. He was not molested by the military police, but his progress was slow. Although thirty people had been baptized there, by November 1853, only seventeen remained faithful. Elder Allan Findlay obtained permission from Colonel Hamilton of the 78th Highlanders for the Mormon soldiers to march to the LDS meetinghouse for Sabbath services.

Both Elders Findlay were grateful for the friendship and support of Sergeant William Tait. Tait was largely responsible for establishing Mormonism as a legal faith in that cantonment. Elder Hugh Findlay described the matter in these words:

> Here every soldier receives pay for each member of his family, the Chaplain's certificate for the *sprinkling* of the new member being the requisite to have it enrolled for pay. Elder Tait of Poona, however, handed in for his son a certificate of Blessing with my name attached, which no one could (or would) receive, till it should go to government. It did go to Government, and the reply received was that all Mormon children are to receive pay the same as any others.[27]

By the end of December, Elder Allan Findlay was still striving to gain hearers in Poona but largely without success. Elder Hugh Findlay had concluded to move to another field, probably Sind, but was waiting to find out how many elders President Jones was going to send from Calcutta and when. What he did not know was that Elder Truman Leonard and I had sailed from Calcutta on December 29th and were on our way to help on the western side of India. Such was the state of affairs in Bombay and Poona at the end of 1853.

Forty days later, Elder Leonard and I arrived at Bombay aboard the *Niobe,* an American ship under Captain Richard Evans.[28] Elder Hugh Findlay was happy to see us, but by that time, he was resigned that little more could be done in Bombay. He yet held hopes for Poona, where his brother, Allan, continued to proselytize the Gospel. After arriving on February 9, 1854, Leonard and I learned from Hugh that he had intended to go to Sind [southern Pakistan], but when he heard that we were planning to go there he rearranged his plans and pointed his hopes south to Belgaum. After only thirteen days in Bombay, on February 22, 1854, we sailed by steamship to Karachi. Our story is told in the next chapter.

HUGH FINDLAY'S MISSION TO BELGAUM

By February 1854, most of the military Mormons in Bombay had been transferred to Aden, Arabia. Although Elder Hugh Findlay continued to teach the Gospel and to distribute tracts, he had no success during the latter part of his stay there. He needed a new area in which to work. Belgaum, although a relatively small post with only one European regiment, Her Majesty's 64th, and one company of artillery (about two hundred men), some pensioners, staff members, and a few civilians, was the second largest cantonment in Bombay Presidency. It seemed to hold the greatest promise as a potential mission field. For some time, Hugh Findlay had studied the Marathi language, mostly under the tutelage of a young Brahmin teacher. This young man had stood at the edge of conversion for some time, but when the moment for decision came, he could not muster the courage to enter the waters of baptism and give up his caste, position, and relationships. Findlay had hoped he would accompany him to Belgaum and assist with translating tracts and perhaps even the Book of Mormon into Marathi, making it possible to introduce the Gospel to Britishers and Indians alike. But this was not to be.

Findlay left the remnants of the Bombay Branch in the hands of Brother Davies and on March 27th sailed south for Vengurla on a *patamar*, a small native sailboat. Vengurla is only a few miles north of the Portuguese territory of Goa. After landing, he traveled east, eighty miles inland, by bullock wagon to Belgaum. The scene was most fertile, "crossing the deep beds of very many mountain streams, some of which were still running, but most of them dry. . . . The mango and locust, both most delicious fruits, hung in abundance by the way-side; with an endless variety of blossomed trees and shrubs casting on the morning breeze their odorous fragrance, presenting the way-farer with a pleasing contrast to the rays of the sultry sun approaching his meridian."[29]

When Elder Findlay arrived in Belgaum, he intended to avoid confrontation with the military by taking a room in the native town. It was so crowded, however, that he had to settle for a ramshackle room in the bazaar inside the cantonment. Before he had unpacked his bags, he was visited by a representative of the superintendent of bazaars who wanted to know by whose authority he was there. This led to an interview with the superintendent, who cited Findlay's expulsion from the cantonment in Poona and used it as precedent to forbid him to stay in the cantonment at Belgaum. From there, Elder Hugh Findlay applied to the quartermaster general for permission to reside and preach in the pensioner's quarters but with the same result. Finally, he went to General Wilson, the brigadier general in charge. His response was initially to deny entrance, but he listened to Findlay's case. Elder Findlay argued that new precedents had been established in Poona and that the general should write to Poona for new references regarding the matter. It took two months for replies to come, but they "were so overwhelming to the prejudices of the General and his colleagues, that [Findlay was] granted all that [he] asked for—to reside in

Part of the cantonment at Belgaum

camp, and exercise all the functions of a minister of the Gospel, in visiting, preaching, &c."[30]

Having received permission to proselytize the Gospel, Hugh Findlay rented "a commodious bungalow" for eight rupees a month, furnished it with benches for meetings, and began teaching. At this point, he also began teaching English classes daily to pay for the meeting place and for other expenses.[31] The classes also gave him entry to the native community. In the evenings, he held two meetings a week with interested Indians and four with British military people. By late July, he had baptized two people, and he had hopes for success to come.[32] Findlay clearly had a gift for "closing the deal." Other elders were able to attract loyal and interested friends but without the ability to get them to enter the waters of baptism.

When Elder Hugh Findlay next reported his work in October 1854, his branch had grown to eighteen members and others were seriously interested in the Church. He was somewhat pleased with the progress of the Church but discouraged that persecutions similar to those he had endured in Bombay and Poona were now afflicting Church members at Belgaum. George Gordon, a devout convert, was taken "before his commanding officer, accused of the notorious crime of having 'renounced Protestantism,' for which, without the pretense of another charge against him, he was deprived of his situation [as assistant schoolmaster], and turned back to the ranks as a private, with the additional stigma hung to his character, that his evidence should not thenceforth be taken in any court-martial."[33] Other Church members were also harassed, and Church books and tracts were burned when found in the barracks. Strange lies and rumors, for example, Mormons purportedly baptizing in brandy, were circulated among the officers, who evidently believed such nonsense and took action against men who attended Mormon meetings or who joined the Church.

Elder Hugh Findlay continued his service in Belgaum into January 1855, when he decided it was time to leave India. His last letter from India that was published in the *Millennial Star* was

The Basilica of Bom Jesus at Goa, which houses the remains of Saint Francis Xavier, an important Jesuit missionary to India and Japan

written March 5, 1855, at Bombay. He had just published a sixteen-page tract titled *To the Marathas of Hindostan! A Treatise on the True and Living God and His Religion,* in the Marathi language, a project he had worked on for a long time. He said it was "suited to the peculiar system of reasoning by the natives of this country, and as far as practicable, the truth is illustrated by the fragments of it still apparent in their traditions and practices, without being so profusely biblical as in addressing those who profess faith in that book."[34] He hoped it would be "an abiding testimony in their own language" even after he and other living witnesses had left the country.

On his way back to Bombay, Elder Hugh Findlay stopped briefly at Panaji, Goa. He visited with the governor-general of that

Portuguese colony and was promised safety as a British subject. But he was strictly forbidden to preach the restored Gospel. After surveying the colony and visiting the Goanese Catholic cathedral, in what is now called Old Goa, he was convinced that there was little difference between the outward rites and worship among the Christians of Goa and those of the Hindus. Throughout the region, he saw Christian shrines in close proximity to Hindu shrines. He said that from their outward appearances there was little difference. Christian images inhabited the one and Hindu gods the other. The flowers, fruits, and liquids (usually *ghee*, clarified butter) used for anointing the images seemed to be the same. Elder Findlay had become familiar with the myths, gods—in this letter he mentioned Vishnu, Gunputte (or Ganesh), Siva, Rama, and Indra—and practices of the Hindus. He also referred to the Muslims and Parsees (Zoroastrians). Seeing that he would not be able to proselytize the Gospel in Goa, he returned to Bombay.

On March 16, 1855, Elder Hugh Findlay concluded his three-year mission to India. He sailed from Bombay on the *Mary Spencer,* an English ship, under Captain Fisher. He did not return home to the British Isles; rather, he gathered to Zion in Utah. With him were seven other members of the Church: Douglas and Helen Davies and their daughter, and William Tait and three of his children from Poona,[35] who were eager to go to Utah. Sister Tait, who was expecting a baby at the time of her family's departure, remained behind at the home of her mother in Bombay. In November 1855, months after the baby daughter's birth, they sailed for England and thence to America. Captain Fisher was an especially kind and generous man. In addition to extending "every kindness while on board," he also returned thirty pounds sterling to the little company of Saints when they reached Hong Kong.

The emigrants remained in Hong Kong from June 8th to the 27th, then sailed for San Francisco under Captain Grove on the ship *Live Yankee.* While in Hong Kong, they baptized the daughter of Brother and Sister Davies. Hers was the first LDS baptism in Hong Kong.[36]

Details of the remainder of the journey to Salt Lake City are not available, but Andrew Jenson lists Elder Hugh Findlay's arrival date as Saturday, December 1, 1855.[37]

On several occasions, Hugh Findlay expressed feelings of failure. This was especially true early in his mission when he compared his number of baptisms with that of William Willes in Calcutta. But it is clear that he had nothing to be ashamed of and much to be pleased with. He baptized more British converts than the rest of the mission combined. Determining exact numbers is difficult, but he, at one time, had close to fifty members in the combined Bombay and Poona branches and later created a branch of eighteen in Belgaum. It appears that he single-handedly brought close to seventy people into the waters of baptism, a wonderful contribution to the kingdom of God.[38] I do not know the date of the emigrant company's arrival in San Francisco, nor is the date of their arrival in Salt Lake City known. Yet the Findlay family documented the arrival in Utah of at least ten of Hugh's converts. There were probably more.

ALLAN FINDLAY'S MISSION INLAND FROM POONA

Not only was Hugh Findlay a fine missionary but his brother, Allan, was as well. From the time he arrived in India in September 1853, he labored diligently to enlarge the branch at Poona. He, like Hugh, developed a deep affection for the Tait family, who ministered to his needs. After fourteen months in Poona, Elder Allan Findlay, the Taits, and other Church members there concluded "no further good could be done among that people."[39]

In the first part of November 1854, he departed from Poona for Ahmadnagar [Ahmednugger], a distance of seventy-six miles northeast. His travels took him over hilly country with occasional rock outcroppings. Most of the terrain had shallow soil and only the occasional rains made the short grass grow. Decent accommodations were unavailable, so he took "a small hut, with an entrance something under four feet high, and it the only medium of lighting the interior, excluding the crevices in the roof."[40] On seeking permission to live and preach in the cantonment, he was subjected to the same kind of interrogation and evaluation that we have described too many times before. Ultimately, he was not allowed to preach there.

From Ahmadnagar, Elder Allan Findlay traveled roads of reddish-black dirt to Jalna [Jaulnah], one hundred miles farther northeast, mostly through high grass, scrub bushes, and jungle. "To accomplish this short journey," he wrote, "took about six days with a pair of bullocks and cart—what can be done in England any day, easily before dinner; but here most everything advances at a very slow pace." He recalled:

> I had an opportunity of meeting with the natives in their true, natural state, European influence not having reached them, so as to make any impression. At nights, when putting up at their villages, I entered into conversation with them, as far as my colloquial knowledge of Marathee would admit, and truly their ignorance and superstition are very great indeed—in fact, not easy to be imagined by a person who has never come in contact with them, or others similarly circumstanced.[41]

At Jalna, a kind man invited Elder Findlay to stay with him. Although far from the city of Madras, Jalna was part of the Madras Presidency. There, Elder Findlay found different customs and rules. To his surprise, he had no difficulty obtaining permission to live in and perform his missionary duties in the cantonment. Amazingly to Elder Allan Findlay, after so many disappointments and so much unkind treatment, Captain Hutchison, superintendent of bazaars, on hearing about Elder Findlay's calling and objectives, said he believed his purposes to be good and offered to donate ten rupees per month for his support for the next twelve months.

Elder Findlay quickly rented a house and furnished it with benches and chairs. He circulated handbills and made his upcoming lectures known to all who would listen. Unfortunately, the pattern established elsewhere too soon erupted in Jalna. The commanding officer over the horse artillery told his men not to attend Elder Findlay's meetings. They being the only Europeans at the post, this brought a fairly quick halt to his work. Sergeant Major McKinzie then invited Elder Findlay to live with him, his wife, and their fourteen children, where he remained for five weeks. The McKinzies believed everything Findlay shared regarding the restored Gospel except the doctrine of plural marriage. Failing to baptize them, he moved on.[42]

From Jalna, Elder Allan Findlay went 260 miles southeast to Secunderabad, only a few miles from Hyderabad, within the Nizam's[43] territory, arriving on February 12, 1855. He found conditions there much different from other parts of the country. "While traveling in the Nizam's territories," wrote Elder Findlay to Elder Franklin D. Richards in England, "one or two things attracted my attention, viz.—to see every traveler armed to the teeth with sword and buckler, and pistols, or match-lock; from the young urchin of twelve or fourteen years, to the hoary-headed old man. Also the walls around the villages are here kept in repair; whereas in the Marathee country, they are generally dilapidated and mouldering to ruin; showing the latter people are living under a feeling of security, to a certain degree, which is not so much the case in the territories of the Nizam."[44] He was now located within a few miles of Hyderabad and Golconda Fortress, even by that time having fallen into ruins.

Golconda Fortress was situated on a granite hill about four hundred feet high. Its great walls and battlement ramparts manifested a powerful military past.

Secunderabad cantonment had an unusual history, having been "established so as to have the British troops available for the Nizams of Hyderabad, who had asked for such assistance."[45] After the usual application procedures, Elder Allan Findlay was granted permission to live and preach in the cantonment. He rented "a pretty large house" and furnished it for meetings. His hopes were fairly high as he published two hundred flyers announcing a series

Ramparts of Golconda Fortress near Secunderabad and Hyderabad

of twelve lectures. Attendance was fairly good at the first two lectures but then became irregular. "I have had numerous inquiries from all the different grades of society," quipped Elder Findlay, "but their appetite for truth in general is very slender, so that very little satisfies it."[46]

Exactly when Elder Findlay left Secunderabad is not clear. A few nights before writing to Elder Richards on March 29th, however, he had an interesting dream:

> I had the pleasure, in a dream, of conversing with President Heber C. Kimball [of the First Presidency]. He had come to the place where I was laboring; when I first saw him, he was sitting apparently in a deep meditative mood, reflecting, as I thought, on the regardlessness of the people around him. After a short time, I went up to and sat down beside him, then putting my right hand on his knee, said—"Brother Heber, there seems to be little likelihood of much good being done in this place?" "No," answered he, "matters are nearly sealed up here." This part of my dream was most firmly impressed on my mind, and while reflecting on it, I instinctively, as it were, asked myself, "Is this also to be an unfruitful place?"[47]

Elder Findlay's dream proved to be an accurate forecast of things to come. He did not have success in Secunderabad and as a result, with the encouragement of a letter from Elder Leonard, decided to go to Belgaum, where his brother, Hugh, had labored.

Shortly after Elder Allan Findlay arrived in Belgaum, George Gordon, an elder who was serving as branch president (Gordon later emigrated to Zion), wrote to Elder Leonard and me in Sind. That letter is the only document we have dealing with Elder Allan Findlay's work in Belgaum:

> [Allan Findlay] arrived here on the 14th May. . . . When he arrived in Belgaum the Brigadier General was absent on a tour of inspection; and Col. LeMeisure was in temporary command of the station. Brother Findlay applied for leave to reside and perform the functions of his office, which was granted him on the 16th, so he issued notice of his arrival and that preaching would be on Sundays, Tuesdays, and Thursdays at 1/2 past 6 o'clock. A few strangers came, and some of the backsliders and

there appeared to be a revival, and I am happy to inform you that such has been the case, for Bro. Perrins that had left off attending our meetings not only begun again to attend, but took Bro. Findlay into his house to live with him, and Bro. Daly got re-baptized. But lo and behold it is not all gold that glitters, the same day I received Bro. Musser's letter, Bro. Findlay received notice to leave the cantonment. The officer that was in temporary command was ordered off to Sholapoor [Sholapur] to take command of that station [which rebelled against the British in 1857] on the 3rd of June, and on the 4th Bro. Findlay's leave was canceled; on the 5th he made application with the General of permission to remain in Camp as a private individual and today received an official thro the Apt. Quarter Ms, General intimating the general non compliance with his request and likewise threatening any authorized camp resident that should be known to harbour him. So you see poor Bro. F.'s in a fix and the monsoon's on. . . . Bro. Perrins and Pate are off this morning to try and get some place in the native town for Bro. F. and I have no fear they will succeed. He will remain at Belgaum until after the rains then proceed to Bombay. We are forbidden to hold meetings of any description in camp by the General, but we are bid to hold meetings whenever we can by our Heavenly Father whom we mean to obey.[48]

Findlay found a place in the native town and stayed there for several months. In August 1855 he wrote that he believed there were three good converts that he had made in Belgaum but that the Belgaum Branch was nearly "extinguished."[50] In September he left Belgaum and arrived in Bombay on the 25th, the same day Elder Leonard and I arrived there from Sind.

NOTES

1. Hugh Findlay, *Missionary Journals of Hugh Findlay, India-Scotland,* comp. Ross Findlay and Linnie Findlay (Ephraim, Utah: n.p., 1973), Pt. 1, 6, 8, 9, 11, 12, 18, 19. Following some introductory front matter, this volume is divided into three parts: Letters of Correspondence Commencing at Hull Concerning the Bombay Mission (Pt. 1); Journal of Events (Pt. 2); and Mission to Scotland (Pt. 3). Each part is separately numbered. Part 1 consists of correspondence, newspaper editorials, and some other items. The title *Missionary Journals* refers to the entire volume, even though only part 2 is actually Findlay's India journal.

2. "The Mormon Challenge," *Bombay Gazette,* June 3, 1852; in Findlay, *Missionary Journals,* Pt. 1, 44.

3. "Lecture on Mormonism," *Bombay Gazette*, June 7, 1852; in Findlay, *Missionary Journals*, Pt. 1, 61.

4. "The Mormon Challenge," *Bombay Gazette*, June 3, 1852; in Findlay, *Missionary Journals*, Pt. 1, 45–46.

5. Hugh Findlay to Lorenzo Snow, May 12, 1852; in Findlay, *Missionary Journals*, Pt. 1, 24–25.

6. "Editorial," *Telegraph and Courier*, June 2, 1852; in Findlay, *Missionary Journals*, Pt. 1, 48.

7. Hugh Findlay, "Success of the Truth in Western Hindostan: Opposition of the Military and Ecclesiastical Authorities—Organization of a Branch of Twelve Members at Poona—Letter from Hugh Findlay" [Findlay to Samuel W. Richards, September 13, 1852, Poona], *Millennial Star* 14 (November 27, 1852): 635.

8. Item in the *Telegraph and Courier*, May 29, 1852; in Findlay, *Missionary Journals*, Pt. 1, 43.

9. William Tait to Hugh Findlay, April 22, 1852; in Findlay, *Missionary Journals*, Pt. 1, 18.

10. Findlay, *Missionary Journals*, Pt. 2, 49.

11. *Millennial Star* 14 (November 27, 1852): 635.

12. Ibid., 636.

13. Findlay, *Missionary Journals*, Pt. 2, 15.

14. Ibid., Pt. 2, 15. See also *Millennial Star* 14 (November 27, 1852): 636.

15. Hugh Findlay's correspondence with Captain Morse and Brigadier Trydell is included in Pt. 2, 16–18. He cited the same documents and added considerable commentary in his letters, Pt. 1, 98–104.

16. Hugh Findlay, "Further Intelligence from Hindustan: Opposition and Baptisms—Letter from Hugh Findlay" [Findlay to Samuel W. Richards, October 13, 1853, Poona], *Millennial Star* 14 (December 4, 1852): 654–55.

17. Findlay, *Missionary Journals*, Pt. 2, 52.

18. Ibid.

19. Ibid., Letter to the Saints at Bombay, March 5, 1853, Pt. 1, 141. Elder Findlay may have borrowed his reasoning from the First Presidency's Sixth General Epistle (September 21, 1852): "The conference voted to observe the words of wisdom, and particularly to dispense with the use of tea, coffee, snuff, and tobacco, and in this thing as well as many others, what is good for the Saints in the mountains, is good for the Saints in other places, and if all who profess to be Saints would appropriate the funds lavished on luxuries, and articles unwise to use, to the benefit of the public works, we would soon see another 'Temple of the Lord'" (Clark, *Messages of the First Presidency*, 2:90).

20. Editorial, "Bombay," *Millennial Star* 15 (July 2, 1853): 426–27.

21. Letter to the President of the Company of Elders from Great Salt Lake City, May 27, 1853; in Findlay, *Missionary Journals*, Pt. 1, 145.

22. Amos Milton Musser to Hugh Findlay, June 2, 1853; in Findlay, *Missionary Journals*, Pt. 1, 146.

23. Hugh Findlay to Musser, June 17, 1853; in Findlay, *Missionary Journals*, Pt. 1, 147. See also S. W. Richards to Hugh Findlay, May 5, 1853; in Findlay, *Missionary Journals*, Pt. 1, 147–48.

24. Hugh Findlay to Musser, June 17, 1853; in Findlay, *Missionary Journals*.

25. Hugh Findlay, "The East India Mission: Illness of Elder H. Findlay—Baptisms—Organization of a Branch in Bombay" [Findlay to S. W. Richards, July 20, 1853, Bombay], *Millennial Star* 15 (September 24, 1853): 639.

26. West, "The India Mission: Ceylon—Bombay—Poona—Arabia," *Deseret News* 5 (September 5, 1855): 206.

27. Hugh Findlay to William Gibson, November 13, 1853; in Findlay, *Missionary*

Journals, Pt. 1, 186. See also Hugh Findlay to A. F. McDonald, November 13, 1853; in Findlay, *Missionary Journals*, Pt. 1, 190.

28. Truman Leonard, "The Bombay Mission: Arrival from Calcutta of Elders Leonard and Musser—Missions to Kurachee and Belgaum—Departure of Elders West and Dewey for Siam" [Leonard to Samuel W. Richards, February 14, 1854, Bombay], *Millennial Star* 16 (April 8, 1854): 223.

29. Hugh Findlay, "Hindostan: Kurrachee and Vengoorly—Permission to Preach at Vengoorly—Baptisms—Ignorance and Superstition of the Natives" [Findlay to Franklin D. Richards, July 26, 1854, Belgaum], *Millennial Star* 16 (November 4, 1854): 701.

30. Ibid., 702.

31. Letter from Hugh Findlay to Amos M. Musser, July 2, 1854, in Britsch, "Missionary Activities in India," 130.

32. Findlay, *Millennial Star* 16 (November 4, 1854): 703.

33. Hugh Findlay, "Hindostan: Intolerance of the Military Authorities at Belgaum—Opening and Baptisms at Kotree—'Review' of an 'Invitation,' &c." [Findlay to Franklin D. Richards, October 22, 1854, Belgaum], *Millennial Star* 17 (January 20, 1855): 42–43.

34. Hugh Findlay, "Hindostan: Superstitions and Idolatry of the Natives—Tract in Mahrattee—Visit to Goa—Elder A. Findlay at Secundrabad—Emigration of Elder H. Findlay and Other Saints. &c." [Findlay to Franklin D. Richards, March 5, 1855, Bombay], *Millennial Star* 17 (May 5, 1855): 281.

35. Truman Leonard to Amos Milton Musser, April 7, 1855, Hyderabad, Sind, India, in Truman Leonard letter collection, Manuscripts and Special Collections, Harold B. Lee Library, Brigham Young University, Provo, Utah. In this and another letter Leonard mentions that the Davies and Taits borrowed money to pay their passage to Hong Kong. For some reason this was considered dishonorable and was published in papers in Bombay, Sind, and other places.

36. Hugh Findlay, "China: Arrival of Elder Findlay and Emigrating Saints at Hong Kong—Baptisms" [Findlay to Franklin D. Richards, June 26, 1855, Hong Kong] *Millennial Star* 17 (September 22, 1855): 607.

37. Jenson, *Church Chronology*, 55.

38. The date of the emigrant company's arrival in San Francisco is not known, nor is the date of their arrival in Salt Lake City; however, the Findlay family documented the arrival in Utah of at least ten of Hugh Findlay's converts. There were probably more.

39. Allan Findlay, "Hindostan: Journey from Poona to Ahmednugger—No Liberty to Reside or Preach in Cantonments—Kind Reception at Jaulnah—Exertions at Secunderabad" [Allan Findlay to Franklin D. Richards, March 29, 1855, Secunderabad], *Millennial Star* 17 (June 16, 1855): 379.

40. Ibid.

41. Ibid., 381.

42. Ibid., 382.

43. *Nizam* means "regulator of the kingdom." It is a Muslim term that refers to the hereditary ruler of the Territory of Hyderabad. This area had been an Islamic stronghold and was by the 1850s under the protection of the East India Company. In later years it was referred to as a native state.

44. *Millennial Star* 17 (June 16, 1855): 382.

45. Veena Maitra, *The Cantonment Administration in India* (New Delhi, India: by the author, 1996), 1.

46. Findlay, *Millennial Star* 17 (June 16, 1855): 383.

47. Ibid.

48. Letter from George Gordon to Amos Milton Musser and Truman Leonard, June 8, 1855, Belgaum, India, in Britsch, "Missionary Activities in India," 144.

49. Letter from Allan Findlay to Amos Milton Musser, August 10, 1855, Belgaum, India, in Britsch, "Missionary Activities in India," 144.

10

EXTENDING THE MISSION TO SIND

On February 12, 1854, President Jones penned a brief letter to Hugh Findlay. His main purpose was to request information regarding the number of branches, members, priesthood holders, and so on, in and around Bombay to include in his April 1st, six-month report to Liverpool. But he also wrote: "No change or alteration since I last wrote. I believe India is determined to reject the offer of salvation from the present appearances." Jones mentioned that Elders Woolley and Fotheringham were on their way back from upper India, having had no success. He added, "Nothing doing in Burmah. No news from Madras."[1] Ballantyne, Owens, and Skelton were still there at this date, although Elder Ballantyne departed for home and Elder Owens for Australia in July 1854. Elder Savage was working in Burma, and Elder Willes, who was at Calcutta with Jones, was to move to Rangoon in March 1854, from which place he departed for home in September. On February 12th, Elder Leonard and I, Elder Musser, had been in Bombay for three days. Within a few days, we would make the decision to sail to Karachi to open missionary work in that desert region of India.

Truman Leonard

THE GOSPEL IS INTRODUCED IN SIND

Elder Truman Leonard and I arrived at Bombay on February 9, 1854, and shipped out for Sind [southern Pakistan] only thirteen days later, on February 22d. We had found Elder Hugh Findlay sick with a fever, and the branch reduced to a small number. Our impressions of the faithful few were positive, but we concluded that it would be best to open a new field.

The last few hours before sailing were quite hurried. The steamer *Bombay* was scheduled to leave at 2:00 P.M., and we were not ready, nor did we have enough rupees to pay our passage. With no other option available, I pawned my watch for twenty-five rupees, twenty-four rupees of which were required to pay our fare. We raced around town picking up our laundry, buying meager provisions, and taking care of other little tasks and made it on board at the appointed time. To our consternation, after all the hustling about, the *Bombay* did not depart until 6:00 P.M.[2]

Captain Bayts and other crewmembers were courteous and quite accommodating later. We did not think anyone was aware of our poverty-stricken condition, when to our surprise an engineer sent us a good meal. Our journals reveal our deep and sincere gratitude to the donors and to the Lord. As always, we improved every opportunity by talking about the Gospel with anyone who would listen. Several members of the crew were quite interested. After settling in Karachi, we often went to visit with the crew of the *Bombay* when it was in port. Such visits were natural because we called at the steamer to pick up our mail.

The *Bombay* arrived at Karachi (sometimes spelled Kurrachee, among other variations) on February 26th, and we went ashore the next morning. The town was situated seven miles from the port. Being almost penniless (we had two rupees and a few annas between us), we had no option but to walk there. The landscape we traversed was bleak desert with mostly dusty roads, although the main road was surfaced. Where crops were growing they were nourished by irrigation water from ancient canals. In locations where farmers lifted water from the Indus River through the use of various animal-powered water wheels, spots of green beautified an otherwise barren scene. This was true throughout Sind. The humidity of Bombay was absent; in its place was dry, often dusty, air.

Camels of various kinds were common (Elder Leonard developed a considerable fascination and respect for the beasts), but the usual Indian bullocks, horses, goats, sheep, donkeys, and elephants were also present. Once we got settled, we learned from our neighbors to be ever watchful for poisonous snakes that were all too common in the area. Scorpions and centipedes, too, brought serious pain to many people.

Elder Leonard and I walked into Karachi to search for a friend to help us, for we needed a room and food. After walking several miles within the town, we became acquainted with a man named Joseph M. Anderson, who with his young family agreed to provide us a room. It was difficult to discern the limits of the cantonment, but Anderson lived within its bounds. Being tired already, we walked the seven miles back to the steamer to get our traps and spent the night on board. We calculated eighteen miles on foot for the day.[3]

Before leaving the steamer, Mr. Gray, the chief mate, gave us breakfast—our last good meal for a while. When we arrived at Anderson's house the next morning, we found our six-by-twelve-foot room cleaned and "a new coat of cow's excrement, reduced by water to a mortar, covered . . . the floor. This they say, is an improvement on dirt floors in this country."[4]

The next day, March 1, 1854, we began our "missioning." First, we visited our neighbors. We found that a large number of them were Muslims. In fact, most of the people in Sind were followers of the prophet Muhammad, as they are today. During our stay in Karachi and Hyderabad, we found many of these people to be generous and kind. But we were soon speaking with military men from various units. The next day, we were into the barracks again. Leonard preached for two hours to a large group of men. But he was not feeling well. On March 3d, we sought out a man named William S. Smith, who owned a building we hoped to rent as a meeting place. We eventually rented the bungalow for ten rupees per month. Leonard was still not healthy.

Days passed and Elder Leonard's health became worse. A contributing factor was our daily diet of bread and water. One day Leonard reported cold feet but a feverish head. He stood in warm water while pouring cool water over his head. Another day, he said he had "every symptom of a severe fit of sickness." His "feet and legs [were] much broken out and bloched." The same day he mentioned discharging a "child's worm 6 or 8 inches in length" from his bowels. On March 16th, he took a dose of sulfur. "I am troubled with bad blood which is apparent from ulcers, boils, and numerous sores upon my body and limbs easily inflamed and attended with considerable pain," he wrote in his journal. We were still living on bread and water. With no fruits or vegetables, it is no wonder he developed sores and boils. It is a wonder he did not die of scurvy. But he also may have been afflicted with malaria. There is little question that he later suffered with that disease.

On March 19th, to our surprise, the Andersons suddenly moved from their house, leaving a debt of forty-five rupees. The Parsee man who owned the place tried to extract from us either money or information about the Anderson's whereabouts, but we could provide neither. The owner told us we had to be out as soon as possible.[5] Fortunately, on March 21st, we closed the deal to rent Mr. Smith's bungalow for meetings and moved into it that day. Mr. Smith was still in the bungalow but moved to a tent as temporary quarters. He did all he could to make us comfortable. Leonard was still sick.

A few days after we began proselytizing in Karachi, we heard rumblings regarding mistreatment of soldiers who were reading our tracts and pamphlets. Then we heard a rumor that anyone who joined the Mormon Church would have to eat only bread and water. Evidently our limited diet was being noised around. But only three days after we moved into our bungalow, before we were really settled in and known in the neighborhood, at 11:00 A.M. a police officer came by and asked for our names. Hardly an hour passed before another policeman was at our door, accompanied by four others who carried clubs, to present us with a written order. It read:

> The attendance of Truman Leonard and Amos M. Musser is required at the police office immediately.
> (Signed) Geo. E. Ashburner
> Capt. &c. of Police
> Bazaar and Police Office
> 24 March 1854

Both of our journals tell essentially the same story. I wrote:

> On our arrival at the [police] office he [Ashburner] was not in, keeping us waiting over one hour for his return, after which he called us and on appearing he asked, "by what authority are you in camp." Before an explanation could be given, he ordered us out of the cantonments forthwith, refusing to give any satisfaction whatever concerning his stern and rigid orders,

not letting us know what law (if any) we had transgressed, or wherein we had done wrong in the least, so as to bring upon ourselves such cruel, uncourteous, and unkind treatment. He ordered 2 *Police* to see that we were outside of cantonments immediately.[6]

In the whole affair, we were handled with contempt and meanness. Like criminals, we were marched to our bungalow, given brief time to gather our belongings, and escorted outside the lines of the cantonment. Now in the native town, we rented a room (twelve feet by twenty-four feet) from a Jewish man and moved in.[7] Our efforts to gain redress of our situation proved fruitless. As had happened in other cantonments, the commanding officers were as determined to keep us away from the troops as were the officers below them, the chaplains and ministers, and hostile newspaper editors.

Regarding chaplains, Protestant missionaries, and ministers, we had several face-to-face encounters with such people individually and as a group. Such interchanges were totally fruitless and bore little more than animosity on both sides. Friendly acquaintances reported to us that several of the ministers were behind our ejection from the cantonment, our inability to find a suitable room to preach in, and the hostile editorials and articles in the local newspapers.

Over the ensuing months, we moved two or three more times in an effort to reduce rent or to improve our circumstances. Life was extremely basic. We hardly had more than our clothes, sleeping cots, bed coverings, and missionary teaching supplies. In our third rented room, we were happy when a native neighbor brought us a rude table and two chairs. Now we had a place to read, write, and eat. Fortunately, our neighbors were generally kind and generous to us. At various times, neighbors took mercy on us and brought fruits, curry and rice, and occasionally other basic foods. Of one of these kindnesses I wrote:

> A native woman brot us *de Basin cha* (2 cups of tea). When we very respectfully declined drinking and told her we did not

make a practice of using tea, she could talk a little English, and offered us some fish &c. But having just bought some bread we thanked her very kindly for her kindness. The natives are very hospitable to Europeans who will converse with and use familiarity, and not consider them beneath their notice. They are very kind one to another also.[8]

Although we had been ordered to remain outside the cantonment, we frequently stole into camp after nightfall, sometimes in disguise, to meet interested soldiers. In these little ventures, we were never detected, probably because the people we were meeting were honestly interested in hearing what we had to say but also because they might have found themselves in trouble if they had been detected meeting with the Mormons. If the military officers had seriously wanted to jail us, luring us into a trap would have been an easy matter. Such a thing never happened.

We left a good deal of evidence of our movements within the cantonment. Most obvious were handwritten notices that we stuck on posts to announce our meetings. We also loaned or sold numerous tracts, pamphlets, and books to our investigators. Occasionally, an anti-Mormon sergeant or officer would find one of these materials and harass its possessor.

Our days were always focused on teaching the principles of the restored Gospel. Often working separately, we tried to turn every conversation into a Gospel discussion. We invited almost everyone we met to drop by and see us or to attend our preaching services. Frequently, we were visited by soldiers, clerks, hospital workers, and occasionally by natives and others who had seen our handbills or overheard our testimonies in barracks or around town. Conversations often went on for one or two hours, and occasionally longer.

Elder Leonard and I each had a love for prose and poetry. Leonard was not much of a speller, but he expressed himself clearly enough. Together and separately, we wrote articles to the *Kossid* and *Sindian*, Karachi newspapers, answering the anti-Mormon articles that were printed therein. Although many columns of print were devoted to the Mormon issue, none were favorable to Mormonism.

Shortly after we settled in Karachi, a man named Thomas Hines, a Roman Catholic Irishman and soldier, made inquiries about the Church. He regularly stopped by to see us and also invited us to meet him within the cantonment. On June 8th, Thomas Willard, the son of an English father and an Indian mother, became interested in the Church and started studying with us regularly. Although we distributed tracts and pamphlets to many people, only Hines and Willard seemed to have a real interest in the Church.

While in Karachi, Elder Leonard expended considerable effort to obtain a suitable room for preaching and to furnish it with chairs. He and I were destitute but continued to operate almost like entrepreneurs. You might say we were unabashed in our requests for assistance, even asking Protestant ministers, who we knew were dead set against us, for help finding a good meeting room. We also went to others, such as a quartermaster sergeant whom we believed might provide chairs. Elder Leonard, a Mason, learned that Sergeant Jones also was a Mason. He used that relationship to gain a commitment for help.

Elder Leonard's status as a Master Mason[9] in the fraternal Masonic order (technically Freemasonry, or the Free and Accepted Masons) was his most useful key to opening doors when he needed help. While yet in Karachi, he became acquainted with at least four other Masons who treated him as a brother. One of these men, William Smith, was the former owner of the first bungalow we rented. He became quite interested in Mormon doctrine and eventually invited Leonard to visit him at his principal home in Kotri, near Hyderabad, 120 miles northeast on the Indus River. Smith promised to "assist us and use his influence in our favor."[10]

The missionary routine fell into a fairly stable pattern. We daily distributed tracts and tried to converse with as many people as possible. Daily, we endured problems finding enough to eat. At that time, an Indian couple named Samuel asked us to teach their seven-year-old daughter English in return for food. A few weeks later, I began teaching a Hindu man the English language for a small monetary reward. Both of us believed this was the right thing to do. As a result, we became good friends with the Samuels and Noorbhoy Abronpee, we helped a little girl and a man learn a useful tool, and we improved our diet in the bargain.

Soon after arriving in Karachi, I decided to study the Hindustani language earnestly. I found a moonshi (teacher) and daily devoted hours to that work. Leonard, too, was interested in the language, but he did not apply himself to the same degree. Before we left Sind to return home, I had developed fluency in Hindustani.

April, May, and June were terribly hot, dry, and dusty (peak temperatures in Sind go above 120 degrees Fahrenheit in the shade). Winds blew blasts of hot air that made our lives almost unbearable. Dust infiltrated every nook and crevice of our room and into all of our belongings. To make matters worse, we were harassed by the Reverend Mr. Seal, a native Christian missionary, who sent a blind man to our room several times to have his sight restored. Elder Leonard began studying the responses of persons who avoided meeting with us. He observed that we sometimes could not gain admittance "because of real or false pretension to sickness or asleep or absent from home. These are common rebuffs if our presence be not agreeable, which has proved itself in several instances and is considered a gentlemanly way of acting the hypocrite." On another occasion, Leonard wrote: "Elder Musser visited some persons or attempted to, but in one instance had the mortification of having to be deprived of a conversation with a man previously friendly but now desires to be excused which was manifested by a retreat upon the Elders approaching the house, sending a message by his Wife that he was engaged, a common way in India of putting an end to friendship."[11]

Elder Leonard developed a practice that he continued until we left Sind. Almost daily, he walked to the seashore or into the desert (or while in Kotri and Hyderabad, to a garden or cemetery) to find quiet, solace, and the opportunity to commune alone with his Heavenly Father. One day he wrote, "In the afternoon I took a walk near the sea shore . . . many curiosities . . . but felt while alone to pour out my desires in prayer to God for his work as also our usefulness in this truly dark and benighted land." On another day, he penned, "Again took a walk a long way towards the sea shore where felt to mourn over the people of this place." And on another occasion, he wrote: "In the afternoon took a walk, repairing to a desert place where I felt to pour out my soul in prayer to God for the few honest in this place that they might be brought to a knowledge of the truth." Another purpose of his long walks was to regain his health and strength, which continued to be a problem.

We devoted as much time as possible to teaching Willard and Hines. Leonard, who had served a mission to Ohio and New York in 1843–44 and had some experience with the conversion process, sometimes counseled them quite frankly regarding the challenges they were facing. Leonard recalled:

> In the evening Mr. Hines called again. . . . He told me that he believed our doctrine but manifested a little delicateness relative to obeying the same. I told him the Devil would endeavor to darken his mind if possible, which he could detect. As there would be and was two invisible powers striving with him, that while with us he felt to rejoice because of the influence of the Spirit in us, and while surrounded by other company the opposite was the result and he would feel miserable, and at times to doubt, adding if he would pray to God that spirit would leave, he again would feel well.[12]

Leonard further taught and encouraged Hines, promising him that if he would be baptized he could be the beginning of a branch among the soldiers. By late May, Hines believed the Church was true but did not yet have the courage to obey it.

From time to time, we had some tender experiences. One afternoon Thomas Hines, following a long meeting with Elder Leonard, gave him two rupees. Leonard was very grateful. On the way home, he called to see Mr. Samuel "who had been feeding us sometime and actually not able to do so and under these considerations [he] offered him one or both of the rupees, which he and also his Wife refused to take. This expression of kindness and hospitality caused me [Leonard] to say may the Lord reward and bless you & further say while you feed us your family shall never be found begging bread." The next day, a Sunday, "we also received a sumptuous meal from a native woman to us a stranger. The Lord reward her." A few days later, I gave Mr. Samuel an old pair of pants and eight annas. The Samuels were more destitute than we were. Then several more days passed, and the Samuels spent some time with us. In the course of conversation, Mrs. Samuel mentioned someone questioning her for feeding the elders without pay. She replied that it was her business, and she would continue to feed us "as long as she had anything and if she had to beg she would divide that with us if we could do no better."[13] Leonard added: "May the Lord reward such by saving them."

On June 11th, Karachi received its first rain in six or eight months. A weak monsoon was finally beginning to cool the temperature and settle the dust of Sind.

In addition to the kindnesses of the few, we expressed almost ecstatic joy when we received letters from home and shipments of the *Millennial Star*, the *Journal of Discourses*, the *Deseret News*, the *Seer*, and other publications from England and home. For the next day or so, we savored every word as we read and re-read each new letter or article. For example, Leonard wrote: "Spent the day in reading further of the glorious news which was truly a feast to our souls sweeter than honey."

On July 12, 1854, Truman received a letter from his wife, Ortentia, that had been written on December 27, 1853, more than six months before. Enclosed within its pages was a letter from a Brother Hughes, who explained that Ortentia and little Helen were living with his family for the winter. The Hugheses were doing their best to make them comfortable and encouraged Leonard by saying "your wife is very prudent and manages well on her part."

If Truman had any questions about an early return home or whether his wife was eager for him to return home before his appointed time, Ortentia put even the possibility of such notions to rest. She admonished:

> Truman! rather than have you come home with the name that most of the Elders have this fall, I would rather never see your face again this side of eternity, but if you can come home as Br. Brigham said that Br. Wheelock had with his garments pure and spotless, that would pay me for your being gone if it were a half dozen years; you may think that I am a stronger Mormon than I used to be, well I am and a better one too I think for I have no one to lean on now as when you are at home. I try to do the very best I know but I need your prayers to help me to do right which I never had stronger desires for, which if I do I feel if I or Helen was sick that I could go before the Lord and claim the blessing pronounced on my head, viz., that I should have the power to issue the destroyer from my house and it has been so, thank the Lord.[14]

With this letter to add strength to his resolve to push onward, Elder Leonard and I decided we should continue working in Karachi for a time but that probably one or the other of us should move to Kotri and Hyderabad to attempt an opening there. We continued regular meetings and made a last attempt to convince the Karachi cantonment commander that we should be allowed to preach in camp. Brigadier General Parr refused our request in most insulting terms and sealed our decision to try to do something up the Indus River.

On August 8th, Thomas Willard made known his desire to be baptized, and the next Sunday was appointed to perform the ordinance. That date did not work out, so the Tuesday following, August 15th, was selected. Even though Willard was not a soldier, we believed it best for the ordinance to be conducted somewhat secretly. Together with Mr. Samuel, who, we hoped, would soon follow Willard's example (Samuel had by this time provided food for the elders for more than four months), we retreated to a lonely arm of the Arabian Sea. There we sang and prayed and then Elder

Leonard immersed Thomas Willard beneath a bright wave. Moving to the deck of a boat nearby, we laid our hands on his head and with me, Elder Musser, as voice, confirmed him a member of The Church of Jesus Christ of Latter-day Saints, the first person to become a member in the area (later to be known as Pakistan).[15]

Thomas Hines was conspicuously absent from Willard's baptism, even though by this time they had become good friends. Hines had been in the cantonment hospital where he had been "greatly reduced" by lance, leaches and other misery-increasing therapies. As soon as he was able, he met again with the three members of the Church and learned of the plan for either Elder Leonard or me to move to Kotri. At the same time, August 17th, Leonard found that he or I could sail by the steamer *Chenaub* at a cost of six or seven rupees. One of the crew had become a good friend and offered to have whoever went stay in his cabin. The following day we decided Leonard should go.

Several spiritual events transpired between Willard's baptism and Leonard's departure, including a healing through a priesthood blessing. But most important was Thomas Hines's decision to be baptized. On Tuesday, August 22d, Hines visited us and expressed his belief in the Church, but said he thought it was too late for Leonard to perform the ordinance since he was leaving the next day. Leonard spoke frankly to his friend: "You will never feel free until you make up your mind to obey the truth; and the sooner you do it the better." Hines said he had been thinking about it for a long time. "Now let me make a proposition," continued Elder Leonard. "Let us go right across here to that tank [reservoir] and appoint the place and meet us this evening at dark and attend to the ordinance at once, which you will never have cause to regret." To this proposition, Hines agreed. In the evening, Elder Leonard and I met Hines at the tank. Leonard baptized him, and I confirmed him.[16] Brother Thomas Hines's was the second of the two baptisms performed in Sind. Other men and women listened intently, discussed the Gospel with us at great length, and read widely in Church literature but did not have the courage to face the derision of their peers and join the Church.

ELDER LEONARD EXTENDS THE MISSION TO KOTRI AND HYDERABAD

When it came time for Elder Leonard to purchase his ticket, he visited the agent, Mr. John Stewart Amos. After Leonard explained who he was and his circumstances, Mr. Amos said, "I am a friend, and an old bachelor and with plenty of money, and now just command me and I will do." Generous Mr. Amos paid Leonard's passage. The *Chenaub* sailed on August 24th at about noon. The trip took most of five days. Mr. Amos paved the way for Elder Leonard to have a comfortable trip. The crew cared well for his needs. When the side-wheel steamer docked at Kotri on August 29th, Leonard figured he had traveled 230 miles by river to accomplish what would have been 120 miles by land.[17] Elder Leonard said the Indus was much like the Missouri River, raucous and energetic with shifting sandbars and many obstacles.

After his arrival at Kotri, Elder Leonard went directly to the home of William S. Smith, who had become his friend in Karachi. Smith welcomed him in and sent servants to the dock to bring Leonard's luggage. This was the beginning of an arrangement that lasted for four months.[18] Smith treated Leonard as if he were a member of the family. He had his own room and enjoyed Smith's generosity. He regained much strength while there.

Smith's home became Leonard's headquarters. His religious beliefs and observations were taken seriously by a number of Smith's friends and acquaintances. Day by day, friends called and held conversations with Elder Leonard. The local clergy as well, who went out of their way to discredit his opinions and work, noted his presence.

Leonard hoped he could convince Mr. Smith that the Mormon religion was true. Smith frequently said he believed most of what Leonard taught, even the doctrine of plural wives, but he continued to have questions on one doctrine, principle, or another. Nevertheless, he made Elder Leonard feel at home.

In an effort to be of some value, in addition to preaching the Gospel, Leonard also used his skills as a carpenter and mechanic to repair items around the bungalow—chairs, a music box, guns— almost anything that was not working. It was evident from being around him, as well as from references in his journals, that Leonard was a skilled carpenter and mechanic. Before he departed from Sind, he had set type for a printing press, fixed machinery for Smith and others (his descriptions of native-built machines are clear and detailed), painted signs (he mixed his own paints and colors), and made and tempered his own chisels for engraving letters on gravestones and other monuments. He accompanied Mr. Smith on two hunting trips and proved himself to be the best marksman in the group. When necessary, he sewed and mended his own clothes. For quite a while, he copied letters for Mr. Smith to partially repay his room and board.

Shortly after Elder Leonard arrived in Kotri, Smith promised to arrange a room for lectures and religious services. But then, even though Leonard touched softly on the matter from time to time, Mr. Smith seemed reluctant to follow through. In his journal, Elder Leonard mentioned several times that he was doing as many favors as possible, such as repairs, in an effort to stay on Smith's good side. But months passed and no progress was made.

On January 1, 1855, Leonard wrote of his determination to move from Kotri across the Indus River to Hyderabad. The distance was short, only three miles from the dock on the Hyderabad side into town, but Leonard hoped for greater success closer to the cantonment. He soon made the move, but he did not have the success he hoped for. He was rejected by the commanding military officer and ejected from the cantonment. He almost starved but was finally given sustenance. The entire story in Hyderabad can be shortened to a sentence: Leonard was unable to convince anyone that his message was true and should be obeyed.

But four observations must be made regarding Leonard's time

in Kotri and Hyderabad. First, he was diligent in his efforts to spread the Gospel through the printed word and in his personal effort to learn all he could from that source. He read voraciously. His journal discloses a list of at least twenty-five printed items (books, pamphlets, tracts, magazines, and journals) in addition to the scriptures that he studied to gain understanding of the restored Gospel, of India, and particularly of Sind, and of Christian and Muslim history.[19] Leonard also read the local newspapers and foreign papers when they were available. He was particularly interested in the Crimean War (1853–56) and its possible effects on India.

Leonard's host, Mr. Smith, owned a small printing press on which Leonard printed a library list for distribution to potential borrowers. Leonard also tried to set the type for a pamphlet he had written but failed to get it into print because of insufficient type.

Second, Elder Leonard developed an impressive group of friends while he lived in Hyderabad. Among these people were sergeants and military officers, a pharmacist, clerks, and others whose occupations are not mentioned. From time to time some of these people contributed to Leonard's livelihood and welfare. Initially, Leonard lived in a very small room, but he eventually rented a house or bungalow. He paid the rent with a rupee from one friend, a few annas from another. Somehow the rent was paid and his needs were met. The bungalow was large enough to become a gathering place for people who were interested in Mormonism. He fitted it out with borrowed chairs and benches for meetings and for a time attracted audiences of forty to sixty people. An interesting side note was his courage to ask a smaller audience of about fifteen if he should give up on them and sail back to Karachi. The congregation voted that he should remain and continue to teach them. When it came time for him to leave, friends held two dinner parties in his honor. He was seated at the head of the table and asked to cut the roast duck. A number of these good friends privately told Elder Leonard that they believed his message and religion to be true, but they did not have the courage to move forward and become Latter-day Saints. It is tragic that Leonard was not able to get these people to share their private expressions of belief with each other. Together they might have formed a small but strong branch of the Church. In May 1855, he wrote: "I have done the best I knew, to get them into the kingdom, but it would seem that nothing but the judgements of God would effect it."[20]

Third, Leonard became friends with a man named Robert Marshall. When Leonard was in need of food, he prayed for help and then went to Marshall. He told him that he, Leonard, had selected him to provide his meals for a season and for this he would be blessed. Marshall accepted this invitation and provided Leonard breakfast, dinner, or both each day for a month or two until Marshall became financially strapped. At that time, Marshall moved into a room in Leonard's home. Their caring for one another was reciprocal.

Robert Marshall had a sincere interest in Mormonism, but he did not have a strong enough testimony at that time to brave the abuse and harassment that was directed against Leonard and the Mormon Church. He bought a number of pamphlets and books, including the Book of Mormon and the Doctrine and Covenants, as well as copies of the *Millennial Star* and the *Journal of Discourses*. When Leonard and I left Sind, Marshall was in Karachi to say goodbye. At that time, he purchased additional issues of the *Star* and *Discourses*. Years passed. Marshall married and settled in Karachi. The Mormon publications stayed on his bookshelves.

Sometime following the American Civil War (1861–65), Marshall remembered Joseph Smith's prophecy that such a war would take place. He had read about this in the Doctrine and Covenants. He became convinced that Joseph Smith was a true prophet and that the Church was as true as Elder Leonard had said it was. From that time, he became known as a Mormon and taught his family about the Church. In 1880, the family contacted the Church in England, but nothing came of it. In 1903, six years after Truman Leonard's death and almost fifty years after Marshall became acquainted with the Church, though old and blind, he was still eager to be baptized. Through a letter sent by a family member to England, a priesthood bearer named John H. Cooper, who was working in Calcutta, was asked by Church authorities to visit Robert Marshall and his family in Karachi. Cooper spent from June to September 1903 in Karachi. Marshall and his family and others were baptized, thirteen in all, and several of the men were ordained to the priesthood, so a branch could be organized.[21] Even though this little unit of the Church gradually faded away, it was a tribute to Robert Marshall's honesty and tenacity and to Truman Leonard's efforts to establish the restored Gospel in Sind.

Fourth, Truman Leonard's courage and faith in the face of terrible sickness can hardly be overstated. Numerous times he briefly noted his fevers and general illnesses. But during the days from March 16th to April 3, 1855, he was in serious danger of losing his life. Some of his journal entries read: "In the afternoon had an attack of the fever with a dreadful headache . . . I passed a restless & painful night." "Quite unwell all day." "Another most dreadful day. Some fever. My bones ached and it seemed that my head would burst open." "This too has been a dreadful day." Fortunately his pharmacist friend, Mr. Thompson, sent some quinine and other medicines at this point, and even though Leonard didn't believe he was getting better, his life might have been preserved by this thoughtful act. Day by day, the miserable reports continued. On Sunday, March 25th, William Smith and a friend called to check on his condition. Smith insisted that he should go to Kotri. He gathered Leonard up, placed him on his camel, and took him to the river. They crossed, and for the next eight days, Smith and his servants gave Leonard the best care they could. He was suffering from a severe case of malaria.[22] Even through all of this, he was eager to return to his place in Hyderabad and continue his work. Feeling somewhat restored, on April 3d, he said goodbye to Smith and returned across the river. But all of this had taken its toll. A few days later, Leonard wrote to me and expressed his eagerness to return home to the Valley.[23]

This was not his only bout with malaria. He had four serious attacks, two of which almost took his life.[24] During his last month in Karachi, before sailing for Bombay and home, he suffered what sounds like a combination of dysentery and malaria. One day he passed what he estimated to be a pint of blood in his stool. Then several days later, he raised the total estimate to three pints. Simultaneously, he suffered with a severe fever, chills, and headache. Again, he was blessed to have survived at all.

While Truman Leonard was sick during April 1855, he received a letter from Elder Hugh Findlay in Bombay. In it, Findlay reported his plans to leave for America within a few hours. He asked Leonard to take charge of Church affairs in the entire west side of India. President Jones had already departed from Calcutta and had left Elder Skelton in charge on that side. Leonard felt burdened by the additional responsibilities, but he did his best to communicate good counsel to Allan Findlay and other members who remained in Belgaum, Poona, and Bombay.

Most of the elders had already left for home. Ballantyne and Owens had left in July 1854; Willes departed in September, and Woolley in November 1854. Jones and Fotheringham had sailed on March 5, 1855, and now Findlay was on his way. By this time the elders were on their own and could either stay or return home depending on their own judgment. On January 26, 1855, I, Elder Musser, had received a letter from T. W. Ellerbeck, a secretary to President Brigham Young, in Salt Lake City. I forwarded the letter on to Leonard. It read:

G. S. L. City Sept. 1/54
Bro Musser

I asked the *President* this morning, if he had anything to say to you, or those Elders in East India. One thing he said was, "*I will dismiss them from there, just as quick as they like to come.*"
Enough—in a hurry—no time.

Above acceptable.

Written by request of Pres. Brigham Young
Yours &c.
T. W. Ellerbeck[25]

On January 27th, I had received a package of *Stars* and read in one of the issues that "The First Presidency say to the Elders in this country [East India], in the Cape of Good Hope, and Australia, 'You can tarry where you are, or go home, as the Spirit may dictate.'"[26]

When Elder Leonard received this news, he wrote the following to me:

> I cannot say that I am sorry to hear that it is the privilege of the Elders of this mission to return if they think best. I will say if things were not so discouraging, I would not consent to leave India yet, but I declare I think my time is too precious to spend to so little advantage as has been the case in this country.[27]

On April 19th, Elder Leonard received a letter from me in which I asked him to return to Karachi. Leonard continued teaching the Gospel but spent considerable time chiseling letters into stone monuments as a means of raising money for the trip down the river. At the end of the month, he went to Kotri to see about steamer schedules. But he was planning one last great meeting on Sunday, May 6th. He placed flyers in prominent places and voiced around his plans. When the appointed hour arrived, only fifteen of his good friends attended, and they came mostly out of courtesy.

Leonard spent the month of May packing, retrieving books and pamphlets and attempting to sell or place them. He did a good deal of socializing, as well as some work lettering stone. On May 31st, nine months after his arrival in Kotri, he purchased his ticket and went on board the *Chenaub*. By nightfall the steamer was eight miles downstream from Kotri and on June 5th, he was back in Karachi, having had a pleasant journey and several opportunities to teach the Gospel to members of the crew.

Two days later, Leonard received a note from Robert Marshall in Hyderabad, saying: "Above all I must say your absence from this place has made us all dull, especially myself. I found that I parted with one of my dear relatives, however, I hope my dear Mr. Leonard soon I may be united in that Brotherhood through

Christ."[28] The following Sunday, Elder Leonard enjoyed a special evening with a group of Saints who had already become members of the Church. Brothers Whiteley, Taylor, and Tomlinson, along with Sister Tomlinson and her sister, joined Brothers Hines and Willard. They had come to Karachi by way of military assignment in Aden, Arabia, and were the fruit of Hugh Findlay's service in Bombay. Hines, Whiteley, and the Tomlinsons eventually emigrated to Utah. For a short time, there were nine Latter-day Saints living in Karachi, including Elder Leonard and me.

THE WORK IN KARACHI

After Elder Leonard left for Kotri in August 1854, I continued the effort to gain permission to preach in Karachi cantonment. My letters and personal meetings with high-ranking military officers proved futile, so I concluded to try another tactic. I would hold tent meetings near the cantonment. To accomplish this goal, I wrote to a Parsee friend named Dinshaw and asked for his help arranging for a large, "cheap" tent. This never worked out.

But while waiting for a reply from Dinshaw, I pursued a number of other activities, most important being contacting people on the streets and visiting soldiers in the cantonment after dark. I looked for a source for chairs to place in my room so I could hold meetings in some degree of comfort. My studies of Hindustani also occupied a considerable amount of my time. By early November, I had completed reading the New Testament in that language. As before Leonard left for Kotri, food remained a problem. For a while, an old woman, whom I called "my old native nanee (grandmother)," brought food to me almost daily. She could not speak English or Hindustani, but she and I communicated by gestures and expressions, and I was grateful for her kindness.[29] Other Indians sent mangos, Muslim friends sent meat and other offerings. The kindnesses offered by native Indians were in character with their way of living life and religion, which in their minds are a seamless whole. Men and women who live lives as humble mendicants, as Elder Leonard and I were doing, are respected and often even worshiped regardless of their religious affiliation. Food offerings to such people are believed to bring good karma to the giver.

In October, I wrote a letter to Mr. Amos, who had paid Leonard's way to Kotri, and asked for a job as a clerk or amanuensis. There were no openings at that time, but I had made my needs known. In November, I sent a similar letter to Mr. R. Taback of the Bombay Steam Navigation Company. Mr. Taback asked me to come to his office because he was impressed with my handwriting. It was decided that I would go to work for thirty-five rupees a month. Taback gave me ten rupees in advance. I was to work from ten until four each day except Sunday. These hours allowed me to continue my mission work in the morning and evening. My salary greatly improved my living conditions, and after Leonard returned to Karachi, both of us lived on my earnings. Not long after I began working, I had some butter on my bread, "the first I [had] tasted for months."[30]

Undoubtedly, my most demanding undertaking was my effort to build a meeting room or chapel. On January 3, 1855, I visited Captain J. B. Dunsterville, a friend, concerning a piece of property on which to build. A few days later, Dunsterville informed me that the land I wanted was available, and he would give it to me for the cost of a yearly tax fee of only one rupee. The property was sixty-five by sixty-five feet.[31] The following day I closed an agreement with a builder for the construction of the meetinghouse. I recorded:

> This morning I closed the bargain for a house, with a Musulman [Muslim] by the name of Dawood Sair Mohumad. The house is to be 20 by 26 feet in size, one story, 10 feet high. (The sides from the foundation to the roof, and the ends 15 feet high.) The whole is to be properly covered with good white tile. There is to be 3 doors and 4 windows in the house. The latter with shutters on the outside, and the walls over the doors and windows are to be made arching. The walls are to be made of good dried brick, and are to be 1–1/2 foot thick, with a good foundation and the whole will be plastered out and inside

Elder Musser's chapel at Karachi

and then whitewashed. He is to complete the whole, even to a new mat by the first of Feb./55, for the sum of rupees one-hundred, and for every day after the above specified time, he forfeits one rupee. (Hundred rupees is exactly $48.)[32]

It did not take me long to learn that this contract was valueless. By the agreed-upon completion date, the building was not yet underway. Finally, on February 23d, I was pleased when the masons started work on the job. Within a week or so, the building was coming up, but to my dismay the contractor was making it larger than the original plan, and it was costing more than budgeted. During April and May, the work moved slowly, and by June 2d, I was getting very discouraged with the project.[33] The doors, windows, and some of the roof tiles were still missing, and the builder was not to be found. I could have jailed him (if I could have found him), but to do so would have been pointless. Fortunately, at this time Elder Leonard returned from Kotri and was able to give me a little advice and help.

After checking with Captain Dunsterville regarding possible legal paths of action, we concluded that our best course was to complete the building ourselves. I got the remaining roof tiles in place on June 20th, but the windows and doors were still missing. The next day we bought some matting and nailed it up over the window spaces and doors. We were determined to move in and stop paying rent. We moved in the next day.[34]

About this time, we started holding meetings in our little meetinghouse, but they were almost invariably small. During our remaining weeks in Karachi, both of us expended much effort to counter foul newspaper articles and unusually great harassment of the few members of the Church in the military. Almost to a man, their rights to religious liberty were greatly curtailed. Brother Whiteley was especially persecuted. In July, he told us that he had not been able to visit us for three weeks because his officers had prohibited him from doing so. They had even broken into his private box and taken all of his books. Leonard's placement of the words to the hymn "Speak no ill!!" immediately following his entry regarding Whiteley may have been intended as irony.[35]

On July 11th, Elder Leonard and I received a letter from Dr. Ely, the American consul in Bombay, informing us that he believed that in about two months he could help us obtain passage home. We had written to him stating we would be willing to work our way home.[36] From that time on, our heads and hearts were turned toward the Valley. But the monsoon kept us captive for the time being. The seas were too rough for most ships. The monsoon, by the way, came terribly hard that year. The mats we had installed over the doors and windows could not hold back the winds and torrential rains.

On August 26th, we ordained Thomas Hines an elder in the Melchizedek priesthood.[37] Although he had faltered a little along the way, he had endured many persecutions from his fellow soldiers and officers in the army and had finally proven himself to be a faithful Latter-day Saint.

On September 15th, I was able, after an earlier disappointment, to sell my house to a Parsee for eighty rupees, sixty rupees under its cost.[38] Five days later the final deed was signed, and we were free to leave for Bombay. Thomas Willard had expressed a desire to go to Utah with us, but a few days before we departed, he declined to make the move because he had debts and other obligations. Both of us worked him over verbally and promised him he would apostatize if he did not gather with the Saints. Although he finally said he would come with us, that was the last we saw of him.

In the evening of September 21st, we shared a tender time with a few members of the Church. Brother Whiteley was especially affected and "could hardly contain himself." Leonard felt to make a prophecy, "agreeable to the Spirit," that "if he was faithful the time should roll away quick to his deliverance when he should go to Zion arriving in safety."[39] Whiteley did eventually emigrate to Utah. Singing "When Shall We All Meet Again" caused the tears to flow.

Leonard and I felt blessed to find a captain of a French ship who would take us to Bombay for a mere ten rupees each. It was leaving the next morning. We arose from bed at 3:30 A.M. and finished packing our things. At daylight, we headed in different directions to find a person or two who still owed us money or books. On the way to the dock, Elder Leonard ran into several people to whom he felt he had to bear his witness one last time. When he arrived at the dock, I was there with our luggage, but the ship was gone. It had sailed earlier than planned, which was frequently true with ships depending on tides and weather.

I was upset, but Elder Leonard believed everything would work out well, which it did. After enjoying a fine breakfast with a Muslim friend, we went to the steamship *Sindian*. Captain Banks was happy to have us on board at a reasonable rate, only eight rupees for deck fare. We sailed at 1:00 P.M. the same day. Before we had been long at sea, we were assigned to a cabin at no extra charge.

While we were standing on the ship visiting with Brother Hines before the ship's departure, Elder Leonard had a devious thought. Hines had a strong desire to gather to Zion, but he yet had an obligation to the military. Leonard figured that if Hines were to go to Bombay by steamer he would be four or five days ahead of the mail, even if Hines's officers got right at spreading word of his departure. In effect, Hines would be absent without leave. Once in Bombay, he would have to sail out immediately in order to successfully escape. Leonard shared this idea with Hines, but he did not know if Hines would try it.[40]

When we arrived at Bombay on September 25th, we found Sister Tait staying with her mother, Mrs. Haer. Sister Tait had remained in Bombay to give birth to a daughter after her husband and family sailed for San Francisco and the Salt Lake Valley with Elder Hugh Findlay. She was, of course, eager to find passage for herself and her five-month-old daughter to either America or Liverpool. Mrs. Haer's home became a headquarters of sorts for the next couple of months. On arriving in Bombay, we found that Elder Allan Findlay had arrived in Bombay earlier the same day. All of our efforts now turned to finding a way home.

LEAVING BOMBAY

We three missionaries (Leonard, Findlay, and I) and Sister Tait and infant, were eager to sail from Bombay as soon as possible. Findlay and I took the lead in looking for a ship's captain who would work with us. Our first success came when we arranged passage for Sister Tait as a servant to the wife of Captain Findlay of the *James White*. She also had to pay two hundred rupees but was pleased with the arrangement. After a tearful farewell from her mother and sister, we elders helped her to the ship on Monday, October 15th. The *James White* sailed for Liverpool the next day.[41] We were happy to have helped her away, but we missed the good dinners we had enjoyed as Sister Tait's guests.

By mid-October, we had a pretty good idea that we would be able to work our way to Liverpool. Two or three ships were at the *bunder* (pier), but they were loading freight slowly and probably would not be away for another month. Leonard had a good chance of sailing as a carpenter. Findlay and I hoped to go as ordinary seamen.

Two days after Sister Tait went on board, we were surprised to meet Brother Hines from Karachi in the street. He had arrived the night before and had looked all over town for us. He had left the army and had to get away from Bombay immediately. We elders found him a room, and he stayed there while we looked for almost any ship that was going anywhere, but preferably to Muscat, for it seemed the most likely destination for a quick retreat. We elders spent most of our time for the next two weeks working on arrangements to get Hines on a ship. On November 1st, after many trips out to the harbor to see Captain Brooster of the ship *Contest*, even though Hines was not qualified, we were able to get him on as an ordinary seaman.[42] He had made his escape. The ship was destined for Massachusetts, where his parents lived at Lowell. I do not know when he arrived there and what happened afterward. His intention was to go to Utah.

Unfortunately, Elder Leonard's journal stops abruptly on November 1, 1855. Elder Allan Findlay's journals are in Pitman shorthand and are unavailable at present. Going back over my own records, I note that I wrote a letter in London to Elder Orson Pratt, in which I mentioned that Leonard and Findlay sailed from Bombay in December 1855. They worked their way to Liverpool on the ship *Yorca*, under Captain Turner. He was the man they had negotiated with most consistently and seriously. I don't know when they reached Liverpool, but on March 23, 1856, Truman Leonard joined in Liverpool a company of 534 Saints who were sailing to Boston on the ship *Enoch Train*, Captain Henry P. Rich, master.[43] The *Enoch Train* was a large, 1618-ton, slow, three-masted square-rigger.[44] Leonard was called to preside over the ship's fifth ward.[45] From Boston, most of the group traveled by railroad to Iowa City, Iowa, where Leonard became part of Daniel D. McArthur's handcart company. That company reached Salt Lake City on

Friday, September 26th. His wife, Ortentia, came to meet him the following day from the new home she had built in Farmington.

Allan M. Findlay has left a hazier trail. He arrived in England with Elder Leonard in February, or at latest, early March, 1856. I do not know what he did in the interim between his arrival in England and his sailing for America. Perhaps he went to Scotland to gather his mother, Mary McPherson Findlay, and to renew an old friendship with Jessie Ireland of Dundee. In any event, on May 3, 1856, he sailed for America on the large, three-masted *Thornton*, under Captain Charles Collins. More important than the ship's captain, however, was the captain of the 764 emigrating Saints—Elder James G. Willie. His name will forever be remembered as the leader of the ill-fated handcart company that bears his name. On May 4th, in Captain Collins's quarters, Elder Millen Atwood married twenty-six-year-old Allan Findlay to twenty-six-year-old Jessie Ireland. Findlay's mother, Mary, James G. Willie, Captain Collins, and others were witnesses. The *Thornton* reached New York on June 14, 1856. Five hundred of those on board went on by train to Iowa City, arriving there on June 26th. The remainder of the tragic story is told in other places and still haunts the hearts of the Saints. Suffice it to say that after almost untold misery and sixty-seven deaths, the Willie Company was brought into Salt Lake City on November 9, 1856. The Allan Findlay family had found its way home to Zion.[46]

I, Elder Musser, sailed from Bombay to Calcutta on November 28, 1855, on the American ship *Lancaster*, Captain John F. Roundy, master. Roundy granted me free cabin passage. The voyage took a long forty-nine days.

When Elder Leonard wrote his last letter from Bombay on November 15, 1855, he said there were those "who still pant for liberty, to the number of 21, all told, in this Presidency, including 2 Elders, 1 Priest, and one Teacher, in tolerable standing."[47] His count included members in Karachi, Poona, and Belgaum. The Taits, the Davies, and Thomas Hines had already emigrated.

Others were to follow. The mission to the Bombay Presidency was closed in December 1855.

NOTES

1. N. V. Jones to Hugh Findlay, February 15, 1854; in Findlay, *Missionary Journals*, 196.

2. Truman Leonard, Journal (typescript, 6); copy in possession of the author. Also available in Manuscripts and Special Collections, Brigham Young University Library, Provo, Utah; spelling standardized.

3. Ibid., 8.

4. Musser, Journals, 4:39.

5. Leonard, Journal, 17.

6. Musser, Journals, 4:50.

7. Leonard, Journal, 21–23.

8. Musser, Journals, 4:55.

9. Glen M. Leonard, "Truman Leonard: Pioneer Mormon Farmer," *Utah Historical Quarterly* 44 (Summer 1976): 243.

10. Leonard, Journal, 34–35.

11. Ibid., 39, 53.

12. Ibid., 38. I have taken some liberties in correcting Leonard's original language. Malcolm R. Thorp discusses the crisis many investigators experienced before fully affiliating with the Church. Although his examples are different from Leonard's counsel, there is clearly a relationship. See Thorp, "The Religious Backgrounds of Mormon Converts in Britain, 1837–52," *Journal of Mormon History* 4 (1977): 57–58.

13. Leonard, Journal, 58–59, 65.

14. Ibid., 99–100.

15. Ibid., 125–26.

16. Ibid., 129–31.

17. Ibid., 130–35.

18. Truman Leonard, "Hindostan: Exertions of Elder Leonard at Hydrabad—Procrastination and Indifference of the People" [Leonard to Franklin D. Richards, May 24, 1855, Hyderabad, Sind], *Millennial Star* 17 (September 15, 1855): 588.

19. The following examples of Leonard's reading material are listed in the order they are found in his journals: *History of Joseph Smith by His Mother; History of the Persecutions of the Saints;* Jones's *Reply to Mormonism Unveiled;* many issues of the *Journal of Discourses;* the *Millennial Star;* the *Seer;* Parley P. Pratt's *The Voice of Warning;* Lorenzo Snow's *The Only Way to Be Saved; Works of Josephus;* Rolins's *Church History;* a history of India; a history of Sind; several of Orson Pratt's works, such as *Divine Authenticity of the Book of Mormon, Divine Authority,* and *The Patriarchal Order of Marriage;* Oliver Cowdery's *First Letter to W. W. Phelps; The Illustrated Mormon; The Voice of Joseph; The Saint's Belief;* Col. Kane's writings, probably in the *Millennial Star;* Parley P. Pratt's *Proclamation, Remarkable Visions,* and *The History of Joseph Smith, the Great Prophet of the 19th Century.* Leonard also mentions a "first rate geography and atlas," a history of Muhammad, Vandoosan's expose of temple secrets, and LDS hymnbooks.

20. *Millennial Star* 17 (September 15, 1855): 589.

21. Henry J. Lilley, "From India's Coral Strand," *Improvement Era* 12 (1908–9): 423–34.

22. The roots of the word *malaria* are *mala aria,* "bad air." In the 1850s the source and transmittal of the disease by mosquito were unknown. On September 1, 1854, Elder Leonard wrote: "The weather here is extremely hot, and much sickness is anticipated, in

fact it has already commenced, the evident reason, is because a vast amount of land has been overflown, which is now drying up, and the poisonous vapour is beginning to rise." Letter from Leonard to Musser in the Gertrude Musser Richards collection.

23. Leonard to Musser, April 7, 1855, Hyderabad, India, in Britsch, "Missionary Activities in India," 138.

24. Truman Leonard, "Hindostan" [Leonard to Franklin D. Richards, November 15, 1855, Bombay], *Millennial Star* 18 (January 19, 1856): 46.

25. Musser, Journals, 5:14.

26. Ibid., and Findlay, *Millennial Star* 16 (November 4, 1854): 721–22. See also "To the Missionaries from Utah," August 31, 1854, in Clark, *Messages of the First Presidency*, 148. The First Presidency invited missionaries to stay or come home as the Spirit dictated.

27. Leonard to Musser, January 30, 1855, Hyderabad, India, in Britsch, "Missionary Activities in India," 138.

28. Leonard, Journal, 275–76.

29. Musser, Journals, 4:160–67.

30. Ibid., 4:173; 5:6.

31. Ibid., 5:11–12.

32. Ibid., 5:12.

33. Amos Milton Musser, "Hindostan: Erection of a Meeting Room at Kurrachee—Corruption of the People" [Musser to Franklin D. Richards, May 8, 1855, Karachi, Sind], *Millennial Star* 17 (September 1, 1855): 557.

34. Leonard, Journal, 283–84.

35. Ibid., 296.

36. Amos Milton Musser, "Hindostan: Preparations for Leaving the Country" [Musser to Franklin D. Richards, August 4, 1855, Karachi, Sind], *Millennial Star* 17 (October 13, 1855): 652.

37. Leonard, Journal, 312.

38. Ibid., 316; Musser, Journals, 5:50.

39. Leonard, Journal, 320.

40. Ibid., 322.

41. Ibid., 330–31.

42. Ibid., 332–39.

43. Sonne, *Saints on the Seas*, appendix 1, 151.

44. Sonne, *Ships, Saints, and Mariners*, 71. Sonne notes that in addition to Leonard there were two converts from India. Perhaps they were Sister Tait and her infant.

45. Leonard, "Truman Leonard," 240–60.

46. Hafen and Hafen, *Handcarts to Zion*, 91–141, 193, and Appendix M. Information for this paragraph is also from Allan McPherson Findlay, Ancestral File, Family History Department, The Church of Jesus Christ of Latter-day Saints, Salt Lake City, Utah; see also Sonne, *Ships, Saints, and Mariners*, 186; *Saints on the Seas*, Appendix 1, 151.

47. *Millennial Star* 18 (January 19, 1856): 46.

11

CLOSING DOWN
THE MISSION

By January 16, 1856, when the *Lancaster* dropped anchor at Garden Reach and I was again in Calcutta, the East India Mission, or Hindustan Mission as it was often called, was working with a skeleton crew. Our mission president, N. V. Jones, and William Fotheringham had left for home on March 5, 1855. I have already recounted the departures of all the missionaries except those of Elders Woolley, Jones, Fotheringham, my own, and that of Elder Skelton, who was the last to leave. Several loose ends that do not fit conveniently with the main story need to be tied together. For example, Elder Fotheringham spent time in the area called Orissa, southwest of Calcutta, building a ship to assist Brother Meik. That story needs to be told. Also, even though James Patrick Meik was not set apart as a missionary, I must say some concluding words regarding him and his family. And there are some other matters, such as my own extended journey and experiences on the way home.

ELDER WOOLLEY'S LAST FEW MONTHS
IN INDIA

We last spoke of Elder Woolley and his companion, Elder Fotheringham, when they had just returned from a seven-month journey up the Ganges plain, having visited almost all of the major cities and cantonments in that vast area. Their travels had taken them three thousand miles, the end of which brought almost complete exhaustion and no baptisms. For a month after their return to Calcutta on March 6, 1854, they had rested at the home of Brother and Sister Meik and regained their strength for the next phase of their missions. Fotheringham remained in Calcutta as Jones's companion (I, President Jones's former companion, had left in December 1853 for Karachi), and Elder Woolley accepted an assignment to watch over the few Saints in Chinsura, twenty or thirty miles north of Calcutta along the west bank of the Hoogly River. In early April 1854, President Jones gave Woolley his release to return home, but he preferred to stay a little longer, not wanting to be among the earliest to leave the mission. Between April and the end of July, Elder Woolley spent most of his time at Chinsura. He lived with and preached at the home of Brother and Sister Sankey. During April, May, and June, Woolley had fair attendance at his preaching meetings. He felt fortunate to baptize two young women, the daughter and stepdaughter of the Sankeys. Those who attended the meetings were almost all soldiers, new recruits who were being trained at the cantonment in Chinsura.[1] But in July, a totally hostile spirit entered his meetings. Soldiers shouted crude words and taunted Elder Woolley when he spoke. "They set a jug of powder and saltpetre on fire right in the midst of the congregation," reported Woolley.[2] The last meeting with the soldiers turned into a mob scene with yelling, threats, and general bad behavior. Eventually, Brother and Sister Sankey, with the help of two corporals, managed to clear the house. The troops then pebbled the corporals and drove them to the barracks.

As a result, two soldiers were put into the guardroom for the night. The next morning the colonel "passed an order not to allow any one to come to brother Sankey's house, not even those who belonged to the Church."[3] This brought an end to Elder Woolley's work in Chinsura. Not long after, the recruits from Chinsura cantonment were transferred to the area where the War of 1857 took place. How they fared is not known, but a good number probably lost their lives in that carnage.

Woolley returned again to Calcutta, where he worked mostly without a missionary companion until he sailed for Boston and thence home on November 1, 1854.[4] By that date the monsoons had ended, and he was able to find a ship that was bound toward the west. Jones was in Burma during this time, and Fotheringham had gone to the area near Cuttack.

Elder Woolley sailed on the American clipper ship the *John Gilpin*, under Captain Ring. After a pleasant voyage, he landed in Boston on February 12, 1855, 104 days out from Calcutta.[5] William F. Carter, it will be remembered, also sailed home on the *John Gilpin* almost two years earlier. Woolley's health was so bad that he could not continue on to Utah that year. Elder John Taylor, who presided over that area, appointed him president of the Delaware conference. On April 9th of the next year, he was ready to move west. Woolley arrived in Salt Lake City on August 15, 1856, almost four years after his departure for India.

ELDER FOTHERINGHAM'S MISSION TO ORISSA

For the first several months after returning from their expedition to the Ganges plain, Elder Fotheringham divided his time between Calcutta and Chinsura, spending the majority of it in Calcutta. But from July until the end of 1854, he was engaged with Brother Meik in a scheme to raise money to help the India Saints emigrate to Zion. The plan involved considerable financial risk on Meik's part and considerable hard work on Fotheringham's part. Fotheringham described the project in these words:

> About this time the railroad schemes in India were just beginning to be developed; and Brother J. P. Meik took an extensive contract to furnish teak, for railroad ties, in Calcutta, from the teak forests in the south-west of India

[actually southwest of Calcutta]. If successful in fulfilling his contract, he would be enabled to secure means to emigrate the few of our people from India. If they were left ungathered they would soon drop back into the slough in which we found them.

To accomplish his object, Brother Meik secured the services of a European . . . who repaired to the Saul forests, in the Orissa country, to superintend squads of natives in getting out the necessary timbers for railroad ties, constructing them into rafts and floating them down the Mahananda [Mahanadi] river to a suitable point, during the rainy season. He was to select such timbers as could be used in constructing a vessel to convey the ties from a suitable point on the river to Calcutta. . . .

In view of this object, President Jones was to manage the affairs . . . in Calcutta, while Brother Meik would take up his quarters at Cuttack, a town on the Mahananda river. . . . The writer, being a ship carpenter, was to accompany Brother Meik to a suitable point on one of the branches of the Mahananda, near the Bay of Bengal, and superintend the construction of the vessel.[6]

Elder Fotheringham's descriptions of his travels two hundred miles into Orissa (published in the Church's Sunday School magazine, the *Juvenile Instructor,* in 1883 and 1884), the customs of the Indian people, his lease from a local rajah (petty king) of land upon which to build his ship, his exasperating efforts to keep Indian carpenters engaged in his ship-building project, his often frightening and uncomfortable experiences in the jungles and on rivers (he carried a pistol to protect himself from the danger of possible encounters with tigers, snakes, jackals, and alligators) make fascinating reading. For example, he wrote:

One evening, one of these scaly monsters kept sporting near the banks of the river where my palanquin stood. [He was living in it at the time.] . . . The night setting in, I felt rather uneasy, with a huge mugger [alligator] close by, and, what was even worse, the indications of a general flood, and no means of moving, and no place to go to. I hired two śhudras the lowest cast of Hindoos, to stand sentry during the night, and if imperiled, by the rising river, to report, that I might wade to the nearest village. . . .

When the morning dawned, the rain had ceased and I was

still on terra firma; but the delta looked like a vast lake, and the sun shone forth hot and sultry.[7]

Elder Fotheringham also spent some time studying Hindu mythology. He was situated near Puri and the temple of Juggernaut. Because it is said to be one of Krishna's four sacred abodes, it is one of India's most important pilgrimage destinations. He and Elder Skelton, who later worked in this same area, described the thousands of Indians who made their way to this sacred site. Juggernaut is a corruption of the word *Jagannātha*, meaning "Lord of the World," and is another name for the god Krishna.[8]

After four months laboring at Manickpatna without a companion, on November 24, 1854, Fotheringham completed his ship and dedicated it to the Lord. His prayer was that it would serve Brother Meik's purposes and speed him to Zion. He left the same day for Cuttack, where Brother and Sister Meik were living. At Cuttack, Fotheringham performed three baptisms, a European couple named Smith and an Indian named Baboo Noben Chander Sarangee, and blessed some children. A few days later he was ready to return to Calcutta, where, after two weeks of travel, he arrived on December 26, 1854. That day Elder Fotheringham penned: "I feel to thank and praise God that He had preserved my life amid the many dangers which I had passed thru and brot me in safety again to Calcutta."[9] Like all who have served in India, his prayer was sincere and filled with underlying meaning. He had left his palki (palanquin) in Cuttack for Sister Meik to use and walked most of the two hundred miles from Cuttack to Calcutta. The jungle was lonely, filled with natural hazards, and difficult to travel for even the native Indians who traveled through it regularly. The enervating heat, uncomfortable humidity, and muddy roads and paths made movement difficult. He truly was thankful to Heavenly Father for his safe return to the civilization and security of Calcutta.

PRESIDENT JONES AND ELDER FOTHERINGHAM RETURN HOME

By the time N. V. Jones had been in India for a year, he was disappointed and discouraged with the mission's prospects. In an effort to get a change of pace and place, he visited Elder Savage in Burma but returned to Calcutta as discouraged as ever. His letters home and to England were very critical of the Europeans and native Indians. He castigated them equally for their stubbornness, dishonesty, and hypocrisy. We all agreed with his assessment of the situation and hoped the Saints throughout the world would not judge us for our poor showing. The people of India, at least those whom we encountered, were simply not ready for the Restored Gospel. Those of European ancestry were simply not of the classes that had provided so many converts in the British Isles and Scandinavia.

Fortunately, when President Jones was wondering what course the mission should take, he received word from the First Presidency through the pages of the *Millennial Star* giving all of the India missionaries their release. I received a copy of the *Millennial Star* announcement, as well as the letter from President Young's secretary while in Karachi, a fact already noted. (The release letter that I received, which was written September 1, 1854, said we were free to return home "as quick" as we wanted to come.)[10] From that time on, President Jones and Elder Fotheringham devoted themselves to getting out of the country.

President Jones wrote to Elder Skelton, who was working alone in Madras at the end of 1854, and asked him to come to Calcutta to take charge of the mission. He arrived in Calcutta on January 17, 1855, and prepared to take care of the affairs of the Church when Jones and Fotheringham left. His special charge was to "gather out the few Saints" who were still in the country and take them to Zion.[11] This proved to be an almost impossible task.

After searching for a number of days, on February 26th, Jones

Banyan in Calcutta Botanic Gardens

and Fotheringham found a captain who would take them to Hong Kong. Captain Chase of the ship *Beverly* agreed to charge them only one hundred twenty-five rupees, the usual price being closer to four hundred rupees. The few members of the Church generously contributed rupees to help defray the cost. From that day until they left, the elders were engaged in final preparations to leave the country, including some tourist-like activities. They bought new clothes in the native part of town (and Brother Booth gave each of them two new coats), visited several local attractions: the Seven Tanks,[12] a botanical garden in which one of the world's largest banyan trees grows,[13] the dry docks, and so on. They also visited some of the members. The only ones remaining faithful were the Booths, Sister McMahon and her daughters, Brother Simeon Aratoon, and the Meiks. Skelton noted visiting Brother Aratoon, an Armenian member of the Church, and criticized the tradition of arranged marriages that would allow a father to cause his son to marry a deranged woman, which was the case with Aratoon.[14]

Through their final days before departure, Fotheringham had a terrible cold, and Jones was seriously ill with a lung infection. Even after leaving India, Jones complained in a letter from Hong Kong that the problem, though temporarily better, had returned. I wonder yet if this illness may have so badly weakened his system that it contributed to his early death by pneumonia at age forty. Nevertheless, he did what had to be done, including speaking in a weak voice to the little branch on his last Sunday in Calcutta. Elder Fotheringham was very supportive in everything that had to be done.

On March 3d, Elders Jones and Fotheringham, along with Skelton, rowed a dinghy out in the river to the ship *Beverly*. While en route, the departing brethren "washed their feet as a testimony against Hindostan, or rather against the inhabitants thereof."[15] Elder Skelton said that even "the waters of the Hoogly will bear record" that the elders had borne a strong testimony of Joseph Smith and the Restored Gospel. Later that month, from Singapore, Jones attested that only those who had endured the India experience could understand the "circumstances that have hindered the progress of the Gospel" in that land.[16]

Many tears were shed before the *Beverly* was pulled by steam tug down the river toward the open sea. Skelton paid a great compliment to Jones when he wrote:

> Being a man of great experience, President Jones is of great utility in family matters, and so much entwined in his feelings are Sis. Meik's that she is sorely grieved at him going home, he having lived with the family most of the time that we have been in India. The affections of the whole family are centered in him. [He] enjoys the most unlimited confidence which he has secured by his upright course in all things. He has acted the part of a father to them.[17]

Similar words could be said of Elder Fotheringham.

At 8:00 on the morning of March 5, 1855, Elders Jones and Fotheringham sailed for home. Their trip took them through Singapore, where they arrived March 28th, after a smooth voyage.

Then, after a few days in port, it was on to Macao, the Portuguese colony near Hong Kong. That part of the journey was miserable. By his own admission, the captain was a grouchy, mean man. The beds were poor and filled with bugs, and the food was inadequate. They were happy to reach Macao on May 1st. But they were even happier when they left the ship and Captain Chase at Hong Kong six days later.

On May 16th, they were safely aboard a French ship called the *Saint Joseph*, bound for San Francisco. They were the last passengers to sign on. Their fare was seventy-five dollars each. The other 347 passengers were all Chinese. While in Hong Kong, they were blessed with the good fortune of meeting Captain Alexander Winsor, the brother of Captain Zenos Winsor of the *Monsoon*, who was the master of the ship *Hussar*. Shortly before they sailed on the *Saint Joseph*, the elders visited Winsor on the *Hussar*. After giving him Fotheringham's own copy of the Book of Mormon, which he had asked for, they explained that they were providing their own provisions on the trip to San Francisco. Fotheringham asked Winsor if he would supply them with some dried apples and two or three pounds of butter. "He immediately told his steward to get ready some apples, butter . . . , a red salmon weighing about 20 lbs.," wrote Fotheringham. "He also gave me a can of fine crackers."[18] By early July, the elders were eager to be on American soil again. Their accommodations had not been the best. A few days out of Hong Kong, Fotheringham wrote: "The sea is becoming rougher and rougher. The smell which proceeds from the hold, combined with that from the Chinese, poultry, hogs, dogs . . . make it almost poisonous enough to kill rats."[19] They were the only English speakers on the ship and had to communicate by sign language. But on July 11th, fifty-six days from Hong Kong, the *Saint Joseph* arrived at San Francisco.

The next project was to get from San Francisco to Salt Lake City. Although the details are interesting, it must suffice to say that because of problems with a horse Fotheringham purchased, he was forced to delay for a time and ended up going south to San

Bernardino and then up the same route the elders had traveled on their way to India. Elder Jones took the route directly east through the Sierra Nevada Mountains and the desert and arrived in Salt Lake City on October 4, 1855.[20] Fotheringham left San Bernardino in late October, in company with Elder Amasa Lyman and others. They suffered cold weather and some snow but arrived in the Valley on December 1, 1855.[21]

AMOS MILTON MUSSER COMPLETES HIS MISSION AND SAILS FOR ENGLAND

Following my arrival in Calcutta from my mission in Sind, I went to the Ice House, where I received several letters, one of which directed me to the home of Sister E. McMahon. She was a grand and faithful lady who cared for my needs in a most saintly manner. What a tragedy that her husband had apostatized. In any event, because the Meiks were now living at Cuttack, her home served as the central gathering place for the few remaining Saints. Elder Skelton, who was now the only other Mormon missionary in the country, was also at Cuttack.

While at Calcutta, I had the pleasure of baptizing David G. McRitchie, chief officer of the *Lancaster*, the ship on which I traveled from Bombay to Calcutta. He was the son of a prominent Presbyterian minister.[22] I'm yet convinced that some of our best missionary work was done on board ships.

I have previously noted that I spent much of my time from my arrival in Calcutta in January until I sailed, caring for Brother William Adams. Following his death, Captain Winsor offered me free first class passage to London on the beautiful clipper ship *Viking*.[23] Why would he be so generous? Elder Skelton said Captain Winsor was "highly honored in taking a servant of God, for he learned by experience the efficacy of the Holy Priesthood, for he testifies to the fulfilment of predictions pronounced upon him by the Elder of Israel."[24] When at London, I wrote: "I cannot speak too eulogistically of Captain Winsor, and, notwithstanding the great length of the voyage from Calcutta [138 days], I must acknowledge, I never before spent a more agreeable time at sea."[25] I maintained Winsor's records and accounts, wrote letters for him, and in general tried to justify my favorable situation.

I arrived in England on July 19, 1856. The Brethren calculated the time required for me to complete my journey home to Utah and concluded I would not have time that season. With my concurrence, President Orson Pratt appointed me to serve for a time as a missionary in that country. I will later write a few words regarding my mission in England and Wales and my experiences traveling the remainder of the way home.

ELDER SKELTON PRESIDES OVER THE MISSION

After President Jones and Elder Fotheringham sailed for home, Elder Skelton was left in charge of the mission. He corresponded regularly with me and with other Church members in Karachi, Bombay, Madras, and Rangoon. Times were difficult and the members, being new in the faith and faced with harassment and temptation every day, found it difficult to hold on to the truth. Brother McCarthy in Madras, for example, took up drinking a few times. And others, who had been sent inland and upcountry for military service, gradually slid into the slough of India. There were, however, a few converts (for example, James Mills in Madras) who were totally committed to their new religion. Among those in other parts of the country were the Meiks, the Booths, the Sankeys, the Saxtons, Sister McMahon, and Brother Aratoon, in the Calcutta area. Mr. McMahon presents a situation difficult to understand. He was so rancorously obnoxious to President Jones that the two men could not get along. But Elder Skelton handled him well and even stayed at his home outside Calcutta on many occasions. Clearly, Skelton found his role as mission president to be delicate if not difficult.

He counseled and encouraged and preached repentance and

endurance the best he could. In mid-April 1855, Elder Skelton baptized Mary Ann Homes, the widowed sister of Hannah Booth. About the same time, he encouraged the faithful members to renew their covenants by being re-baptized. Whether Skelton had heard of the "reformation" that was taking place in Zion, I do not know. But the result was the same. He re-baptized seven souls but was delicate about re-baptizing the eighth, Sister Meik. "Sister Meik being pregnant," penned the good elder, "I requested Bro. Meik to re-baptise her: he being better acquainted in the matters of this kind: I thought better not to risk it myself, she being a very stout woman as well."[26]

Elder Skelton was faced with some unusual problems. Brother Sankey came to him from Chinsura and asked how he felt about his son, John, marrying his stepdaughter. Skelton was not concerned about the social ramifications of such a union, but he was against the marriage because John was "a gentile." He was not a member of the Church and his proposed spouse was. John, Skelton learned, was favorable to every doctrine of the Church except plural marriage. Elder Skelton was convinced that he could easily resolve that problem. He met with John and cleared his thinking on the matter. Even though the rain was falling in torrents when their meeting ended, John insisted on being baptized immediately, and was.[27]

In late April 1855, Brother Meik concluded to move his family to Cuttack to be closer to his business. He had invested more than fifteen thousand rupees in his lumber enterprise, in addition to forty thousand rupees that had been advanced by the railroad company. About this time, Meik was forced to take an Indian partner, an arrangement that Elder Skelton considered totally unfair. Unfortunately, Meik's projects and investments continued to falter. He moved out of his house on Lower Circular Road about May 1st. (That place had served as mission headquarters since the Meiks's removal from their place on Jaun Bazaar Street in June 1854.) Skelton helped them on their way. When they had gone, he complained:

I took leave of our worthy friends, being very sorry to part with them. On returning to the house, found it to be truly a forlorn place: desolate, and still as death! Where once the prattling children made the hall echo in their playful glee, was in one night changed into a gloomy, desolate, and forsaken abode! At this my heart was grieved within me, and I can safely say that I never before in all my life realized a keener pain on parting with my friends.[28]

After seeing the Meiks off, Skelton still had much to do to aid them. He was responsible to help in the sale of their household furniture. When the sale was ended, Skelton believed the merchant had sold the goods too low. His journal reflected his anger at the blatant and constant dishonesty he saw around him. "In attending to Bro Meik's business," wrote Skelton, "I have great vexation of spirit owing to the roguish propensities of the natives with whom I have to deal. Their avarice for money is beyond all description, which, coupled with right-out lying, gives me an utter abhorrence to them. (And I cannot help it.)"[29]

The departure of the Booth family for America brought a moment of joy to Elder Skelton. The little emigrant company consisted of Charles L. Booth, his wife, Louisa, and their infant, Charles's mother, Hannah, and her sister, Mary Ann Homes. They had been making preparations to emigrate to America for some time. Charles had "sold all their favorite family Jewels in order to make up their passage money." They even sold gold bracelets that his wife's mother had given the baby. When she learned of this, she bought them back. She would have gone to America, too, but she had two other daughters living in India. Elder Skelton ordained Charles a priest in the Aaronic Priesthood so he could preside "in that capacity, while on board" the ship.[30] The *Frank Johnson*, under Captain Asa Lothrop, sailed down the Hoogly River on May 28, 1855, bearing the second Mormon emigrant company from India.[31] (Elder Hugh Findlay had led the first group from Bombay in March 1855.)

Incidentally, there was an additional passenger on board,

Brother Johnson. His name is absent from other records, and I never met the man, but he stowed away on the *Frank Johnson*. To his discomfort and Elder Skelton's, he was discovered before the ship weighed anchor. Skelton explained to Captain Lothrop that our Church did not approve of such behavior. The kindly captain allowed Johnson to work his passage to San Francisco as an ordinary seaman.

The *Frank Johnson* sailed southeast to Singapore, where it stopped for a few days, and then on to San Francisco. The entire voyage took about one hundred twelve days. The small, three-masted ship dropped anchor in San Francisco harbor about September 18, 1855.[32] Details regarding the remainder of the Booths' travels to Zion are few; however, Elder Skelton mentioned his joy in seeing the Booth family in San Bernardino on July 24, 1856, while on his homeward journey.[33] Family records indicate that the Booths settled in San Bernardino until Brigham Young called the Saints in from the colonial peripheries in 1857 because of the threat of war in Utah. At that time, they sold their home at a great loss and migrated to Beaver City, in central Utah.[34] Hannah Booth had given up her position as an aristocrat—fine house, affluence, and luxury—in India and her husband, a British army officer named John William Booth, to become a member of the Church. He refused to have anything to do with her after she was baptized. In addition to Charles Lovell Booth, second engineer on a river steamer, who was the first to accept the Restored Gospel, Grandma Booth was mother to George Henry Booth, a medical doctor, who was baptized in Burma while on duty there. George emigrated to Utah in 1886. Both Charles and George have posterity in the Church.

ELDER SKELTON'S EXPERIENCES IN ORISSA

In May, Elder Skelton wrote to Elder Savage in Burma and asked him to come to Calcutta to watch over the members there. Skelton had decided to go to Cuttack in the province of Orissa to help Brother Meik with his timber-cutting business. Savage did as he was asked but arrived there after Skelton departed for Cuttack on June 1st.

Brother Skelton was growing tired and critical of his surroundings. Small wonder, for everyone he dealt with seemed determined to take his last rupee. My task in writing this history has been to summarize his writings and those of others. But sometimes it is best to let the writer speak for himself. Following are a few lines from Skelton's journal. They deal with his efforts to travel the two hundred miles from Calcutta to Cuttack.

> Today [June 1st] I made the second start for Cuttack, having been disappointed by the boatmen, who are a mean, contemptible race and will do nothing without asking extortionate prices. . . . After making all necessary preparations, I embarked on board a dinghy and proceeded down the river. [It] was very rough. [We pulled into a creek for the night. In the morning] we proceeded on our journey [to Tamluk]. . . .
>
> I immediately set about to hire carts, in order to load up Bro. Meik's furniture and stoves. . . . After toiling till midnight getting ready . . . the old man owning them backed out. . . . [H]e would not start unless I would advance him all the pay. . . . I, however, did not give in to them. . . . I had rather cradle three acres of wheat or undertake to start a camp of fifty wagons over the plains of America than to procure a dozen halting Bengal or rather Orissa carts. . . .
>
> The weather being excessively hot, suffered greatly from heat and fatigue in traveling,[35] my cart being only two feet broad and 6 feet in length, the cover made of palm leaf. Continuing my journey, passing through a great number of native villages that as a general thing are built in a line on either side of the road, the street between being exceedingly narrow and filthy. The water [is] very bad which is only to be found in tanks which at this season of the year are very low, and the dregs only left.[36] Excavating the earth, on which they build their houses . . . , of course forms a tank of necessity. At the back door (or rather what I shall properly term a hole in the wall, which is seldom more than three feet high), all the broken earthenware and filth is deposited, which as the rains fall is washed into the tank. Here all the village wash their clothes and bathe: and in fact every filthy vessel is washed in it. There

A *typical Indian cart*

being no better water, I am of necessity compelled to drink it or go without. The latter is impossible in this hot climate, and owing to my short stay at each village, [I] have not time to filter it—besides which I am generally so much fatigued as to indispose me from doing anything but rest.[37]

At Midnapur, a minor place, Skelton stopped at a travelers' bungalow. There, to his dismay, but not really to his surprise, he found an anti-Mormon tract. "It is really marvelous how that falsehoods spread as it were to the ends of the earth; we cannot go anywhere but we are confronted with such abominable trash so that the minds of the people are prejudiced against us wherever we go."

After traveling through monotonous country—"From this to Calcutta is one continual Paddy field"—he arrived at Cuttack on June 17, 1855. The latter part of his trip he was on a larger road, one that was traveled by thousands of pilgrims who were bound for Puri and the temple of Juggernaut. The entire Meik family warmly greeted him. Sister Meik had only recently given birth to another son, Thomas Nathaniel—Nathaniel after President N. V.

Jones. Joyfully, Elder Skelton wrote: "She presented me a plump healthy and pretty child, with that same affectionate glee, that is so peculiar to every dignified mother in Israel, who alone can appreciate the blessings of having children, the Lord's heritage!"[38]

Skelton rested and surveyed his surroundings in Cuttack. The city lay on an island surrounded by the mighty Mahanadi River. The British compound was arranged with houses facing each other along the main road. "Cleanliness and order is observed." Such could not be said regarding the native part of town: "The lanes very narrow and filthy; right in the face and eyes of their neighbors, the Hindoos deposit all their filth [so that] passers by are of necessity compelled to trample over it."[39]

After resting a few days, Elder Skelton announced a series of fifteen lectures. But as had happened so many times before in India, a diligent Mormon elder failed to attract a crowd that had any interest in his message. By this time in his mission, he had long since left behind the reticent demeanor that stood aside while Elder Ballantyne did most of the preaching. Skelton was now confident, conversant with the scriptures and doctrines of the Church, and constantly ready to boldly proclaim the truth. But the opportunity to preach had steadily dwindled. By this time, there was little more that he could accomplish. In July and August, he visited every European house in Cuttack: every colonel, captain, minister, missionary, priest, and civilian. He visited "rich and poor, high and low," distributing copies of Elder Snow's *The Only Way to Be Saved*, Pratt's *Proclamation*, and so forth. But he was rejected by all as an imposter, deceiver, and fanatic. Elder Skelton recognized that he may have been overzealous in some of his conversations, "but by His grace," said he, "I am resolved to do my duty to the best of my ability, ridding my garments of the blood of my fellow men; unto whom I have been sent with the Gospel."[40]

He went on, saying,

> the utter neglect on the part of people, relative to the sacred truths of heaven, is a source of grief to me. Not one soul out of millions in number can bear truth but lies. Novels and current

press reports are law and Gospel to this people. They will not believe that good angels visit the earth but admit bad ones do. God, say they, no more speaks, yet with the same breath acknowledge the devil does it through spiritual mediums. [They] will not acknowledge the Holy Spirit is given whereby to speak in tongues, prophesy, heal the sick, &c. &c. But say they the heathen are possessed of the Devil, but will not admit power is given on earth to cast them out. So it is with this generation, who put light for darkness and darkness for light; good for evil and evil for good; bitter for sweet and sweet for bitter; vain traditions call they the truth; truth they call blasphemy.

Ah me! I would to God, I were among a people who would receive the truth, where my time could be profitably improved.[41]

Skelton enjoyed himself most when he was teaching Brother and Sister Meik's children. He considered them of "uncommon wild dispositions" but loved them and taught them geography, English grammar, arithmetic, and so on. He was grateful that he now had the ability to do this. When he left home for India he "could scarcely write [his] own name." The only education he had was what he had "assiduously attained" himself.[42]

On July 19, 1855, Elder Skelton received a letter from President Brigham Young. It was addressed to President N. V. Jones. It said: "Come home, and bring as many of the Saints with you as are ready to come and leave the rest in the best possible state you can." Skelton said President Young intimated that the way "may be blocked up" before long, and that it is "enough." This set Skelton into remembrances of how hard he had tried to convince the Saints of India to save, to put something aside, and to prepare to emigrate. He said they had "no idea of saving." Almost everyone in India was in debt, including the members of the Church.

The Booths were an exception, but they had already left for Zion. The Meiks, too, were expending every effort to leave the country. Skelton felt his responsibility to them. President Jones had told Skelton not to leave the Meiks behind. But Brother

Temple of Juggernaut, at Puri

Meik's business was in terrible shape. How, asked Elder Skelton, was he going to accomplish the gathering? Perhaps he could not.

In September, Elder Skelton received another release from President Franklin D. Richards in Liverpool. "When I have gathered up the few remaining Saints, I may consider my work finished," penned Skelton. He certainly knew he was at liberty to return home, as did I. But finding the means to leave was a difficult matter.

Before leaving for home, or even for Calcutta, Skelton traveled further in Orissa. His journey took from October 6th to November 3d. He visited a number of cities, including Puri, the great temple city. He hoped to encourage Brother Burgess and his family, who were living at Berhampur, close to the coast south of Cuttack, to emigrate to Zion. His trip to that city was more interesting than his travels to Cuttack from Calcutta, but he was not successful in gathering that family. As he had done in Cuttack, Skelton made every effort to preach the Gospel to the European inhabitants of Berhampur and some other small military camps, again without success.

While returning to Cuttack, Elder Skelton rode in a small boat the length of Lake Chilka and then visited Puri and the grand temple of Juggernaut, which was only a few miles farther north. A wall twenty feet high and twenty-four hundred feet in length surrounded the main temple. Skelton's description was interesting and manifested his wonder at such a place. But he was most amazed at the sculptural work on the various temples. He wrote:

> These are literally covered over with hideous imagery, of man, beast, Soul & Serpent, and indeed some facsimiles that are here represented have no place in the animal kingdom of this earth. I am perfectly astonished and at a loss to know how, when, or where such indescribable animals originated. Thousands of these obscene images are carved in the sides and on the top of temples, exhibiting to say the least of it, a most peculiar depraved genius, which must have taxed the mind of the inventor to no small degree.[43]

Artists and historians from throughout the world have found the temples at Puri to be magnificent examples of Hindu art and architecture, but Elder Skelton's attitude is not surprising considering his calling and his negative observations regarding pilgrimage activities in Puri.

Elder Skelton's main reason for going to Cuttack was to help Brother Meik raise money to emigrate to Zion. He devoted much time to taking care of the Meik family and overseeing their affairs while Brother Meik traveled and worked in the timber area. When Skelton returned from Puri, he counseled Meik to return to Calcutta and try to get release from his partnership in the timber contract. Meik did so and successfully escaped from that contract but still needed to raise money to go to Zion.

Meik's next project was to manufacture small shovels. He hoped to obtain a government contract. This required mining the ore to smelt and to make into the *cudals*, or native shovels. Eventually, Meik arranged a contract to make picks instead.

Between November 1855 and February 1856, Skelton spent his time with the Meik family in the wilds of the Talcher district of Orissa on the banks of the Brahmani River, "entirely outside of civilization right in the jungles."[44] They lived in a shack under the most humble of conditions. Finally, on February 18th, Skelton decided he had done all he could to help and encourage the Meiks and that they were not going to be able to leave for at least a year. He had received another letter from an Apostle, this time from Elder Ezra T. Benson, telling him to come home. So, even though he was disappointed to leave the Meiks in India, as Elder Jones had told him not to do, on February 20th, Elder Skelton started back toward Calcutta and home. Again, he was almost torn apart to leave his beloved friends. "They have on their hands a large family from the Lord," wrote Skelton, "and a better little host were never I believe entrusted to the care of any mortal man."[45]

After two or three false starts and twelve days of difficult but relatively rapid travel by river and by bullock cart, Elder Skelton arrived again at Calcutta on March 4, 1856. He came to the home of Sister McMahon and found me ready to load my traps on the ship *Viking*. Desiring to spend some time together after three years apart in different regions of India, he came on board with me and sailed down the river until March 8th, when he left the ship and returned by foot to Calcutta.

After my departure, Elder Skelton spent his time writing to Church members asking them to come to Calcutta and leave with him for Zion. He was singularly unsuccessful. Not another Church member was ready at that time to go. He contacted many captains trying to find one who would take him at a reduced fare. Brother Skelton even enlisted his old friend Captain Scott to help him in his quest. Some captains treated him rudely, but on May 1st, Skelton found Captain James Simpson Hutton of the 1200-ton square-rigger, the *Earl of Eglinton,* who welcomed him as a passenger for one hundred fifty rupees, about one-third the normal cost to Hong Kong. The ship was departing the next morning, so Skelton had to hurry to be ready to leave. By five in the afternoon, he had his traps together and took them to the ship at Garden Reach, a little south of Calcutta.

After spending the night on board, he returned the next morning to meet briefly with Sister McMahon and a few others. He charged them to be faithful in keeping the commandments and to make every effort to "get away from 'Babylon.'" "I took leave of Sist McMahon, procured a boat and drop't down with the tide to Garden Reach," wrote Skelton. "As I passed down the river, I attended to the ordinance Viz, the 'washing of feet' as a testimony [against] the inhabitants thereof for rejecting the fulness of the everlasting Gospel and the testimony of Joseph Smith the Prophet. I feel justified in leaving them in the hands of God, and leave all judgment and justice for Him to execute according to the attributes of His divine perfections."[46]

When Elder Skelton sailed down the wide waters of the Hoogly River that day, May 2, 1856, the East India Mission of The Church of Jesus Christ of Latter-day Saints was closed.

ELDER SKELTON'S JOURNEY HOME

The *Earl of Eglington* encountered stiff resistance from the winds and tides. The small steam tug could not stem the torrent. Finally, after eight days the ship reached the open seas of the Bay of Bengal, and the voyage to Hong Kong was fully under way. But the trip to Singapore was slow. Days dragged on in calms or with little wind until they finally reached that port on June 3d, thirty-five days from Calcutta. Robert Skelton relished his days studying Parley P. Pratt's *Key to Theology* and other doctrinal works. He wrote of his hopes that when he married he could create a fine library in his home to refine and educate his children. After five days at Singapore, the ship sailed into the South China Sea and on to Macao, arriving there on June 18th. Captain Hutton boarded Skelton while they were in port at Macao. After nine days, Skelton took a steamboat to Hong Kong. Within two hours of his arrival, he arranged cabin passage to San Francisco on the bark *Caesar*, at a cost of sixty dollars. Four days later, on June 30, 1856, Captain Graham took the *Caesar* out to sea. Fifty-one days later, on August 19th, the small ship dropped anchor in San Francisco harbor.

At San Francisco, Elder Skelton stayed with George Q. Cannon and his wife for two weeks, during which time he gave some public lectures on East India. He then sailed down the coast to San Pedro on the steamship *Sea Bird*. He was at San Bernardino by mid-September. He enjoyed himself immensely with his old friends there. A month later, on October 12th, he left for the Valley, where he arrived thirty-seven days later on November 18, 1856. He had been away from home for more than four years. After reporting to Church authorities, he wrote: "I am perfectly reconciled to do whatever I may in future be told by them to do."[47]

NOTES

1. Samuel Amos Woolley, "The East India Mission: Travels from Agra to Cawnpore, Allahabad, Calcutta, and Chinsurah—Course of Lectures at Chinsurah—Baptisms—

Healing" [Woolley to Samuel W. Richards, June 27, 1854, Calcutta], *Millennial Star* 16 (September 9, 1854): 573–74.

2. Samuel Amos Woolley, "Hindostan: Baptisms—Mobbing" [Woolley to Franklin D. Richards, August 1, 1854, Calcutta], *Millennial Star* 16 (October 14, 1854): 651. For a slightly different description see Fotheringham, "Travels in India," *Juvenile Instructor* 16 (October 15, 1881): 231.

3. Ibid., Woolley, 652–53.

4. Nathaniel V. Jones, "Hindostan: Voyage of Elder Jones to Birmah . . . Departure of Elder Willes and Woolley for Zion" [Jones to Franklin D. Richards, November 7, 1854, Calcutta], *Millennial Star* 17 (February 10, 1855): 94.

5. Sonne, *Ships, Saints, and Mariners,* 119.

6. Fotheringham, "Travels in India," *Juvenile Instructor* 16 (October 15, 1881): 231.

7. Ibid., *Juvenile Instructor* 17 (January 1, 1882): 2.

8. Ibid., *Juvenile Instructor* 17 (June 15, 1882): 191.

9. William Fotheringham, Excerpts from the Journal of William Fotheringham, by date, in possession of the author; hereafter cited as Journal.

10. Musser, Journals, 5:14.

11. Skelton, Journal, 258 (typescript, 149).

12. A series of beautiful pools where the Victoria Memorial now stands.

13. The tree was still alive in 1998.

14. Skelton, Journal, 258–71 (typescript, 148–52).

15. Ibid., 276 (typescript, 155–56). See also Fotheringham, "Travels in India," *Juvenile Instructor* 15 (May 1, 1880): 100. Fotheringham devoted a number of lines to the topic of washing of feet against those whom reject the elders' testimony. Scriptural backing is found in D&C 24:15; 75:20; and 84:92–95, among others.

16. Nathaniel Vary Jones, "Hindustan: Prospects of the Work—Departure from Calcutta of Elders Jones and Fotheringham" [Jones to Franklin D. Richards, March 30, 1855, Singapore], *Millennial Star* 17 (July 7, 1855): 428–29.

17. Skelton, Journal, 275 (typescript, 155); some grammar and punctuation standardized.

18. Fotheringham, Journal, May 16, 1855.

19. Ibid., May 19, 1855.

20. Rebecca M. Jones, "Extracts from the Life Sketch of Nathaniel V. Jones," *Utah Historical Quarterly* 4 (January 1931): 4.

21. William Fotheringham, Part of My History, Book A (typescript, 10), in possession of the author. I acquired this material from Carol Lloyd, whose deceased husband, Robert, was a direct descendant of Fotheringham.

22. Amos Milton Musser, "London" [Musser to Orson Pratt, July 29, 1856, London], *Millennial Star* 18 (September 6, 1856): 570.

23. Sonne, *Ships, Saints, and Mariners,* 194–95.

24. Robert Skelton, "Hindostan" [Skelton to Franklin D. Richards, March 8, 1856, Calcutta], *Millennial Star* 18 (May 31, 1856): 349.

25. Musser, *Millennial Star* 18 (September 6, 1856): 569.

26. Skelton, Journal, 293 (typescript, 166).

27. Ibid., 291 (typescript, 165).

28. Ibid., 295 (typescript, 167); punctuation standardized.

29. Ibid., 296 (typescript, 168); some spelling and punctuation standardized.

30. Ibid., 298–99 (typescript, 170). Skelton's journal says he ordained Booth a teacher; however, family records assert that he was ordained a priest.

31. Sonne, *Ships, Saints, and Mariners,* 77. Sonne says the *Frank Johnson* sailed on May 29, while Skelton, who was there to see it off, says it was May 28.

32. Ibid.

33. Skelton, Journal, 599 (typescript, 280).

34. At Beaver City, Hannah Booth practiced medicine and midwifery. She was known as Grandma Booth. After William Fotheringham moved to that city in 1865, she occasionally prepared Indian dishes (curry and rice or curried lamb or chicken) for him and Amos Milton Musser, who lived there temporarily. She was described as being of dark complexion, short, heavy, and with small hands. Her father, Pascal Peters, was Portuguese and her mother, Nancy, was from Manila. She was clearly loved by her neighbors and provided remedies for people's ills. (Family records of Nora White Brown of Cedar City, Utah, a direct descendant of Hannah Peters Booth.)

35. Robert Skelton, "Hindostan" [Skelton to Franklin D. Richards, November 3, 1855, Cuttack, Orissa, India], *Millennial Star* 18 (March 1, 1856): 142. Regarding the excessive heat, Skelton said it "ranged from 100° to 112° in the shade of the Banyan tree, which was my chief shelter by the way; in the sun the thermometer stood 135 degrees."

36. Skelton, Journal, 300–302 (typescript, 171–72).

37. Ibid., 303–4 (typescript, 173); grammar, syntax, and punctuation standardized.

38. Ibid., 317 (typescript, 181).

39. Ibid., 318 (typescript, 182).

40. Ibid., 342 (typescript, 198).

41. Ibid., 343–44 (typescript, 199–200); punctuation, spelling, and syntax standardized.

42. Ibid., 321 (typescript, 184).

43. Ibid., 394–95 (typescript, 228–29); punctuation, spelling, and syntax standardized.

44. Ibid., 533 (typescript, 246).

45. Ibid.

46. Ibid., 552 (typescript, 258).

47. Ibid., 602 (typescript, 281).

12

GOING HOME

I arrived in England on July 19, 1856, and was soon assigned by President Orson Pratt, who had replaced Elder Franklin D. Richards as the president of the mission, to serve a brief mission in England and Wales. I traveled from city to city and met with the Saints. In addition to lectures on the East India Mission, I also encouraged the members to hold fast to the kingdom of God and to repent of their sins. Led by Elders Pratt and Ezra T. Benson, we re-baptized many of the Saints, effecting a reformation similar to that in Utah. On March 21, 1857, I was re-baptized and soon after was released to return home.

I joined a company of 817 Saints, who were traveling with support from the Perpetual Emigration Fund, and thirteen other missionaries. Our leader was Elder James P. Park. I served in my usual capacity as clerk and secretary to the company. We sailed on the *George Washington*, a 1534-ton square-rigger, under Captain Josiah S. Cummings on March 28, 1857.[1] Less than a month later, on April 20th, we arrived at Boston. Eight days following, I sailed on the steamer *Connecticut* for New York City. From there, I went to Albany and on to Chicago. By railroad I made it to Iowa City, where I saw many of the group who had been my fellow passengers on the *George Washington*.

At Iowa City, I met with Elders John Taylor and Erastus Snow, who asked me to remain at that place to assist them in organizing companies to take the overland journey. Many who were leaving then were going by handcart. After Taylor and Snow left, I was in charge of preparing the last companies and getting them on their way. By the time I started west, there were 1,214 souls on the plains. I joined the last group that year. We left Florence, Nebraska, on July 12th.[2] Only twelve days later, Brigham Young and all of Utah learned that the United States government was sending an army to Utah to quell a supposed rebellion. Fortunately, we were ahead of that armed force. To my amazement and delight, in Wyoming I saw my old missionary companions, Colonels N. V. Jones and Chauncey Walker West, and William Fotheringham at Fort Bridger. They were part of a seventy-man force that Brother Brigham had sent out under the command of Colonel Robert Taylor Burton to slow the advance of the United States Army. They remained in Wyoming, and our company continued on to Salt Lake City. We arrived there on September 23, 1857. I was the last of the East India missionaries to return home.

Salt Lake City had changed considerably during my five-year absence. There were more houses, small and large, such as the Lion House. More businesses had been established. And the trees that were young and small in 1852 were now much larger. My mother was again a widow and my sister, Elizabeth, had died in 1853, leaving behind one child. I immediately missed her. Within a week of my return home, President Young called me into his office and asked me to work again in the Tithing Office. He also told me to look for a wife. Being twenty-six years old, I hardly needed his advice and counsel on that matter.[3]

THE MISSION IN MARCH 1856

When Elder Skelton was sailing down the Hoogly River on his way home, he summarized the state of the mission. That record, like many others that had been submitted to the presidency in England on a regular basis, was printed in the *Millennial Star*.

Skelton regretted his inability to gather the few Saints to Zion. Their temporal conditions were generally very humble. Most of the Indian members were in debt and seemed not to understand how to save and gain their freedom. Most, too, were scattered across the country and unable to give each other strength. Elder James P. Meik, the one man who had some means to share, tried to raise more money to help, but failed in the process and had a difficult time leaving the country with part of his own family.

Elder Skelton gave several members positive marks in his final report. He wrote:

> There are a number of faithful brethren in this land; most of whom have more than ordinary abilities, whose services will tend greatly to the building up of the kingdom of God. Among them may be mentioned Elders J. P. Meik, McCune, Smith, Mills, McCarthy, and Hefferan, who have taken a lively part in the ministry in their several spheres.[4]

Elder Skelton left Elder Meik in charge of the mission and Elder McCune in charge of the Church in Burma. There were in March 1856, sixty-one members of the Church in India. By Skelton's count, eleven had already emigrated to America. There were twenty-one members in Calcutta and Bengal; eight in Rangoon (mostly the McCune family); twelve in Madras; twenty in Bombay; and two brethren currently in Bangalore with the military. Skelton was pleased to report that two of his converts, Elder James Mills and Elder John McCarthy, were still active and expanding the Church in Madras. Mills was about to baptize Dr. Geils and his family. Elder Skelton had worked with them, taught the Geils children the songs of Zion, and hoped for their eventual entry into the Lord's kingdom. Mills had just completed a Tamil translation of Elder Lorenzo Snow's pamphlet *The Only Way to Be Saved*.[5]

That is where matters stood when the mission closed. There were, in addition to the sixty-one members Skelton mentioned, an unknown number of members who had drifted away and been lost when they were transferred with their military units or simply because they could not stand the fire of adversity. There were undoubtedly a few members in places like Karachi, Belgaum, and Poona who were faithful to their baptismal covenants but out of touch with the Church. We prayed for all of them.

WHAT WE FACED IN INDIA AND HOW WE RESPONDED

I have attempted within the body of this history to introduce and explain the major problems and issues we faced throughout the country. Without question, the single greatest deterrent to our work was the doctrine of plural marriage. Everywhere we went we were criticized and scoffed at for defending the practice. But it was then the doctrine of the Church, and we neither hedged on the matter nor apologized for it.

An almost equally difficult deterrent to our success was the almost uniform refusal of the military commanders to allow us to teach the Gospel in the cantonments. We were vigorous in our condemnation of them for their refusal to grant us what we believed was our right to religious liberty under the laws of Great Britain. But I don't believe any of us elders understood the long-standing policy of the government and military in India to insist on religious toleration and non-interference in the religious affairs of the people, especially among the sepoys. The British imposed this policy to maintain peace among the various Indian castes and groups. Missionary work was forbidden among the sepoys.[6] We were most interested in preaching to the Europeans, but European and Indian troops interacted constantly, and had we been granted permission to preach the Restored Gospel to the European troops, that same permission would have had ramifications among the sepoys. That was a risk the cantonment commanders were not willing to take. To us it appeared to be discrimination against the Mormons. There was some truth in this. The generals, colonels, and other officers with whom we dealt were encouraged in their prejudice against us by the ministers and chaplains of the Anglican

Church and other Protestant denominations. Nevertheless, the policy of religious toleration had been in effect for a number of decades before we arrived in the country and was not directed toward our mission alone.

We missionaries penned frequent judgments against British government and society in India. We were convinced that the East India Company (which was by our time totally under the control of the British government) and the British overlords in India were the "dark satanic colonial empire." Ironically, however, we were dependent upon that government for our protection and for the general peace that existed throughout the land. Our mission would not have been possible had it not been for the presence of the British and their administration.

Closely related to the problems we had in the cantonments was the wholesale rejection we received from most of the Europeans throughout the country. They were a unique breed, really quite different from their counterparts in England, Scotland, Ireland, and Wales. For the most part, they were of two groups: those who were born in India and partakers of the spirit of aristocracy that set them apart from the native population, and those who were military recruits who had been sent to India as part of the Queen's forces. The term *nabob* was no longer strictly appropriate when applied to the people of European ancestry, but snobbery was far more common than gentility or humility. Even some Church members suffered in their adjustment to life without a corps of servants to take care of their every comfort and need. Sister Hannah Booth, whom I loved as if she were my mother, had never cooked before she reached California and had to learn how to use a common stove and oven when she arrived. And the McCune's were always convinced that they were of the aristocracy, even though Matthew was simply a sergeant. It was far more commonplace for Europeans to treat us as the dregs of society than to accept us as equals.

It was our uniform view that the Indians were better people when they had no contact with European civilization and

Christians. Too often we saw Indian women offering themselves for sale in broad daylight, the result, we believed, of British influence. In towns and villages where Europeans were absent, the standard of morality was much higher. There was no question that too many British soldiers spent their lives in grog shops and houses of prostitution and died young as a result. Ironically, these same people accused us of immoral behavior and gross sins because of our belief in plural marriage.

Native Indian Christians were a problem and an enigma. We were critical of these people because we believed they were worse, less honest, than the rest of the Indian population. We probably overreacted because of our disappointments among them. There were many "old Christians" in other parts of the country, particularly in the south, who had been Christians since the time of Saint Thomas and who had a better reputation for integrity. They had become a caste, or castes, of their own. But our impressions were largely developed in Bengal, where Elder Willes's early converts so quickly fell away when they learned that they would not be paid to be members of our church. They were bought back by the Baptists, from which denomination most of them had come.

The situation with the Indian Christians was complex. As mentioned earlier, Indian converts became outcasts when they became Christians. They lost their place in society. They had no former social relationships, no occupation, no means of financial support, no place to live, no community political rights or power. When they became Christians, they in effect became part of a Christian quasi-caste. Their occupation was to be Christians, with all that implied. To be Christians was now their work. Conceivably, if asked what they did for a living, they might have answered, "I am a Christian." When they went from denomination to denomination or from mission to mission seeking higher compensation, they were doing a somewhat reasonable thing within the context of their own experience and beliefs. They wanted the best pay they could get for doing their new caste occupation—being Christian.

The Churuk puja, or swinging ceremony

As we traveled throughout India and Burma, we observed firsthand the religious rites and practices of the people. We saw the tender and loving concern of mothers teaching their children how to perform *puja* (worship and prayer) and devotional rites. We wandered around in many sacred cities of the Hindus, such as Benares [Varanasi], and viewed their temples, statues, images, and paintings. The elders noted marriage customs such as child marriage and the refusal to allow widows to remarry. Having spent more than a year in Karachi, where the majority of the population was Muslim, I was particularly interested in the life of Muhammad, the founder of the Islamic faith. We found ourselves confused at times and critical at others. For example, the Churuk puja, or hook swinging ceremony, revolted our sensibilities. Hindu stubbornness to perform certain tasks, such as hauling our traps beyond a certain geographical point, made us angry. But we gradually learned that each caste had its rules and limits, beyond which its members would not go. Some of the festivals we observed were extremely colorful and entertaining, even though we did not fully understand their underlying meanings.

Most of the elders read widely in books on Hinduism, Buddhism, and Islam. We were not uninformed regarding the culture and religious practices of the native Indians. Our major problem with them was our inability to gain the language fluency necessary to communicate effectively with them. I agree with Elder Skelton, who wrote: "In my estimation, the natives as a nation have not rejected the Gospel, not having heard it in purity by a legally authorized ministry."[7] Our inability to carry our message to the Indians notwithstanding, we made a vigilant effort to learn some of the languages of the country: Hindustani (Hindi and Urdu), Tamil, and Marathee received the greatest attention. I became fluent in Hindustani, having read the New Testament in that language three times. We also published some tracts and pamphlets in various Indian languages. But because of our limitations in numbers of missionaries, the vast amount of territory there was to cover, and the limited time in which we had to do it, we were unable to make even a small impression on the great mass of the people. Other messengers will yet have to do that work.

Even though we were unable to make an impression on India, we were convinced that God's judgements were imminent upon the peoples of that part of the earth. Years later, Elder Fotheringham shared his belief that the Mutiny of 1857 was God's judgment upon the British of India. Elder Leonard saw the Santal Insurrection of 1855 in the same light. As we viewed famines, diseases, minor earthquakes, and destructive storms, we considered these natural occurrences to be signs and warnings from God, as indeed they are. All of us expected the Millennium to come fairly soon. We saw ourselves as bearers of the Lord's message to the world for the last time. In Matthew we read: "And this Gospel of the Kingdom shall be preached in all the world for a witness to all nations, and then shall the end come" (Matthew 24:14). We accepted such scriptures as timely and looked forward with hope to the Lord's Second Coming.

Most of us suffered much from tropical diseases, steamy heat, the poverty of our situations, and the humbleness of our condition. But we were keenly aware that the Lord's hand was over us, and His blessings were evident every day. Our journals are replete with prayers of thanksgiving to our Heavenly Father for His watch care and for food to eat. As Elder Skelton said in his journal, the only reason for his ever going hungry was his unwillingness to ask for food. The Lord always raised up merciful friends.

Food and shelter were very important to our welfare. So was transportation. Ship captains were in many instances incredibly kind and generous to us. I, for example, went around the world without purse or scrip. This was also true of five others in our group. And others were allowed to travel at much reduced rates. Although only Captain Trail, who took Elder Luddington from Singapore to Bangkok, was baptized, many of the captains allowed us to preach the Gospel to them, to their crews, and to the passengers on board. These captive audiences were conducive to making converts. Also, the long acquaintances that developed aboard ship gave us the opportunity to prove that we were not the horrible people the worldwide press was painting us to be.

Our greatest benefactors were the handful of members who provided shelter, food, clothing, places to worship, money for printing our tracts and pamphlets, a supporting voice of counsel, and more. Those who stand out are the McCunes, Sister McMahon, the Taits, the Davies, the Mills, and the McCarthys. But the East India Mission might have ended much sooner than it did had it not been for the endless generosity of James Patrick and Mary Ann Meik. Their home was the mission home and headquarters through most of the period of the mission's existence. The Gospel thoroughly engulfed their lives. They were true Latter-day Saints. They never stopped spending their own funds for the benefit of the Church. Among the many tributes I could present in testimony to their service to the Lord's servants, I include the following from the pen of Elder Skelton:

> In justice to our worthy brother Meik, I must say that he has borne the burthen of the whole, with very few exceptions, the exact account of which I am not able to find out, no record having been kept of these things [tithing and Perpetual Emigration Fund offerings], for which I am very sorry. But, to my personal knowledge, during my stay at Calcutta he has paid £200, and how much more during my mission to Madras, I cannot tell, besides supporting all the Elders, and keeping up a meetinghouse at the rate of £10 per month for the last year, and ever since the first Elders arrived; were I to form an estimate of the whole, I should say £400 at the very least.[8]

In closing, what can be said of this the East India Mission? What importance could a mission have that did not produce large numbers of converts and that certainly did not change India? Most importantly, it made our testimonies of the Gospel firm and fast. In all of our journals and letters there was not a word questioning the wisdom or inspiration of the leaders of the Church in sending us to India. We accepted our calls from the Lord and did our best to establish the Restored Gospel in India. We were obedient. We warned the people everywhere we went so their sins would not be upon our garments. Because we loved the Church, we did our best to share the responsibility the Lord had placed on its leaders to take the Gospel to every nation.

Over the past half century, I have been asked many times whether the mission should have been attempted. How can I doubt the will of the Lord? What does the Lord say? "Prove the nations." "Gather the wheat from the tares." "Gather scattered Israel before the time of His coming." "Take the Gospel to every nation, kindred, tongue and people." Who should do this? If not us, who? If not then, when? God's command was to go everywhere, including India, Burma, and Siam.

Was our mission difficult? Of course. The record attests to that. But Latter-day Saints have always believed that "sacrifice brings forth the blessings of heaven." We placed our sacrifice on the altar of faith. In the *Lectures on Faith*, the Prophet Joseph said: "Let us here observe, that a religion that does not require the sacrifice of all things never has power sufficient to produce the faith necessary unto life and salvation."⁹ We believed this principle then and to a man we have believed it unto death.

Looking back from the vantage point of fifty years, I feel some pride in the work our mission accomplished. When we left India, we did not feel that we had accomplished much. We were keenly aware of the accomplishments of missionaries in Britain and Scandinavia. Every issue of the *Millennial Star* seemed to tell us that others were doing well, and we were accomplishing little. The small number of souls we baptized seemed like a paltry offering at the Master's feet. But considering our circumstances, we did not fail. We covered the Indian subcontinent with our witness and message. We introduced the Restored Gospel to Burma. We made an honest attempt at taking the message to Ceylon and Siam. To that time, no group of missionaries from the Church had faced such challenges: physical, legal, religious, or cultural. But none of us faltered in our knowledge that the Prophet Joseph Smith was the prophet of the Restoration and that Jesus Christ lives and is the Savior of the world. And none of us lost our lives. The Lord said, "Take no thought for your life, what ye shall eat, or what ye shall drink; nor yet for your body, what ye shall put on."¹⁰ The fowls of the air don't sow, yet Heavenly Father feeds them. And through our faith in Him, He fed, clothed, comforted, and healed us. And He allowed us to gain a few converts. Even though we would have liked more success, Heavenly Father would not give us control over the agency of other men.

In spite of our trials, we came home filled with the desire to do the will of the Lord and to accept whatever His leaders asked us to do. We have served in many responsible positions in the Church and in our communities, and we have reared worthy families who continue to serve the Lord. Looking back at our challenges in India, we have everything to be proud of.

NOTES

1. Sonne, *Ships, Saints, and Mariners*, 86.

2. Most of the information for this section is from Brooks, *Life of Amos Milton Musser*, chap. 4.

3. That is the point at which he concluded the record of his life.

4. Robert Skelton, "Hindostan" [Skelton to Franklin D. Richards, May 4, 1856, Ship *Earl of Eglington*, River Hoogley, Hindostan], *Millennial Star* 18 (August 16, 1856): 522.

5. Ibid., 523.

6. See Ramsey Muir, *The Making of British India, 1756–1858* (Manchester, England: University Press, 1923); and Douglas M. Peers, *Between Mars and Mammon: Colonial Armies and the Garrison State in India, 1819–1835* (London: I. Botarus Publishers, 1995), 91.

7. Skelton, *Millennial Star* 18 (August 16, 1856): 523.

8. Skelton, *Millennial Star* 18 (March 1, 1856): 143.

9. Joseph Smith, *Lectures on Faith* (Salt Lake City: Deseret Book, 1985), 69.

10. Matthew 6:25; see also vv. 25–34.

Appendix

LIFE SKETCHES OF THE MISSIONARIES

The men who accepted the call from the Lord to establish the restored gospel in India, Burma, and Siam did their best to fulfill that mission. After they left Asia, they continued to serve in a variety of responsible callings in the Church, to help build their communities, and to rear strong families. Their lives stand as a testimony of their love for Heavenly Father, his Son, Jesus Christ, and his Restored Church.

RICHARD BALLANTYNE

Richard Ballantyne was born on August 26, 1817, in Whitridgebog, Roxburgshire, Scotland, and died in Ogden, Utah, a community he helped develop, on November 8, 1898. In Latter-day Saint history, he is best known as the founder of the Sunday School in the Church. While this was an important contribution, his full life was a gift to his family, his Church, and the communities in which he lived and served. His parents were devoted to the Lord Jesus Christ and shared that devotion with him. His father, David, died in 1829, before the Church was organized, but his mother, Ann Bannerman, joined the Church along with Richard and the rest of their family. They emigrated to Nauvoo, Illinois, in

1843. From that time on, Richard and his family were part of the main events in LDS Church history.

Following his mission to India, Richard married two more women, Mary Pearce on November 27, 1855, and Caroline Sanderson on March 6, 1857. He was the father of twenty-two children, and grandfather to more than one hundred grandchildren. During his life, he was a baker, farmer, railroad construction worker, newspaperman, schoolteacher, and lumberyard owner. In the Church, he continued his work in the Sunday School and served for seventeen years on the Weber Stake high council. He saw no need for a distinct line between his sacred and secular interests. Most of his projects were altruistic in nature, such as building schools and organizing school districts, and constructing the Davis and Weber Counties Canal. He served as an alderman in Ogden for several terms and in other civic positions (see Sonne, *Knight of the Kingdom;* Jenson, *LDS Biographical Encyclopedia,* 1:703–6.)

WILLIAM FURLSBURY CARTER

William F. Carter was born May 1, 1811, in Newry, Maine. He spent his early years in Maine, where he joined the Church on November 17, 1834. Three years before, in 1831, he had married Sarah York. From the time of their baptism, the Carters' life and fate was intimately connected with that of the Church. In 1836, the Carters moved to Kirtland, Ohio, and a year later they moved on to Far West, Missouri. In 1839, at Quincy, Illinois, Carter was ordained a seventy. About that time, the Carters moved to Nauvoo, Illinois. In early 1846, William and Sarah received their endowment in the Nauvoo Temple. When the Saints were forced out of Nauvoo, Carter took his family to Council Bluffs, Iowa, where they remained until the spring of 1851, when they migrated to the Salt Lake Valley. They arrived there in June. Until that time, he had blacksmithed to help the Saints get ready for the cross-country trip. In 1852, the Carters moved to Provo, from which place he was called to India.

After his mission, Carter lived in Provo until 1864, when he moved his family to Mona, in Juab County. Over the years, he lived in Goshen, Santaquin, and Benjamin, Utah. He was a skilled blacksmith, an excellent mechanic, and a successful farmer. He eventually married four plural wives: sisters Roxena and Sally Ann Mecham, Elizabeth Howard, and Cordilia Hannah Mecham. He was the father of at least thirteen children, three by Sarah and ten by Sally Ann. He died on October 11, 1888, in Santaquin, Utah, at age seventy-seven (see Carter, "Life Sketch of William Furlsbury Carter"; Black, *Early LDS Membership Data*).

BENJAMIN FRANKLIN DEWEY

Benjamin F. Dewey was born on May 5, 1829, in Westfield, Massachusetts, and was baptized by Wilford Woodruff at Winter Quarters, Nebraska, on April 5, 1847. Dewey was one of the original pioneers to enter the Great Salt Lake Valley with Brigham Young. He was twenty-three years of age when called to Siam. A carpenter by trade, he also spent years of his life in mining. Dewey married Disey Parallee Russel and Eliza Smithson (the recorded dates are confused). In 1860, he had a household of five. He died at Chloride, Arizona, on February 23, 1904 (see Jenson, *LDS Biographical Encyclopedia*, 4:698; Black, *Early LDS Membership Data*).

ALLAN McPHERSON FINDLAY

Allan M. Findlay was born January 1, 1830, to James and Mary McPherson Findlay in New Milns, Ayrshire, Scotland. He was baptized November 6, 1846. After he and his bride, Jessie Ireland, arrived in Salt Lake City, they were endowed and sealed on March 13, 1857, in the Endowment House. They were parents to seven children. Allan died on February 11, 1891, at the age of sixty-one.

HUGH FINDLAY

Hugh Findlay was born June 9, 1822, in New Milns, Ayrshire, Scotland. In addition to his mission to India, he also served a mission to Scotland from 1878 to 1880, served in responsible positions in the Church before and after his mission to India, spoke on two occasions at general conferences of the Church, participated in civic affairs in Rich County, Utah, and was on the board of directors of the Fish Haven Branch United Order in Franklin County, Idaho. In addition to his first wife, Isabella Ratray, he married three other wives. His final calling in the priesthood was that of patriarch. He died at his home in Fish Haven, near Bear Lake, on March 5, 1900, leaving a numerous posterity (see Findlay, *Missionary Journals*, i–vii).

WILLIAM FOTHERINGHAM

From the time of his baptism in November 1847, until his final day, William Fotheringham never faltered in his devotion to the Restored Church. He was born at Clackmannan, Scotland, on April 6, 1826. Soon after he joined the Church, his parents and other members of his family followed suit. Along with about sixty members of his branch and family, he emigrated to America in 1848. The family spent some time in St. Louis and Council Bluffs and then traveled to Salt Lake City, arriving in late September 1850. William and his parents were among the first settlers of Lehi, in Utah Valley.

After his mission to India, he married Elizabeth Hardy in Salt Lake City in April 1856. A year later, on May 25, 1857, William married Mary Wardrope. In 1861, he was called to preside over the Church's mission in South Africa. He returned in 1864. A year later, at the request of President Brigham Young, the Fotheringhams sold their farm in Lehi and moved to Beaver, in central Utah. Later that year, on October 10th, he married his third wife, Harriet

Electra Hales. According to Andrew Jenson, Fotheringham was the father of thirty children, eighteen sons and twelve daughters.

Over the years, Fotheringham served as justice of the peace, county clerk, member of the territorial legislature, and mayor of Beaver City. In the Church, in addition to his missions, he served as bishop, high councilor, temple ordinance worker, counselor in the stake presidency, and patriarch. Fotheringham founded and nurtured the Sunday Schools of his area for forty years. He was an unusually good writer, as has been noted in the body of this work. At the age of eighty-six, William Fotheringham died in Milford, Utah, on February 27, 1913 (see Jenson, *LDS Biographical Encyclopedia*, 2:190; Black, *Early LDS Membership Data*, and Fotheringham family records in possession of the author).

NATHANIEL VARY JONES

Nathaniel V. Jones was born in Rochester, New York, on October 13, 1822. During his early life, he worked as a ship carpenter. Later, he worked at several other professions, most of them relating to mining and metals. He joined the Church on April 6, 1842, at Potosi, Wisconsin. In the spring of 1842, he moved to Nauvoo, Illinois, where he was ordained an elder on June 11, 1843. In that same month, he left on a mission to Ohio, a mission that actually extended beyond that territory. His companion was Elder Robert Taylor Burton. In March 1845, Jones married Burton's sister, Rebecca Maria. He received his endowment in the Nauvoo Temple on February 3, 1846.

His life was remarkable in its number of accomplishments. Among other things, he was first sergeant in the first company of the Mormon Battalion; bishop of Salt Lake City Fifteenth Ward; mission president in India at age thirty; member of the Salt Lake City council; missionary to England; developer of the lead and iron ore industries in Utah and neighboring states; and colonel in the defense force against Johnston's Army during the war of 1857–58. When he left Salt Lake City for India in the fall of 1852, he left behind his wife, Rebecca, and four children; the fifth child was born a week after his departure.

After his mission to India, he married Caroline M. Garr, Mary E. Brown, and Eliza Reed. He was the father of fourteen children. Jones died February 15, 1863, at the age of forty in Salt Lake City (see Jenson, *LDS Biographical Encyclopedia*, 2:368–69; Jones, "Extracts from the Life Sketch of Nathaniel V. Jones," 2–6; Black, *Early LDS Membership Data*).

TRUMAN LEONARD

Truman Leonard, Jr., was born September 17, 1820, in Pottertown, New York. He was baptized into the Church on March 25, 1843, and was called on a mission four months later. He met and married Ortentia White in Nauvoo, Illinois. Their marriage in the Nauvoo Temple on January 1, 1846, was the first performed there. At his departure for India, he was thirty-two years old and left behind his wife and one child. Three other children had died at birth or in their early months.

After his mission he married Margaret Bourne and Mary Ann Meadows on January 6, 1857. He had met these sisters on his journey from England. Mary Ann bore seven children, but Margaret remained childless. His first wife, Ortentia, gave birth to ten children, only three of whom reached maturity. Truman spent most of his life as a farmer in Farmington, Utah, but served two additional missions in the United States and hid out for a time in Canada during the worst of the anti-polygamy campaigns. He was senior president of his seventies quorum most of his life. He died on November 20, 1897, at the age of seventy-seven (see Leonard, "Truman Leonard," 240–60; Black, *Early LDS Membership Data*).

ELAM LUDDINGTON

Elam Luddington was born November 23, 1806, and died in Salt Lake City on March 22, 1893, at the age of eighty-six. Elam was baptized into the Church on May 16, 1840. Joseph Smith, Sr., ordained him a high priest. He was the eldest of the India-Siam missionaries, being forty-five years of age at the time of his call. He left behind his wife, Mary Eliza, and two children. This seems to be the extent of his family. He was first lieutenant of Company B of the Mormon Battalion. Luddington served for a time as city marshal but spent most of his life as a farmer (see Black, *Early LDS Membership Data*).

MATTHEW McCUNE

Matthew McCune was born July 27, 1811, on the Isle of Man, Great Britain, and died October 27, 1889, at age seventy-eight, in Nephi, Utah. His first wife, Sarah Elizabeth Caroline Scott, was born January 28, 1812, in London, England. She died on July 17, 1877, in Nephi, at the age of sixty-five. Although he was not set apart as a missionary in India and Burma, he served valiantly in that calling and considered himself a missionary. McCune had a relatively large number of convert baptisms.

After emigrating to Utah, he spent most of his life in Nephi, working as a druggist, homeopathic physician, and farmer. He served two missions in England and was on the Juab Stake high council for almost twenty-five years. He also married Ann Midgley, Isabella Bailey, and Ann Chalmers and was the father of nineteen children.

JAMES PATRICK MEIK

James P. Meik was born in Secrole, three miles west of Benares, India, on December 9, 1807. His wife, Mary Ann Francis, was also born in India, in 1818. They were among the first four converts baptized into the Church in all of Asia. They had a large family, probably ten children. Complications of Mary Ann's eleventh pregnancy took her life on October 24, 1857.

After the mission closed and the missionaries departed, Meik corresponded occasionally with Elders Musser and Jones, each letter indicating his intention to leave for Zion as soon as possible. Notes in the *Deseret News* of May 24, 1869, and September 14, 1869, indicate that he had finally left India for England and from there to Salt Lake City. He received his blessings in the Endowment House on September 27, 1869, soon after his arrival. He was unable to induce any of his children to emigrate with him, although one child had preceded him to Utah and lived for a time with the McCune family in Nephi.

Within a year or two of his arrival in Salt Lake City, Meik married Susannah McAndrew Hutchison, a Scottish woman thirty-nine years his junior. Only one of their four children, Francis Thomas Meik, lived to maturity. According to family recollection, Meik did not do well financially in Utah. He died at age sixty-eight on September 6, 1876, in Salt Lake City.

AMOS MILTON MUSSER

By any measure, A. Milton Musser was a remarkable man. In 1858, President Brigham Young called him to serve as Traveling Bishop of the Church, a position he held until he was called on a mission to Pennsylvania in 1876. "His duty," wrote Orson F. Whitney in Andrew Jenson's *LDS Biographical Encyclopedia*, "was to visit the various stakes and wards, with instructions to attend to all matters pertaining to the collecting, forwarding and reporting of the tithes and offerings of the Saints; to collect moneys due the Church and the Perpetual Emigrating fund, and attend to other Church business under the direction of the First Presidency and the Presiding Bishopric" (1:382). During the period while he was serving as Traveling Bishop, Musser was also engaged as a founding partner in a number of other important enterprises, including the Deseret Telegraph Company, Zion's Savings Bank and Trust Company, the State Bank of Utah, the Great Western Iron Company, and several Utah railroads. Musser introduced the telephone to Salt Lake City.

After his mission to the East, Musser worked in the Church historian's office as a clerk. On April 4, 1902, at general conference, he was sustained as an assistant Church historian, which position he held until his death on September 24, 1909.

Musser married four wives and was a vigorous defender of the principle of plural marriage. His wives were Ann Leaver, married January 9, 1858; Mary Elizabeth White, married October 1, 1864; Belinda Pratt, married September 4, 1872; and Annie Seegmiller, married January 30, 1874. These women were the mothers of his twenty sons and fifteen daughters. In April 1885, Musser was found guilty of unlawful cohabitation, fined three hundred dollars, and sentenced to six months in the penitentiary, which term he served.

On his death, the *Deseret Evening News* wrote: "Elder Musser never tired of speaking of his experiences during his mission [in India], and the wonderful manner in which the Lord opened the way for him, traveling, as he did, literally without money. He used to say that at no time did he have to beg for food, clothing or transportation. He opened his heart in prayer to his Father in Heaven, and the way was always prepared for him" (see Jenson, *LDS Biographical Encyclopedia*, 1:381–86; 3:765).

ROBERT OWENS

Robert Owens was born July 10, 1818, in Dover, Maryland. He married Catherine Ann Williams in 1837, in Franklin County, Ohio. He was baptized into the Church on September 21, 1844. He received his endowment in the Nauvoo Temple on February 7, 1846, the last day that ordinances were performed in that temple. After leaving for the West with the body of the Saints, Owens served as a private in Company B of the Mormon Battalion.

The Owens family settled in the Big Cottonwood area of Salt Lake Valley. On March 7, 1850, Robert married a second wife, Martha Evins Allen. When he departed for India, he left behind nine children, and both of his wives were pregnant. Catherine delivered on December 12, 1852, and Martha on February 6, 1853.

When Owens completed his mission in India, he sailed for Melbourne, Australia, as an ordinary seaman on the British ship *Hyderabad*. It was a medium-sized, three-masted square-rigger under Captain Frederick A. Castle. Although Owens served for a time as a missionary in Australia and reportedly was the first Latter-day Saint elder to attempt to preach the Gospel in Tasmania, nothing more is known about that venture. On April 27, 1855, Owens, among seventy-two LDS emigrants (including missionaries) sailed from Melbourne on the small brig *Tarquinia*. (It weighed 210 tons; the *Mayflower*, by comparison, weighed 180 tons.) The trip was ill-fated. The brig developed leaks and had to put into harbor at Papeete, Tahiti, for repairs. It made it to Honolulu, where further repairs were needed. Soon after leaving that port, the *Tarquinia* ran into a storm and being in danger of sinking was forced back to Hawaii. The ship was condemned, and its passengers had to find other means of reaching California. How or when Owens got there is not known.

A later reference to him is found in Robert Skelton's journal. Writing in San Bernardino, he says: "Learning that Robert Owens was in this place I sought diligently to see him who was glad to see me altho in a lukewarm condition. He began as he always does to relate over his troubles and injuries sustained by [?] Brethren &c and that he had been sick most all summer. I exhorted him earnestly to return by all means to his family with a view to provide for & school them. Feeling impressed he promised to do so" (Skelton, Journal [August or September 1856], 598 [typescript, 279]).

Robert Owens died November 9, 1883, in Los Angeles, California (see Black, *Early LDS Membership Data;* Sonne, *Ships, Saints, and Mariners*, 101, 185–86).

JOSEPH RICHARDS

Little information is available about Joseph Richards beyond the comments Willes made in his reminiscences. In 1884, Willes noted that Richards was living as "a pensioner in the Sailors' Snug Harbor [probably a retirement home], Staten Island, New York." He had been there for several years by that date. Willes said Richards was then nearly eighty-three years old. That would place Richards's birth around 1801 and his first arrival in Calcutta as a missionary at age fifty. Nothing is said regarding family. Presumably he died within the next few years or by 1890.

LEVI SAVAGE

Levi Savage, Jr., was born March 23, 1820, in Greenfield, Ohio, and died on December 13, 1910, in Toquerville, Utah. He joined the Church in 1846, was a member of the Mormon Battalion, and was an early Utah pioneer, arriving in the Salt Lake Valley on October 16, 1847. On January 23, 1848, he married Jane Mathers, who gave birth to their only child, Levi Mathers Savage, three years later in January 1851. She died on December 29, 1851. Only eight months later, in August 1852, while the pain of losing his wife had to remain severe, he was called to missionary service in Siam. Savage left his toddler son with his sister, Hannah M. Eldredge, while he served his mission. After his return to Utah, he married Ann Brummel Cooper, an English widow, in 1858. Ten years later, he married Ann's daughters by her first marriage, Adelaide and Mary Ann Cooper, a week apart. Mary Ann bore him three children. He worked in farming, gardening, and dairying. Savage remained faithful to the Church until the time of his passing.

ROBERT HODGSON SKELTON

Robert H. Skelton was born November 28, 1824, in Burgh, Cumberland County, England. He and his five siblings were left orphans when he was six years of age. His early life was difficult. Coldhearted neighbors provided for him, but their cruel abuse led him to go on his own by age thirteen. He worked from place to place as a farmer. At age twenty-three, Robert emigrated to America on the ship *Lord Maidstone* and found his way to Saint Louis, Missouri. It was there he was introduced to the Church and baptized in March 1849.

In that same year, he joined a group of pioneers heading for the Salt Lake Valley, led by Elder Ezra T. Benson. Skelton served as the driver of Elder Benson's team. From that time on, Skelton enjoyed a close relationship with the Bensons. They arrived in Salt Lake City on October 11, 1849. Soon afterward, Skelton joined the Bensons and others as the first settlers of Tooele, Utah.

After his mission to India, Robert married Eliza Angeline Gollaher in the Endowment House in Salt Lake City on January 17, 1857, only three months after his return home. They became the parents of twelve children. Over the years he served in various civic and Church callings. Among them were mayor of Tooele and counselor in the bishopric of the Tooele Ward. He was faithful to the Church until his death on February 1, 1895, in Tooele (see Whittaker, Register to the Robert H. Skelton Collection, MSS 1597; Black, *Early LDS Membership Data*).

CHAUNCEY WALKER WEST

Chauncey W. West was born February 6, 1827, in Orange, Pennsylvania. He joined the Church at age sixteen. Only a year later, he was ordained a seventy in the Melchizedek Priesthood. With his family, he gathered to Nauvoo. West married his first wife, Mary Hoagland, on May 16, 1846. They lived for a time at Winter Quarters and settled in the Salt Lake Valley in the fall of 1847. He was twenty-five years of age when he was called to Siam. Chauncey and Mary were the parents of three children at the time of his call to India.

In the year of his return from Asia, he was called as bishop of the Ogden First Ward and the next spring as presiding bishop of Weber County, Utah, which position he held until his untimely death on January 9, 1870, at age forty-four. In 1863, he was called to replace (for sixteen months) Elder George Q. Cannon as president of the European Mission in England. He also served in the Utah House of Representatives. He was colonel of the Weber military district. Of him, George Q. Cannon wrote: "He was a man of untiring energy and industry. He was remarkable for these qualities and for his great hopefulness. I do not think he ever had a feeling of discouragement in his life" (see Jenson, *LDS Biographical Encyclopedia*, 1:753).

At his death he left a number of wives (perhaps ten) and thirty-six children (see Jenson, *LDS Biographical Encyclopedia*, 1:749–54; Black, *Early LDS Membership Data*).

WILLIAM WILLES

William Willes is an intriguing figure who deserves more research and a full biography. Willes was a teacher, writer, and poet. At least two of his poems, "The Prophet, Joseph Smith" and "Come, Haste to the Valley," appeared in the *Millennial Star* in July 1852 and June 1855, respectively. His article entitled "The Castes of India" was printed in the *Juvenile Instructor* on July 15, 1882. A prolific writer, in 1872, Willes published a collection of his own lyrics along with those of other writers in a 128-page book titled *The Mountain Warbler*. For several years after its publication he stumped up and down Utah and Idaho to sell the five thousand copies he had printed. His texts for two hymns, "Come Along, Come Along" and "Thanks for the Sabbath School" appear in *Hymns of The Church of Jesus Christ of Latter-day Saints*, 1985 edition. Willes's literary talents gained him appointments to the Deseret Dramatic Association and the Board of Regents of Deseret University (now the University of Utah). He also served as Territorial Superintendent of Common Schools.

But his talents as a writer-scholar-educator did not serve him as well as they might have. He moved many times to maintain employment as a schoolteacher and was unemployed every few years. He tried running a store and various other occupations but never did well financially. His fourth wife, Elizabeth Wyatt, ran a store successfully to support him and their five children during the later years of his life.

William was ordained a seventy shortly after immigrating to Utah. Beginning in 1862, he filled a mission to England. His most memorable Church calling was as a Sunday School missionary. In 1875, he was called to move forward the work of the Sunday School Union of the Church. Along with George Goddard, he traveled Utah, Idaho, and Arizona, singing, preaching, doing recitations and in other ways encouraging Sunday School work. He was released from that calling in 1882 but picked it up again after his second mission to India from 1884 to 1886.

Willes was born July 5, 1814, in Woolwich, a suburb of London, England. His father, who was a plumber, painter, and glazier, died when William was twelve, and his mother when he was sixteen years old. They had placed him in school at a young age. He eventually attended normal school and became a teacher. When he joined the Church in 1848, he lost his position and struggled after that time. After his mission to India and his migration to Utah, he married Sarah Jane Walters in November 1856 and Mary Patricia Griffiths in January 1857. They each bore him a child but both divorced him within a year or two. He seems not to have reestablished his home with his first wife, Ann Kibby, for very long after his mission. In May 1866, he married Elizabeth Wyatt, whom he considered his wife from that point on. She was twenty years his junior.

He was the father of twelve children, several of whom died in infancy or early childhood. He died of pneumonia on November 2, 1890, in Salt Lake City, at age seventy-six.

SAMUEL AMOS WOOLLEY

Like most of his India Mission companions, Samuel A. Woolley lived a remarkably full life. He was born in Pennsylvania on September 11, 1825. Orphaned at a young age, he tried his hand at many occupations. In his adult life, he worked as a pail maker, in the lumber business, as a storekeeper, and at farming, among other things. He was introduced to the Church in 1836 and was baptized on October 7, 1840. He helped quarry stone for the Nauvoo Temple. As a young man he was among those youths known as the "whittling and whistling brigade" who warded off an unfriendly law officer who had intended to arrest the Prophet Joseph Smith. "After the martyrdom of Joseph and Hyrum Smith," wrote Elder Woolley, "I was present at the important meeting where Pres. Brigham Young first spoke to the Saints of Joseph's death, and I received a testimony that the mantle of Joseph had fallen upon Brigham Young's shoulder, for when he spoke it seemed as if Joseph himself were speaking, his voice and gestures being exactly like those of the martyred Prophet" (Jenson, *LDS Biographical Encyclopedia*, 1:781).

He was ordained a seventy in October 1845. On May 21, 1846, he married his first wife, Catherine Elizabeth Mehring. Two years later, they emigrated to the Salt Lake Valley, arriving in September. He was one of the original settlers of Parowan but spent most of his life in Salt Lake City. After his mission to India, he was ordained a high priest and served in the bishopric of the Ninth Ward in Salt Lake City, where he later served as bishop for many years. In addition to India, he served two other missions, both in the United States.

The record is not clear regarding the number of his wives. One, Rachel, died in childbirth. Another left him. But he lived with Catherine Elizabeth until her death in 1880. His wife, Frances Ann Phillips, whom he married in 1867, died in 1883. Two years later, in 1885, he married Elizabeth Ann Stephenson. Three of his wives bore him twenty-one children, ten of whom survived

him. Bishop Woolley died in Salt Lake City on March 23, 1900 (see
Jenson, *LDS Biographical Encyclopedia,* 1:781–82; Black, *Early LDS
Membership Data*).

BIBLIOGRAPHY

BOOKS AND PAMPHLETS

Black, Susan Easton, comp. *Membership of the Church of Jesus Christ of Latter-day Saints, 1830–1848.* 36 vols. Provo, Utah: Religious Studies Center, 1984–87. This multivolume work attempts to list and provide family and demographic data on all members of the Church from 1830 to 1848. The series has been included in Infobases CD-ROM productions, under the title *Early LDS Membership Data* in *The LDS Collectors Library* (Salt Lake City: Infobases, 1995), which was the source of the information I used in this book.

Britsch, R. Lanier. *From the East: The History of the Latter-day Saints in Asia, 1851–1996.* Salt Lake City: Deseret Book, 1998.

Brooks, Karl. *The Life of Amos Milton Musser.* Provo, Utah: Stevenson's Genealogical Center, 1980. Revised reprint of Brooks's master's thesis, Brigham Young University, 1961.

Caunter, Hobart. *Lives of the Moghul Emperors,* The Oriental Annual Series. London: Samuel Bentley, 1837.

———. *Scenes in India,* The Oriental Annual Series. London: Samuel Bentley, 1838.

Chislett, John. "Mr. Chislett's Narrative." In T. B. H. Stenhouse. *The*

297

Rocky Mountain Saints: A Full and Complete History of the Mormons, from the First Vision of Joseph Smith to the Last Courtship of Brigham Young. New York: D. Appleton, 1883.

Clark, James R., comp. *Messages of the First Presidency of The Church of Jesus Christ of Latter-day Saints.* 6 vols. Salt Lake City: Bookcraft, 1965–75.

Esshom, Frank E. *Pioneers and Prominent Men of Utah.* Salt Lake City: Pioneer Book Publishing Co., 1913.

Hafen, LeRoy R., and Ann W. Hafen. *Handcarts to Zion: The Story of a Unique Western Migration, 1856–1860.* Glendale, California: Arthur H. Clark Company, 1960. Reprint, Lincoln: University of Nebraska Press, 1992.

Jenson, Andrew. *Church Chronology.* 2d ed., rev. & enl. Salt Lake City: Deseret News Press, 1899.

———. *LDS Biographical Encyclopedia.* 4 vols. Salt Lake City: Arrow Press, 1920.

Mahajan, Jagmohan. *The Raj Landscape.* Surrey, Eng.: Spantech Publishers, 1988.

Maitra, Veena. *The Cantonment Administration in India.* New Delhi: by the author, 1996.

Moffett, Samuel Hugh. *A History of Christianity in Asia, Beginnings to 1500, Vol. 1.* San Francisco: Harper, 1992.

Moorhouse, Geoffrey. *Calcutta* New York: Holt, Rinehart and Winston, 1971.

Muir, Ramsey. *The Making of British India, 1756–1858.* Manchester, England: University Press, 1923.

Neill, Stephen. *The History of Christianity in India, The Beginnings to 1707.* Cambridge, England: Cambridge University Press, 1984.

Peers, Douglas M. *Between Mars and Mammon: Colonial Armies and the Garrison State in India, 1819–1835.* London: I. Botarus Publishers, 1995.

Pratt, Orson. *Remarkable Visions.* Edinburgh: Ballantyne and Hughes, 1840.

Pratt, Parley Parker. *The Voice of Warning.* New York: W. Sanford, 1837.

Roberts, B[righam] H[enry]. *A Comprehensive History of The Church of Jesus Christ of Latter-day Saints, Century One.* 6 vols. Salt Lake City: The Church of Jesus Christ of Latter-day Saints, 1930.

Schmidt, Karl J. *An Atlas and Survey of South Asian History.* Armonk, N.Y.: M. E. Sharpe, 1995.

Smith, Joseph. *Lectures on Faith.* Salt Lake City: Deseret Book, 1985. Originally delivered 1834–35.

Smith, Joseph Fielding. *Essentials in Church History,* 13th ed. Salt Lake City: Deseret Book, 1953.

Sonne, Conway B. *Knight of the Kingdom: The Story of Richard Ballantyne.* Salt Lake City: Deseret Book, 1949; 2d ed., 1989.

———. *Saints on the Seas: A Maritime History of Mormon Migration, 1830–1890.* Salt Lake City: University of Utah Press, 1983.

———. *Ships, Saints, and Mariners: A Maritime Encyclopedia of Mormon Migration, 1830–1890.* Salt Lake City: University of Utah Press, 1987.

Spencer, Orson. *Letters.* Liverpool: Orson Spencer, 1848.

Stegner, Wallace. *The Gathering of Saints: The Story of the Mormon Trail.* New York: McGraw-Hill Book Co., 1964.

Urwick, W. *India Illustrated.* New York: Hurst and Company, 1891.

Ward, Andrew. *Our Bones Are Scattered: The Cawnpore Massacre and the Indian Mutiny of 1857.* New York: Henry Holt and Company, 1996.

Wolpert, Stanley. *A New History of India.* 5th ed. New York: Oxford University Press, 1997.

Yule, Henry, and A. C. Burnell. *Hobson-Jobson: The Anglo-Indian Dictionary.* 1886. Reprint. Hertfordshire: Wordsworth Editions Ltd., 1996.

ARTICLES

Ballantyne, Richard. "A Promise Fulfilled." *Improvement Era* 6 (June 1903): 590–93.

Britsch, R. Lanier. "Church Beginnings in China." *Brigham Young University Studies* 10 (1970): 161–72.

Christy, Howard A. "Weather, Disaster, and Responsibility: An Essay on the Willie and Martin Handcart Story." *Brigham Young University Studies* 37, no. 1 (1997–98): 6–74.

Harris, Jan G. "Mormons in Victorian Manchester." *Brigham Young University Studies* 27 (Winter 1987): 46–56.

Jones, Rebecca M. "Extracts from the Life Sketch of Nathaniel V. Jones." *Utah Historical Quarterly* 4 (January 1931): 2–6.

Leonard, Glen M. "Truman Leonard: Pioneer Mormon Farmer." *Utah Historical Quarterly* 44 (Summer 1976): 240–60.

Lilley, Henry J. "From India's Coral Strand." *Improvement Era* 12 (1908–9): 423–34.

McCune, Henry F. ["Life Sketch."] *Utah Genealogical and Historical Magazine* 6 (October 1925): 144–52.

Peterson, Paul H. "They Came by Handcart." *Ensign* 27 (August 1997): 30–37.

Tanner, John S. "Milton and the Early Mormon Defense of Polygamy." *Milton Quarterly* 21 (May 1987): 41–46.

Thorp, Malcolm R. "The Religious Backgrounds of Mormon Converts in Britain, 1837–52." *Journal of Mormon History* 4 (1977): 51–65.

Whittaker, David J. "Richard Ballantyne and the Defense of Mormonism in India in the 1850s." In Donald Q. Cannon and David J. Whittaker, eds. *Supporting Saints: Life Stories of Nineteenth-Century Mormons*. Provo, Utah: Brigham Young University Religious Studies Center, 1985, 175–212.

JOURNALS (PUBLISHED AND UNPUBLISHED) AND UNPUBLISHED SOURCES

Ancestral File. Family History Department. The Church of Jesus Christ of Latter-day Saints. Salt Lake City, Utah.

Ballantyne, Richard. Journals. 7 vols. Archives of The Church of Jesus Christ of Latter-day Saints. Salt Lake City, Utah. These journals are the primary sources on Ballantyne.

Booth Family Records. In possession of Nora White Brown, Cedar City, Utah.

Britsch, R. Lanier. "A History of the Missionary Activities of The Church of Jesus Christ of Latter-day Saints in India, 1849–1856. Master's thesis, Brigham Young University, 1964.

Carter, William F. "Incidents from the Life of William F. Carter." In *Heart Throbs of the West*, comp. Kate B. Carter, 4:204–20. Salt Lake City: Daughters of Utah Pioneers, 1943.

Carter, William Furlsbury. Journal, October 1852–December 1853. Archives of The Church of Jesus Christ of Latter-day Saints, Salt Lake City, Utah.

Carter, Nora W. "Life Sketch of William Furlsbury Carter." Copy in possession of the author.

East India Mission Index. Minutes of Conference Held in Calcutta. 1853. Archives of The Church of Jesus Christ of Latter-day Saints. Salt Lake City, Utah.

Findlay, Hugh. *Missionary Journals of Hugh Findlay, India - Scotland.* Comp. Ross Findlay and Linnie Findlay. Ephraim, Utah: n.p, 1973.

Fotheringham, William. Part of My History, Book A. Typescript in possession of the author.

———. "Travels in India." *Juvenile Instructor.* Fotheringham's auto-biographical series on his mission to India ran from 1877 to 1884.

Fotheringham, William. Journal, 1854–55.

Fotheringham Family Records. In possession of the author.

Journal History of the East India Mission. Branch Record, 1851. Archives of The Church of Jesus Christ of Latter-day Saints. Salt Lake City, Utah.

Leonard, Truman. Letters. Copies in possession of author.

Manuscript History of the East India Mission. Archives of The Church of Jesus Christ of Latter-day Saints. Salt Lake City, Utah.

McCune, George M. "Henry Frederick McCune, Autobiography and Biography of His Life and Works, A.D. May 31, 1840 to

December 15, 1924." Typescript, 1971. Archives of The Church of Jesus Christ of Latter-day Saints. Salt Lake City, Utah.

McCune, Matthew. Journal, 1851–1856. Daughters of Utah Pioneers Library. Salt Lake City, Utah; microfilm, Archives of The Church of Jesus Christ of Latter-day Saints. Salt Lake City, Utah.

Meik Family Records. In possession of the author. I am grateful to Julie Kay Petersen, a direct descendent of James Patrick Meik and Mary Ann Meik, for providing information.

Musser, Amos Milton. Private Journals and Memos, 23 vols. Typescript. Archives of The Church of Jesus Christ of Latter-day Saints. Salt Lake City, Utah.

Savage, Levi, Jr. Diaries, 1852–1903, 4 vols. Mission Journals—Calcutta, India, Burma, Siam, 1852–1853. Manuscripts and Special Collections. Brigham Young University Library. Provo, Utah.

———. *Levi Savage Jr. Journal.* Comp. Lynn M. Hilton. Salt Lake City: John Savage Family Organization, 1966.

Skelton, Robert H. Journal and Papers. Manuscripts and Special Collections. Brigham Young University Library. Provo, Utah.

Whittaker, David J. "Early Mormon Pamphleteering." Ph.D. diss., Brigham Young University, 1982.

———, comp. Register to the Robert H. Skelton Collection, MSS 1597. Manuscripts and Special Collections. Brigham Young University Library, Provo, Utah.

Willes Family Records.

Willes, William. Journal and Reminiscences, 1851–1885. Archives of The Church of Jesus Christ of Latter-day Saints. Salt Lake City, Utah.

PERIODICALS

The Contributor
Deseret News
Juvenile Instructor
The Latter-day Saints' Millennial Star
The Mormon

INDEX

Pages on which illustrations or photos appear are shown in *italic* type.

organizes Poona Branch, 190;
builds Poona meetinghouse,
193–94; debates James Michel,
194–95; deals with member
problems in Bombay, 195–97;
accomplishments of, 197, 206;
health problems of, 198; organizes
Bombay Branch, 198; journey to
Belgaum, 201; in Belgaum, 201–4;
in Panaji, 204–5; emigrates to
America, 205–6; life sketch of,
284
Findlay, Isabella Ratray, 284
Findlay, James, 283
Findlay, Jessie Ireland, 241, 283
Findlay, Mary McPherson, 241, 283
Fire Queen (ship), 100–101, 115, 172,
177
Fisher, Captain, 205
Forest of Masts, 16
Fort Saint George, 125–26, *128*,
141–45, *142*
Fotheringham, Elizabeth Hardy, 284
Fotheringham, Harriet Electra
Hales, 284–85
Fotheringham, Mary Wardrope, 284
Fotheringham, William: mission call,
9–10; age and marital status at
time of call, 17; assigned to labor
in Dinapore, 33; on the
challenges of conversion, 65; in
Chunar, 65; in Mirzapore, 65;
journey to Dinapore, 69–72;
portrait of, *70;* in Dinapore, 72,
74; in Chunar, 74, 76; in
Mirzapore, 76–77; voyage to
Calcutta, 77–78; health problems
of, 84; journey to Secundrabad,
85–86; in Secundrabad, 86; in
Meerut, 86–88; in Delhi, 90–91,
93; on British-Indian relations, 93;
in Kurnaul, 93–94; in Agra, 94;
faith of, 95–96; in Cawnpore, 97;
in Allahabad, 97–98; rests in
Calcutta after Ganges plain
travels, 244–45; in Calcutta and
Chinsura, 246; attempts to raise
money for Saints' emigration,
246–47; in Orissa, 246–48; in

Cuttack, 248; journey to Calcutta,
248; in Manickpatna, 248; voyage
to Hong Kong, 249–52; voyage to
America, 252; returns to Salt
Lake City, 252–53; life sketch of,
284–85
Frank Johnson (ship), 256–57
Frost, Burr, 14
Fuller, Mr., 170

Gallay, Moning, 169
Gamble, Captain, 108
Gazelle (ship), 117, 163–64
Gee, 97
Geils, Dr., 145–46, 271
Geils, Mrs., 145–46
George Washington (ship), 269
Gloriosa (ship), 40, 41
Golconda Fortress, 208, *209*
Goodyear, Sister, 65, 76
Gordon, George, 203, 210
Government, Indian: British
administration of, 1–3; three
presidencies of, 121; attitude of
missionaries toward, 273
Governor's mansion, *83*
Graham, Captain, 266
Gray, Mr., 217
Green, Mr., 64, 76
Grove, Captain, 205
Grundy, John, 43, 52
Grundy, Maria, 43

Haer, Mrs., 239
Hamilton, Colonel, 199
Hanks, Ebenezer, 114
Harris, Captain, 117–19
Hayes, Mr., 87
Hayes, Mrs., 87
Health problems. *See under*
individual missionary
Hefferan, John, 161, 168–69, 170,
174
Helios (ship), 140
Herbert (ship), 174
Hewett, John Z., 190, 196
Hiageer (ship), 111, 113
Hindostan Mission, 102
Hindustan, 12

attempts to raise money for
saints' emigration fund, 246–47,
255; faithfulness of, 250; moves to
Cuttack, 255–56; assisted by
Robert H. Skelton in effort to
emigrate, 261, 264; as mission
leader after closure, 271;
generosity of, 277–78; life sketch
of, 287–88
Meik, Mary Ann: reaction to plural
marriage, 31; introduction to the
Gospel, 40; baptized by Joseph
Richards, 40–41; assists William F.
Carter and William
Fotheringham, 70; faithfulness of,
250; re-baptism of, 255;
generosity of, 277–78
Meik, Susannah McAndrew
Hutchison, 288
Meik, Thomas N., 259
Metcalf, Thomas, 37–38, 84
Michel, James, 194–95
Midnapur, 259
Miller, Captain, 112
Mills, James, 144–45, 254, 271
Mirzapore, 65, 76–77
Mohumad, Dawood Sair, 235–36
Monsoon (ship), 18–22, 196
Morse, T.R., 191
Moulmein, 160, 163, 165–66
Musser, A. Milton: arrival in
Calcutta, 5; birth and childhood
of, 5–8; portrait of, *6;* in Nauvoo,
7–8; conversion of, 8; works in
Tithing Office, 8; mission call,
9–12; journey to California, 13,
14–15; preparations for mission,
13; set apart as missionary, 13–14;
clerk of missionary company, 14;
arrival in San Francisco, 15–16;
age and marital status at time of
call, 17; solicits travel funds, 17;
voyage to India, 18–22; on
Calcutta, 25, 27; assigned to labor
in Calcutta, 33; in Calcutta,
100–102; assists Hugh Findlay in
Bombay, 200; voyage to Karachi,
215–16; in Karachi, 216–27,
234–38; treated kindly by Karachi

neighbors, 219–20, 234–35; love
for prose and poetry, 220; learns
Hindustani, 222; confirms first
Karachi members, 226; builds
chapel in Karachi, 235–37; voyage
to Bombay, 238–39; voyage to
Calcutta, 241; voyage to England,
253–54; labors in England and
Wales, 269; re-baptism of, 269;
voyage to America, 269; returns to
Salt Lake City, 269–70; assists in
organizing handcart companies,
270; meets former companions at
Fort Bridger, 270; returns to work
in the Tithing Office, 270; on
challenges to the work, 272–73,
276, 277; on receptivity of the
Europeans, 273; on Indian
government and society, 273–74,
275–76; on native Indian
Christians, 274; on the difficulties
of communication, 276; on God's
judgments upon India, 276; on
the generosity of ship captains,
277; on the many kindnesses of
the members, 277; on physical
hardships of the mission, 277; on
the generosity of the Meiks,
277–78; on the accomplishments
of the mission, 278–79; on the
blessings of the work, 278–79; life
sketch of, 288–89
Musser, Ann, 5–8
Musser, Annie Seegmiller, 289
Musser, Ann Leaver, 289
Musser, Belinda Pratt, 289
Musser, Mary Elizabeth White, 289
Musser, Samuel, 5

Neff, John, 6–7
Niobe (ship), 200
Nixon, Mr., 91
Norris, David, 7

Orissa, 246–48
Owens, Catherine Ann Williams,
289–90
Owens, Martha Evins Allen, 289–90
Owens, Robert: mission call, 9–10;